RHONA SNELLING

SPEAK YOUR MIND

TEACHER'S EDITION
+ access to Teacher's App

S
STARTER

macmillan education

Macmillan Education
4 Crinan Street
London N1 9XW
A division of Macmillan Education Limited

Companies and representatives throughout the world

Speak Your Mind Starter Level Teacher's Book
ISBN 978-1-380-03099-3
Speak Your Mind Starter Level Teacher's Book + access to Teacher's App ISBN 978-1-380-03667-4

Written by Rhona Snelling
Additional material by Mickey Rogers and Tony Prince.

The author has asserted her right to be identified as the author of this work in accordance with the Copyright, Designs, and Patents Act 1988.

First published 2020

Teacher's Edition credits:
Designed by QBS Learning
Original cover design by therestless.co.uk
Cover adaptation by Roberto Martínez

Author's acknowledgements
Rhona would like to thank the wonderful editorial team at Macmillan Education for their enthusiasm and positivity during the development of this course. She hopes that the course will be beneficial and enjoyable to teachers and students alike. She would also like to thank her lovely family and friends for their kind support.

The publishers would like to thank all the teachers that piloted and reviewed the series.

The author and publishers would like to thank the following for permission to reproduce their photographs:
NILE p. xxviii; **Macmillan Education Limited**/Getty Images/iStockphoto/zentilia p. xxv, Macmillan Education Limited/iStockphoto/alexsl pp. xxvi–xxvii.

Student's Book credits:

Written by Rhona Snelling

The author has asserted her right to be identified as the author of this work in accordance with the Copyright, Designs, and Patents Act 1988.

Designed by QBS Learning
Illustrated by Jerome Brasseur/Beehive Illustration pp. 16(t), 57(r); Daniel Deamo/Lemonade Illustration pp. 16(b), 68, 69; Bunky Hurter/Mendola Artists pp. 28(b), 67; Zhen Liu/Shannon Associates p. 56, Keith Favazza/Wendy Lynn & Co. pp. 4, 34, 57(l), 65, 69; Lon Eric Craven/Wendy Lynn & Co.; QBS Learning pp. 4, 20, 28(t), 38, 42, 50, 54, 63, 66, 79, 90, 102, 104, 106(t), Greg Paprocki; Martina Farrow.
Picture research by Fernanda Rocha / Ikonia LLC and Emily Taylor

Full acknowledgements for illustrations and photographs in the facsimile pages can be found in the *Speak Your Mind* Starter Student's Book & Workbook ISBN 978-1-380-03090-0.

The author and publishers are grateful for permission to reprint the following copyright material:
"Macmillan English Dictionary Online" © Macmillan Education Limited 2019, Published by Macmillan Education, a division of Macmillan Education Limited. Used by Permission. All Rights Reserved

Printed and bound in Brazil

2025
33

Table of Contents

Speak Your Mind Philosophy

In the 21st century, it is no longer enough just to teach subject matter. Teachers need to help their students develop important skills that can lead to success in whatever they choose to do.

The core objective of ***Speak Your Mind*** is to help students become confident communicators. The focus is on using English to communicate in both local and global contexts. Most students may not live in an English-speaking country, but it is probable they will need to use English in the course of their academic and professional lives. Being a confident and competent communicator involves going beyond language skills. Students need to think critically and creatively, work effectively in teams, and solve problems.

Job readiness consists of more than just a strong academic performance. The ability to communicate effectively in English and to use 21st-century skills are essential in order for young adults to enter successfully into or advance within the complex, global world in which they live. ***Speak Your Mind*** is designed to help students achieve their goals.

UNIT 2 My Place

WHAT DO YOU ALREADY KNOW?

1 Think about rooms in your home. Write words that you know in the box.
2 IN PAIRS Share and compare your information. Add more words to the box, if possible.

Living room: sofa
Bedroom: bed
Kitchen: oven

DISCUSS & SHARE

VIDEO

3 IN GROUPS Watch the video and answer the question.
SYM City or country?

In this unit, you will ...

- introduce your partner, talk about classroom objects and talk about where items are in a room.
- use thinking skills: analyze, evaluate and brainstorm.
- read about college student rooms.
- use strategies to give extra information and ask about new words to continue a conversation and check understanding.
- use communication skills to book a hotel room and write a text message.
- follow an online teacher to learn about their job and the skills needed to be in this industry.

Unit 2 My Place 15

Speak Your Mind has a number of features that help students in their academic, professional, and everyday lives:

- Every lesson in ***Speak Your Mind*** ends with a specific communicative outcome. Students do a collaborative task in which they use target language from the lesson to communicate their ideas and express their opinions on a topic related to the subject of the lesson.
- Students learn skills that transfer from the classroom to real life. The lessons contain critical and creative thinking activities that help improve their thinking skills as they learn English. The last lesson in every unit (Language and Life) develops real-life skills by taking students through a step-by-step process in which they read or listen to an example of a real-life task. Students then work together to carry out the task.
- Young-adult students already have a great deal of knowledge about the world, and they are encouraged to transfer their real-life knowledge to the classroom. The topics in ***Speak Your Mind*** allow students to express their opinions on real-world events and issues and to learn more about those topics. Students are often asked to give opinions or to say what they already know about a topic before listening to or reading a text on the subject.
- Most young adults will have at least some previous knowledge of English. They are encouraged to share that knowledge and to build on it according to their personal needs and interests. *Unit Openers* help them be aware of how many words they already know in English and to share their knowledge with their classmates. *Make It Yours* boxes allow them to build their own personal vocabulary lists.
- Videos further help students connect their language learning to real life. For each unit, there is a video that focuses on the Unit Opener topic and acts as a prompt for discussion. There are also documentary-style videos that follow a day in the life of a person in a particular profession.

Overview

***Speak Your Mind* Student's Book Starter** consists of 6 units of 10 pages each. Every unit begins with a one-page Unit Opener designed to introduce the unit topic and to elicit vocabulary and other language that students are already familiar with. Each Unit Opener features a video that can be used to prompt a discussion.

Unit Structure

The Unit Opener is followed by four double-page lessons. Lessons 1–3 contain the core GRAMMAR, VOCABULARY, READING, SPEAKING, LISTENING, PRONUNCIATION, and WRITING sections for the unit. Lesson 4 is called Language and Life. It also includes a reading, but its purpose is to provide students with a task that will help them develop key 21st-century skills.

At the end of each unit, there is a REVIEW page with additional practice of the target vocabulary and grammar. This page also contains a section to introduce a study skill (in odd-numbered units) or a profession related to the topic of the unit (in even-numbered units).

At the end of each **Student's Book**, there is also a list of common irregular verbs, as well as further practice of the target grammar in the book.

Apart from the **Student's Book**, there is a **Workbook** available in print or digital form. The **Student's Resource Center** contains *Reading Worksheets* for extra reading practice, as well as lesson plans adapted from Macmillan's *OneStopEnglish lessons* and *CEFR correlations* that map the course outcomes and objectives to the CEFR scale.

For more information on each feature mentioned in this Introduction, please see the relevant sections that follow.

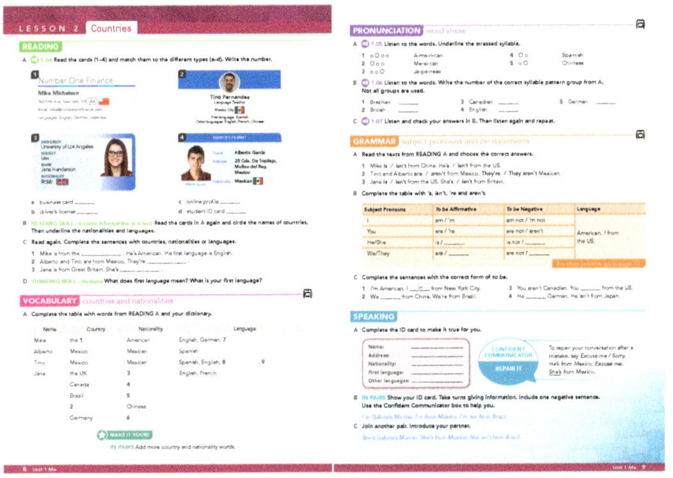

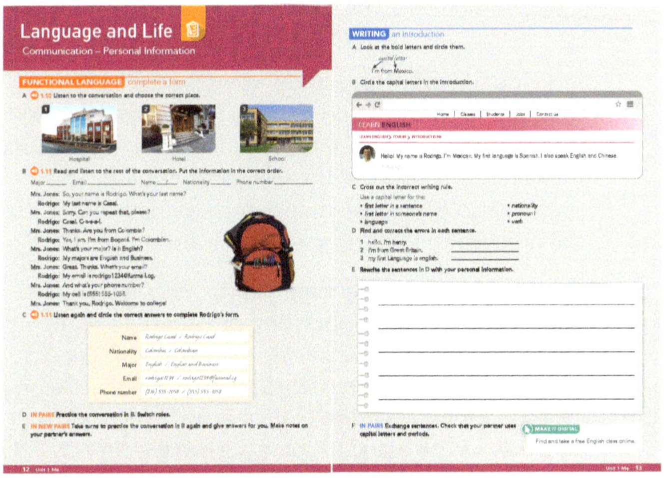

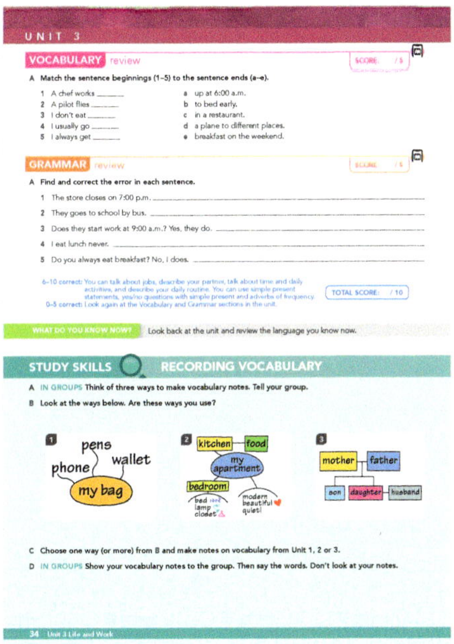

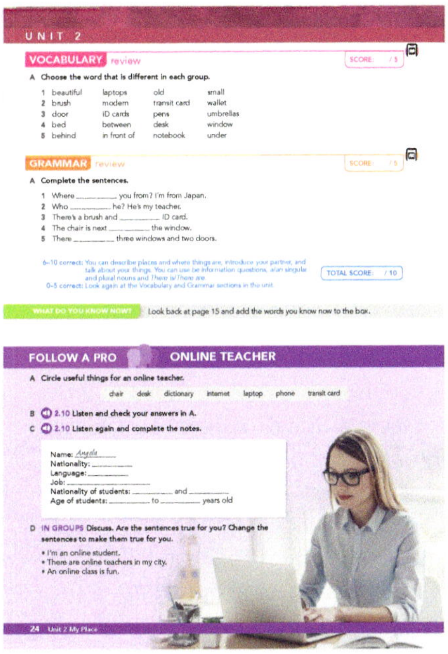

Unit Opener

The ability to use prior knowledge to support the acquisition of new knowledge is an important learning strategy. Having students think about language they already know or knowledge they already have helps them approach new material with greater confidence.

Another important concept in today's classrooms is cooperative learning. Students begin by thinking about something or doing a task individually, then work in pairs to share and build on their individual work. Finally, they work in groups to apply what they have learned individually and in pairs.

Each Unit Opener in ***Speak Your Mind*** introduces the general topic of the unit in a way that will stimulate the interest and curiosity of young adults. The Unit Openers give students the opportunity to think about topic-related words and phrases they already know and to discuss a question they can think about as they work through the unit. Each Unit Opener features a video to support this discussion.

PROCEDURE: Teaching the **Unit Opener** in *Speak Your Mind*

① **Individual work.** Have students work individually to list familiar words and phrases related to the unit topic. This helps build their confidence by highlighting the fact that they already know some English. This section also gives them the chance to think about how the unit topic relates to their own lives.

② **Peer teaching and learning.** Put students in pairs and ask them to share the words and phrases they wrote. At the beginning of the course, explain that working together and sharing what they know allows them to increase their knowledge. Note that at the end of the unit, they will be asked to come back to the Unit Opener and add new words they have learned in the unit.

③ **Video.** A short, optional video accompanies each *DISCUSS & SHARE* section. The purpose of these videos is to provide input that can support students in their discussion of the ***Speak Your Mind*** *Question*. Note that the videos are intended to provide information and context for the discussion, but the ***Speak Your Mind*** *Question* can easily be discussed without viewing them. Teachers are strongly encouraged to use them, as they provide fun and interesting contexts for the discussion, as well as input from both sides of the issue to help students form opinions.

④ **Speak Your Mind Question.** Ask students to work in groups to discuss the ***Speak Your Mind*** *Question*. Explain that the questions do not have specific right or wrong answers because the purpose is to make students think and allow them to express their opinions. Note that these questions are part of the critical-thinking thread in ***Speak Your Mind***. Students should think in terms of a continuum. For example, in Unit 3 Life and Work, some students may think it is better to celebrate their birthdays with a birthday party, some students may think it is better to celebrate their birthdays doing something else.

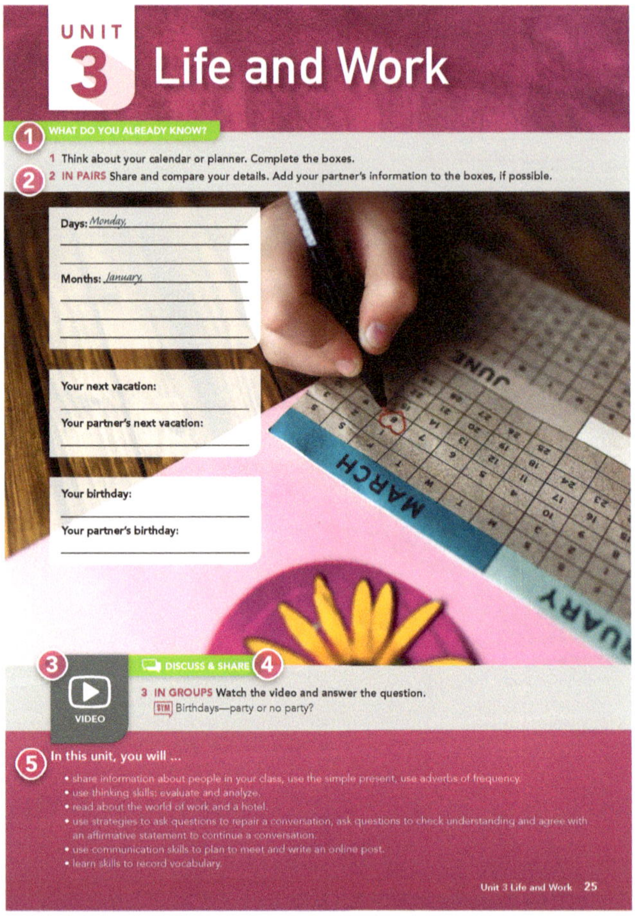

⑤ **Unit Summary.** At the bottom of the *Unit Opener* page, there is a summary of what students will learn in the unit. You may want to go over this so students know what they will learn in the unit.

Vocabulary

Vocabulary plays a very prominent role in ***Speak Your Mind***. Every unit begins with a focus on vocabulary through Unit Opener activities that elicit familiar vocabulary related to the unit topic. Students build on that knowledge through peer sharing. In Lessons 1–3, there is a VOCABULARY section to present and practice new vocabulary related to the specific lesson topic. In Lesson 4, there are opportunities for students to use vocabulary from the unit in the context of the tasks in the lesson.

In ***Speak Your Mind***, vocabulary is presented within the context of the reading or listening text in the lesson. Sometimes the vocabulary is pre-taught in order to help the students understand it when they encounter it as they read or listen. Other times, the VOCABULARY section follows the READING or LISTENING section, and students are encouraged to use the context of the text to help them figure out the meaning of the words.

PROCEDURE: Teaching **Vocabulary** in *Speak Your Mind*

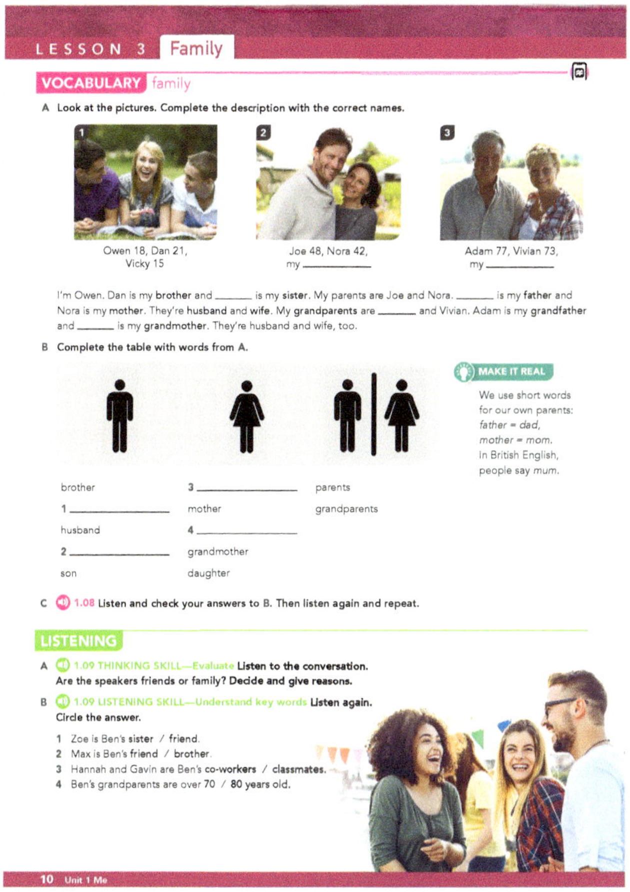
LESSON 3 Family

VOCABULARY family

A Look at the pictures. Complete the description with the correct names.

1 Owen 18, Dan 21, Vicky 15

2 Joe 48, Nora 42, my ______

3 Adam 77, Vivian 73, my ______

I'm Owen. Dan is my **brother** and ______ is my **sister**. My parents are Joe and Nora. ______ is my **father** and Nora is my **mother**. They're **husband** and **wife**. My **grandparents** are ______ and Vivian. Adam is my **grandfather** and ______ is my **grandmother**. They're husband and wife, too.

B Complete the table with words from A.

brother	3 ______	parents
1 ______	mother	grandparents
husband	4 ______	
2 ______	grandmother	
son	daughter	

MAKE IT REAL

We use short words for our own parents: *father = dad*, *mother = mom*. In British English, people say *mum*.

C 1.08 Listen and check your answers to B. Then listen again and repeat.

LISTENING

A 1.09 THINKING SKILL—Evaluate Listen to the conversation. Are the speakers friends or family? Decide and give reasons.

B 1.09 LISTENING SKILL—Understand key words Listen again. Circle the answer.

1 Zoe is Ben's sister / friend.
2 Max is Ben's friend / brother.
3 Hannah and Gavin are Ben's co-workers / classmates.
4 Ben's grandparents are over 70 / 80 years old.

10 Unit 1 Me

Lexical sets. These are particularly relevant at lower levels—when students need a great deal of basic vocabulary related to topics such as food or sports. The lexical sets are often presented through visuals, and students are asked to match the words to the pictures.

When a lexical set is presented, ask students if they know or want to know any other words related to the set. This is a good way to utilize peer teaching, to make students feel that they are participating in the learning process, and to expand the target vocabulary to include words that the students are interested in knowing.

Remember to have students practice saying vocabulary words that are intended for active use. It is also important for them to learn how to spell the words.

Topic-related vocabulary. Words or phrases that are related to the topic of the reading or listening are frequently presented by asking students to look at sentences from the text and match the target words to their definitions, or use them to complete sentences or a short text.

When the VOCABULARY section comes after a reading text, encourage students to go back to the text and look at the words in context to help them confirm their answers to the vocabulary exercise.

When the vocabulary is presented before a LISTENING section, encourage students to listen for the words during the listening activity. Either before or after students listen, you may want to write the sentences with the vocabulary words on the board and check that they understand how each word is used.

Synonyms and antonyms. Learning synonyms and antonyms helps students expand the range and variety of their vocabulary.

There are vocabulary lessons on synonyms and antonyms in ***Speak Your Mind***, but you can teach synonyms or antonyms appropriate to the level as an extension to any vocabulary lesson. For example, if students learn *delicious*, also teach *tasty* or the slang word *yummy*. If they see *shiny* in a text, you can teach them that the opposite is *dull*.

Grammar

Grammar in ***Speak Your Mind*** is taught through an inductive approach in which students are encouraged to observe grammatical structures in context and to go through an analytical process that allows them to figure out rules of structure and function. Each unit has three *GRAMMAR* sections: one in Lesson 1, one in Lesson 2, and one in Lesson 3. In Lesson 4, students have opportunities to use the grammar they have just learned.

The grammar is also used in the *SPEAKING* section at the end of each lesson, which gives students communicative practice with the target structure. Remind them that they should use the grammar as much as possible in the speaking activities in order to become comfortable with it. You may want to elicit some examples of how they can use the grammar before they start the speaking activity.

GRAMMAR and *VOCABULARY* sections are often accompanied by a *Make It Real* box. The purpose of this feature is to provide students with examples of language that they may not be formally taught but that is commonly used by native speakers. This helps them understand more easily when they listen to a native speaker, and it can help them sound more natural when they speak English.

PROCEDURE: Teaching **Grammar** in *Speak Your Mind*

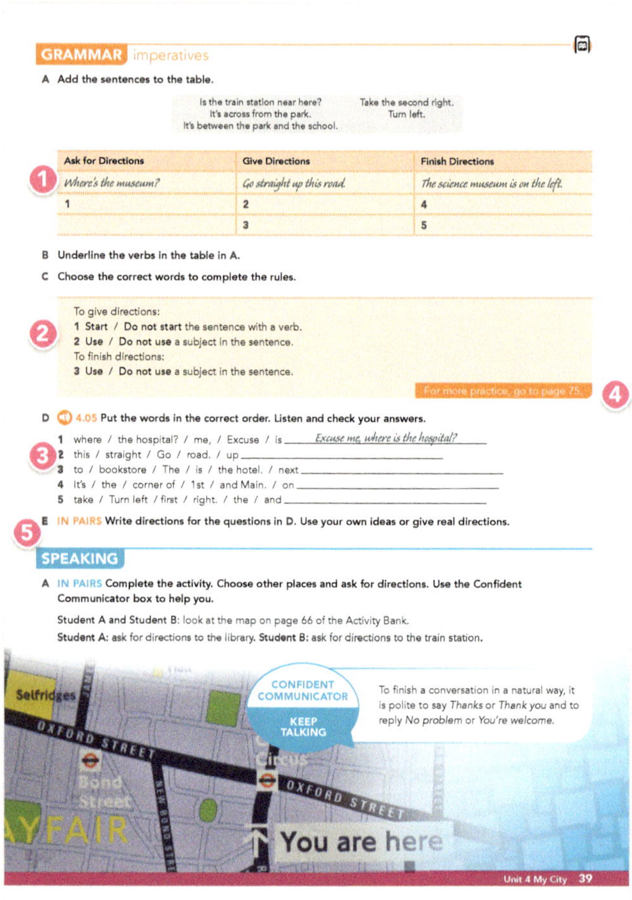

GRAMMAR imperatives

A Add the sentences to the table.

Is the train station near here? It's across from the park. It's between the park and the school. Take the second right. Turn left.

Ask for Directions	Give Directions	Finish Directions
Where's the museum?	*Go straight up this road.*	*The science museum is on the left.*
1	2	4
	3	5

B Underline the verbs in the table in A.

C Choose the correct words to complete the rules.

To give directions:
1 **Start** / **Do not start** the sentence with a verb.
2 **Use** / **Do not use** a subject in the sentence.
To finish directions:
3 **Use** / **Do not use** a subject in the sentence.

For more practice, go to page 75.

D 4.05 Put the words in the correct order. Listen and check your answers.

1 where / the hospital? / me, / Excuse / is *Excuse me, where is the hospital?*
2 this / straight / Go / road. / up ____
3 to / bookstore / The / is / the hotel. / next ____
4 It's / the / corner of / 1st / and Main. / on ____
5 take / Turn left / first / right. / the / and ____

E IN PAIRS Write directions for the questions in D. Use your own ideas or give real directions.

SPEAKING

A IN PAIRS Complete the activity. Choose other places and ask for directions. Use the Confident Communicator box to help you.

Student A and Student B: look at the map on page 66 of the Activity Bank.

Student A: ask for directions to the library. Student B: ask for directions to the train station.

CONFIDENT COMMUNICATOR
KEEP TALKING
To finish a conversation in a natural way, it is polite to say *Thanks* or *Thank you* and to reply *No problem* or *You're welcome.*

Unit 4 My City 39

① **Notice the grammar in context.** Students are exposed to the new grammar structure in the context of a reading or listening text before they are asked to study and work with the grammar itself. You may want to point out one or two examples of the new structure in a reading text or explain that students will hear examples of new grammar in a listening text, but it is not necessary to pre-teach the grammar in order for them to understand the text. Part of learning a new language is learning to use context to understand the meaning of new grammar or vocabulary.

② **Complete the rule.** Ask students to look at examples of the grammar from the reading or listening text. The examples are usually included in the GRAMMAR section, but sometimes students are asked to look for examples in the text. Explain that they should notice the form of the grammar and also think about the meaning, or the function, of the grammatical structure. One of the grammar exercises asks them to complete grammar rules or answer questions about the grammar in order to show that they have understood it. When going over the rules, have students point out the grammar structures in the example sentences or texts that confirm the rules.

At the beginning of the course, explain to students that they will be asked to actively participate in their own learning by using observation and thinking skills to figure out grammar rules about form and function. Point out that we tend to learn more effectively when we figure something out for ourselves rather than just being told.

③ **Practice.** The analysis of the grammar rules is followed by one or more written exercises to practice the new structure. You may want to let students compare their answers in pairs before checking answers as a class. This will provide an opportunity for cooperative learning. If students have had trouble with an exercise, refer back to the grammar rules as you go over each answer to make sure that students understand why the answer is what it is.

④ **Further practice.** In the majority of the highlighted boxes, there is a reference to further practice in the *Grammar Reference* section at the back of the book. These exercises could be done in class if you feel that students need more practice right away to help them understand the grammar, or they could be done as homework or as review before an exam. At the end of this section, there is a list of suggestions for further grammar practice.

④ **Oral practice.** The GRAMMAR sections often include a short pair or group communicative activity to practice the new grammar. Make sure that everyone has an opportunity to use several examples of all forms of the new grammar. For example, if they are learning questions and answers with a verb tense, make sure that the students are practicing both the question forms and the answer forms.

Speak Your Mind provides a number of opportunities for further practice of the grammar:

- The *Student Practice* section in the ***Student's* App** contains grammar practice. An icon indicates where there is practice in the app.
- A *Grammar Review* section at the end of the book reviews grammar from every unit.
- A *Grammar Reference* section at the end of the **Student's Book** gives further explanations and practice exercises for the grammar points in each unit.
- Grammar practice exercises in the **Workbook** reinforce the GRAMMAR sections in the lessons.

Pronunciation

In ***Speak Your Mind***, pronunciation is taught through a combination of observation and practice. There is a PRONUNCIATION section in each unit, and three main areas are emphasized: specific sounds, specific words, and stress and intonation.

Students are usually asked to listen to examples and to notice a pattern or confirm a rule. It is important to allow them to listen and understand the pronunciation point before asking them to try to produce it.

The noticing activity is followed by practice of the pronunciation point, sometimes as a whole class and other times in pairs.

PROCEDURE: Teaching **Pronunciation** in *Speak Your Mind*

1

PRONUNCIATION vowel sounds 1

A 4.07 **Listen to the vowel sound and the words. Then listen again and repeat.**

æ	ɜ	ɝ	iː	uː
jacket	dress	skirt	jeans	shoes

B 4.08 **Listen and match the words (1–4) to the correct vowel sound (a–d).**

1 boots 2 pants 3 shirt 4 T-shirt

a æ b ɝ c iː d uː

2

PRONUNCIATION plural nouns

A 2.05 **Listen to the words and the final –s sound. Repeat.**

/s/	/z/	/ɪz/
laptops	phones	watches
1	3	5
2	4	6

B 2.06 **Listen and add the words to the table in A. Then listen again, check and repeat.**

brushes ID cards notebooks sandwiches umbrellas wallets

3

PRONUNCIATION word stress in questions

A 3.06 **Listen to the conversations and underline the stressed words.**

Conversation 1
Do they speak English?
Yes, they do. / No, they don't.

Conversation 2
Does it open in the mornings?
Yes, it does. / No, it doesn't.

B 3.06 **Listen again and repeat.**

1. **Specific sounds.** Make sure students understand the rule and can distinguish the sound. Model the sound for them, first with the sound only and then using the sound in a word. Allow them to practice the sound a number of times until they feel comfortable with it.
2. **Specific words.** When students have to recognize specific words in a sentence, you may want to let them listen to the sentences more than once. If they are asked to notice a sound within a word, make sure they can all distinguish it.
3. **Stress and intonation.** You may want to read the sentences yourself before students practice them. In this way, you can exaggerate the stressed words or the intonation pattern to make sure students can recognize the pattern.

Reading

Good readers unconsciously use a number of different skills when they read in their own language. When people learn a second language, they often need to become aware of those skills and learn how to use them when reading in the second language. Reading is considered a receptive skill, but that does not mean that it is a passive activity. Reading involves interacting with a text by reading it with questions in mind, comparing one's own knowledge or opinions to the information in the text, and applying skills to help one understand and interpret the text.

In the classroom, reading is usually done to develop reading skills, and/or as a vehicle for language study. However, a text will be more effective for academic purposes if the students find it interesting. In ***Speak Your Mind***, reading texts on a wide variety of topics in a number of different genres are designed to engage students' interest while providing work on key reading skills and general reading comprehension.

After students have done the activities in the READING section, you may want to close by asking follow-up questions about main ideas and supporting details or by asking students to summarize what they learned or understood from the text.

For further practice of reading skills and general reading comprehension, there are *Reading Worksheets* available in the **Student's Resource Center**.

PROCEDURE: Teaching **Reading** in *Speak Your Mind*

Every READING section begins with a pre-reading activity. Before students read the text, have them look at the title and any visual elements. Ask them to think about what they know and what they would like to know about the topic. Students can predict what information they think will be in the text or have them give their opinions about the topic. The objective is to get them to start thinking about the topic before they read. After they have read the text, you could ask them whether they predicted correctly or they changed their opinions after reading.

1. **Reading.** The ***Speak Your Mind*** reading texts are included in the audio recordings in case you would like students to listen to a text. This may be particularly useful in cases where the reading text is in the form of an interview.

There are two types of comprehension activities that accompany reading texts: exercises for general comprehension and exercises to develop specific reading skills. For general comprehension exercises, it is a good idea to have students read the questions before reading the text in order to help them identify key information while reading. Good readers usually have an idea of what information they want to get from a text before they begin reading. Students can underline key words and information as they read, make notes, or write questions in the margin.

2. **Reading Skill.** For READING SKILL activities, check that students understand what the skill is and why it is useful before asking them to do the exercise. Each unit of the **Workbook** has further practice of the skill. You may want to direct students to the explanation in the **Workbook** before having them do the exercise in the **Student's Book**.

3. **Thinking Skill.** The THINKING SKILL activity is usually found in the READING section. This activity encourages students to further analyze a text, express their opinions about a text, or extend and apply the ideas from a text to their own context. While the thinking skills questions are an opportunity for students to express themselves orally, the main objective is not accuracy. Help students if they are having difficulty expressing themselves, but don't spend a lot of time on correction. The purpose of these questions is to allow them to think critically and to express themselves freely.

LESSON 2 Countries

READING

1 A 1.04 Read the cards (1–4) and match them to the different types (a–d). Write the number.

a business card ______ c online profile ______

b driver's license ______ d student ID card ______

2 B READING SKILL—Locate information in a text Read the cards in A again and circle the names of countries. Then underline the nationalities and languages.

C Read again. Complete the sentences with countries, nationalities or languages.

1 Mike is from the ________ . He's American. His first language is English.
2 Alberto and Tino are from Mexico. They're ________ .
3 Jane is from Great Britain. She's ________ .

3 D THINKING SKILL—Analyze What does *first language* mean? What is your first language?

VOCABULARY countries and nationalities

A Complete the table with words from READING A and your dictionary.

Name	Country	Nationality	Language
Mike	the 1	American	English, German, 7
Alberto	Mexico	Mexican	Spanish
Tino	Mexico	Mexican	Spanish, English, 8 , 9
Jane	the UK	3	English, French
	Canada	4	
	Brazil	5	
	2	Chinese	
	Germany	6	

MAKE IT YOURS

IN PAIRS Add more country and nationality words.

8 Unit 1 Me

Listening

The importance of good listening skills cannot be over-emphasized, as listening represents 45% of adult communication. In ***Speak Your Mind***, there are listening comprehension sections in two of the four lessons in each unit. These sections are designed to help students develop key listening skills, as well as general comprehension skills. The listening texts represent a variety of genres, including conversations, radio broadcasts, and podcasts, in order to give students exposure to as many different listening situations as possible.

Like reading, listening is a receptive skill, but it is not a passive activity. Listeners rely on their own prior knowledge of a topic, their expectations about what a speaker will say, as well as contextual clues like body language to help them predict what will be said. Listeners also employ a variety of skills while listening, such as identifying key words to help them understand both the gist of a conversation and important details.

There are a number of things that teachers can do to help students improve their listening comprehension:

- Do not speak too slowly or enunciate too perfectly. This will make it easier for students to understand in the classroom but much more difficult when they encounter English outside the classroom. You may want to slow down a word or a sentence occasionally, but in general, you should use normal speech.
- Remind students not to worry if they do not understand every word in a listening text. Point out that we often miss words even when listening in our own language. Encourage them to identify key words to help them understand the gist of a listening text, as well as important details.
- As students develop specific listening skills, remind them to use those skills when they are listening to the teacher or to their classmates. Point out that they get listening practice not only in the *LISTENING* sections of their textbooks but also during speaking activities and classroom interactions.

PROCEDURE: Teaching **Listening** in *Speak Your Mind*

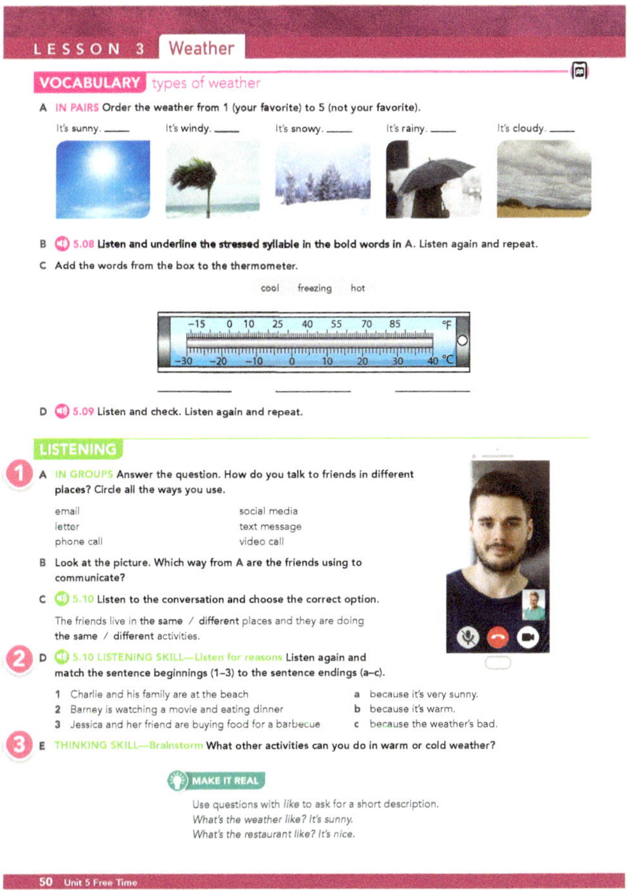
LESSON 3 Weather

VOCABULARY types of weather

A IN PAIRS Order the weather from 1 (your favorite) to 5 (not your favorite).

It's sunny. ____ It's windy. ____ It's snowy. ____ It's rainy. ____ It's cloudy. ____

B 5.08 Listen and underline the stressed syllable in the bold words in A. Listen again and repeat.

C Add the words from the box to the thermometer.

cool freezing hot

–15 0 10 25 40 55 70 85 °F

–30 –20 –10 0 10 20 30 40 °C

D 5.09 Listen and check. Listen again and repeat.

LISTENING

1 A IN GROUPS Answer the question. How do you talk to friends in different places? Circle all the ways you use.

email social media
letter text message
phone call video call

B Look at the picture. Which way from A are the friends using to communicate?

C 5.10 Listen to the conversation and choose the correct option.

The friends live in the same / different places and they are doing the same / different activities.

2 D 5.10 LISTENING SKILL—Listen for reasons Listen again and match the sentence beginnings (1–3) to the sentence endings (a–c).

1 Charlie and his family are at the beach
2 Barney is watching a movie and eating dinner
3 Jessica and her friend are buying food for a barbecue

a because it's very sunny.
b because it's warm.
c because the weather's bad.

3 E THINKING SKILL—Brainstorm What other activities can you do in warm or cold weather?

MAKE IT REAL

Use questions with *like* to ask for a short description.
What's the weather like? It's sunny.
What's the restaurant like? It's nice.

50 Unit 5 Free Time

(1) **Pre-Listening.** Pre-listening activities help students prepare for listening by asking them to predict what speakers will say or to talk about what they already know about a topic. If students have difficulty with the pre-listening activity, do the activity with the whole class. If students have a lot to say about it, do the activity in pairs or groups so that everyone will have a chance to speak.

(2) **Listening Skill.** As with reading, every LISTENING section of ***Speak Your Mind*** includes the development of a listening skill. Check that students understand what the skill is and why it is useful. You may want to refer students to the explanation of the listening skill in the relevant unit of the **Workbook**.

LISTENING sections also include general comprehension exercises. Especially at beginning levels, students often need a lot of support for listening comprehension. It is a good idea to allow them to read through a comprehension exercise before listening in order to give them an idea of what to listen for. You may want to ask them to listen to the recording once before attempting to do the exercise. After they listen, give them a few minutes to do the exercise and then play the recording again for them to check their work.

(3) **Thinking Skill.** In each LISTENING section of ***Speak Your Mind***, there is a thinking activity that encourages students to further analyze what they've heard and to express their opinions or to extend and apply the ideas in the listening text to their own context. You may want to refer back to the procedure notes on page x.

Speaking

Foreign-language teachers often comment that students just don't want to speak. There are a number of reasons for this. Sometimes they are afraid of making mistakes. This is especially true of young-adult and adult students, who are used to thinking of themselves as competent adults. Other times students are just not prepared when asked to speak. It can be very difficult for them to think of what to say and how to say it if they are not able to prepare beforehand, especially at lower levels. It is important to create a classroom environment in which students feel confident and motivated to communicate in English.

Not every student will want to or be able to participate fully in every discussion, so it is important to provide frequent opportunities for students to speak. In ***Speak Your Mind***, there is a strong emphasis on speaking, and students are given many opportunities throughout the lessons to voice their ideas and to practice the language that they are learning:

- Unit Openers have cooperative learning opportunities and group discussion questions.
- Pre-reading and pre-listening activities often involve class discussions.
- Thinking skills sections often have questions for group or class discussions.
- GRAMMAR and VOCABULARY sections frequently include group or pair speaking activities.
- Lessons 1–3 end with a SPEAKING section, which allows students to use the grammar and vocabulary of the lesson to talk about a related topic.
- Language and Life lessons (Lesson 4 in every unit) are designed as collaborative tasks that involve a variety of interactive pair, group, and class activities.

Be sure to allow plenty of time for the speaking activities, as this is the communicative outcome of the lesson. The SPEAKING section frequently takes up less space on the page than other sections in the lesson, so it is easy to make the mistake of thinking that the activity is very short. It is important to allow enough time for preparation and for each student to have the chance to speak.

When students are working in groups or pairs, listen for common errors, especially in the target language of the lesson. Have a short review session after the speaking activity. This generally works better than interrupting students while they are speaking. If you have a large class, you may not be able to listen to every pair or group, but you can get a good idea of things they may need more practice with by listening to as many of them as possible.

PROCEDURE: Teaching **Speaking** in *Speak Your Mind*

1. **Preparation.** SPEAKING sections are scaffolded in order to give students the support they need when they speak. They first think about the topic, make notes, fill in a form, or in some other way prepare for what they are going to say. It is important to give them enough time to do this so that they feel confident when they start speaking. You may want to add a class preparation stage before asking students to work on their own—have a class brainstorming session to help them come up with ideas, or you could elicit vocabulary and grammar structures that they may need for the speaking activity.
2. **Practice.** Once students have had a chance to prepare, they work in pairs or groups to share their ideas. Make sure that students understand what they are going to do and exactly what their roles are before you put them in their groups or pairs. You may want to model the activity with a student or ask two students to model it.

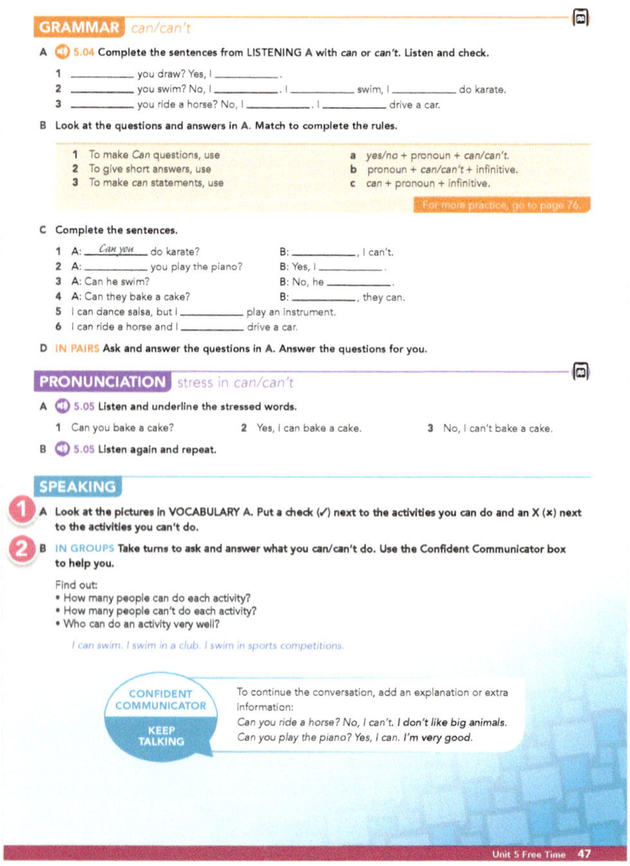
GRAMMAR can/can't

A 5.04 Complete the sentences from LISTENING A with *can* or *can't*. Listen and check.

1 ________ you draw? Yes, I ________.
2 ________ you swim? No, I ________. I ________ swim, I ________ do karate.
3 ________ you ride a horse? No, I ________. I ________ drive a car.

B Look at the questions and answers in A. Match to complete the rules.

1 To make *Can* questions, use — a *yes/no* + pronoun + *can/can't*.
2 To give short answers, use — b pronoun + *can/can't* + infinitive.
3 To make *can* statements, use — c *can* + pronoun + infinitive.

For more practice, go to page 76.

C Complete the sentences.

1 A: *Can you* do karate? B: ________, I can't.
2 A: ________ you play the piano? B: Yes, I ________.
3 A: Can he swim? B: No, he ________.
4 A: Can they bake a cake? B: ________, they can.
5 I can dance salsa, but I ________ play an instrument.
6 I can ride a horse and I ________ drive a car.

D IN PAIRS Ask and answer the questions in A. Answer the questions for you.

PRONUNCIATION stress in can/can't

A 5.05 Listen and underline the stressed words.

1 Can you bake a cake? 2 Yes, I can bake a cake. 3 No, I can't bake a cake.

B 5.05 Listen again and repeat.

SPEAKING

1 A Look at the pictures in VOCABULARY A. Put a check (✓) next to the activities you can do and an X (×) next to the activities you can't do.

2 B IN GROUPS Take turns to ask and answer what you can/can't do. Use the Confident Communicator box to help you.

Find out:
- How many people can do each activity?
- How many people can't do each activity?
- Who can do an activity very well?

I can swim. I swim in a club. I swim in sports competitions.

CONFIDENT COMMUNICATOR
KEEP TALKING
To continue the conversation, add an explanation or extra information:
Can you ride a horse? No, I can't. ***I don't like big animals.***
Can you play the piano? Yes, I can. ***I'm very good.***

Unit 5 Free Time 47

Confident Communicator

One of the core objectives of ***Speak Your Mind*** is that students should become confident users of English—that is, Confident Communicators. Every *SPEAKING* section in ***Speak Your Mind*** includes a *Confident Communicator* box that gives students tips on what to say and how to say it. Some of the tips focus on functional language, which includes words and phrases used in specific situations, such as greeting someone or asking directions. Others focus on speaking strategies, such as taking time to think or explaining what you mean. The subheadings *Start Talking*, *Keep Talking*, and *Repair It* indicate how the language in the *Confident Communicator* box functions in a conversation.

Before students get into pairs or groups to do the interactive part of the *SPEAKING* section, go over the language in the *Confident Communicator* box to make sure they understand how to use it. You may want to practice a few short interactions with some or all of the phrases before they start working together.

When applied to language learning, the old saying "Practice makes perfect" should probably be changed to "Practice makes perfectly adequate." Wanting students to be confident communicators does not mean that everything they say should be perfectly constructed. In our own languages, we often communicate with incomplete sentences or even just facial expressions or gestures. The goal is to give students the confidence to express their ideas in English, and the best way to do that is through a combination of frequent opportunities to speak and support with the language.

Confident Communicator feature in *Speak Your Mind*

With the *Start Talking* boxes, students learn phrases for initiating a conversation or topic.

CONFIDENT COMMUNICATOR
START TALKING

To join a conversation, use the following phrases:
Excuse me, can I join you?
Hi there, can I join you?

With the *Keep Talking* boxes, students learn strategies and phrases to keep a conversation going even when they are not yet very proficient in the language.

CONFIDENT COMMUNICATOR
KEEP TALKING

To continue the game after your partner gives his or her answer, say: *Yes, that's the correct answer! Good job!*
No, sorry. That's not the right answer. Try again.

With the *Repair It* boxes, students learn phrases to use when there is a problem in communication.

CONFIDENT COMMUNICATOR
REPAIR IT

To repair your conversation after a mistake, say *Excuse me / Sorry.*
He's from Mexico. Excuse me.
<u>She's</u> from Mexico.

Writing

The ability to communicate effectively in writing is more important than ever for professional success. In the past, a great deal of business communication was conducted on the phone, but now most business communication is done via email. Email is no longer considered just an informal mode of written communication. Emails, like letters in the past, can have varying degrees of informality or formality, and young adults who are about to enter a very competitive professional world will have to be able to communicate competently in writing.

Teaching students to communicate in written English is complicated by the fact that many students do not have good writing skills—even in their own language. In ***Speak Your Mind***, students are taught basic writing skills like planning before starting to write, reviewing and editing their work after they write, and how to construct different genres of written communication. Learning to write short texts in different genres gives students practice in skills such as writing a short introduction, sending a text message, or describing a place. While the topics they write about may not be directly related to a profession, the skills they learn can be applied later on in business communications, both in English and in their own language. There is a WRITING section in Lesson 4 of every unit in ***Speak Your Mind***.

Remember that the purpose of writing is to communicate ideas, so it is always a good idea to have students share their finished work. You could have them read their texts aloud in small groups and then have a discussion, or you could have them work with a partner and read each other's texts. They can then get together to discuss their ideas or report on each other's texts to different partners.

There is further practice in writing mechanics and editing skills in the **Workbook**. In ***Speak Your Mind***, students are given the support and the practice they need in order for them to become competent writers in English.

PROCEDURE: Teaching **Writing** in *Speak Your Mind*

① **Read the model.** A model text is provided in the WRITING section of the Language and Life lesson. Students read the text and do an exercise that asks them to notice elements of content, organization, or language commonly used in a specific genre. You may want to have students read the text and then ask some general comprehension questions before having them do the exercise.

② **Organize [Pre-writing].** After students have worked with the model text, they are given a framework to provide them with cues and help them organize their ideas for their own text. You may want to start with a class brainstorming session to help generate ideas. As they work, give individual help with ideas and vocabulary as needed.

③ **Write and share.** Once students have written their texts, give them time to review and correct their work. This may be done individually or in pairs. If it is done in pairs, it is a good opportunity for cooperative learning. You may want to go over some common grammar or spelling errors before they start editing their work in order to help them spot their own errors.

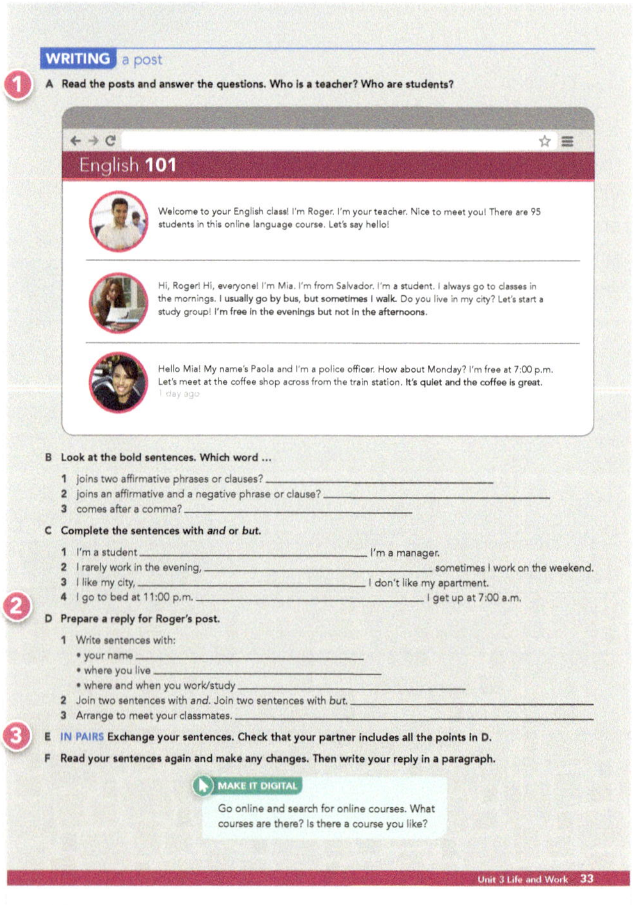
WRITING a post

① A **Read the posts and answer the questions. Who is a teacher? Who are students?**

English **101**

Welcome to your English class! I'm Roger. I'm your teacher. Nice to meet you! There are 95 students in this online language course. Let's say hello!

Hi, Roger! Hi, everyone! I'm Mia. I'm from Salvador. I'm a student. I always go to classes in the mornings. **I usually go by bus, but sometimes I walk.** Do you live in my city? Let's start a study group! **I'm free in the evenings but not in the afternoons.**

Hello Mia! My name's Paola and I'm a police officer. How about Monday? I'm free at 7:00 p.m. Let's meet at the coffee shop across from the train station. **It's quiet and the coffee is great.**
1 day ago

B **Look at the bold sentences. Which word ...**

1 joins two affirmative phrases or clauses? ______
2 joins an affirmative and a negative phrase or clause? ______
3 comes after a comma? ______

C **Complete the sentences with *and* or *but*.**

1 I'm a student ______ I'm a manager.
2 I rarely work in the evening, ______ sometimes I work on the weekend.
3 I like my city, ______ I don't like my apartment.
4 I go to bed at 11:00 p.m. ______ I get up at 7:00 a.m.

② D **Prepare a reply for Roger's post.**

1 Write sentences with:
• your name ______
• where you live ______
• where and when you work/study ______
2 Join two sentences with *and*. Join two sentences with *but*. ______
3 Arrange to meet your classmates. ______

③ E IN PAIRS **Exchange your sentences. Check that your partner includes all the points in D.**

F **Read your sentences again and make any changes. Then write your reply in a paragraph.**

MAKE IT DIGITAL
Go online and search for online courses. What courses are there? Is there a course you like?

Unit 3 Life and Work 33

Language and Life

21st-Century Skills

In the 21st century, the teaching of academic subjects is accompanied by the development of the types of skills that are necessary for success in academics, work, and life. These skills for success include communication, collaboration, problem-solving, creativity, self-direction, critical thinking, and media literacy.

In ***Speak Your Mind***, these skills are developed throughout each unit through collaborative activities, training in effective communication, and tasks that require critical thinking and problem-solving. The last lesson in each unit is specifically designed to focus on the development of 21st-century skills while recycling key grammar and vocabulary from the unit.

PROCEDURE: Teaching **Language and Life** in *Speak Your Mind*

The heading is in two parts. The first part indicates the target 21st-century skill. The second part indicates the main topic of the lesson. Check that students understand both the skill and the objective of the task.

The FUNCTIONAL LANGUAGE section allows students to experience different real-life scenarios, where they are required to communicate with others to perform a professional or social function. For much more on functional language, see "Functional Language" by Tony Prince on pages xxviii–xxxi of this book.

1. **Read the text.** Students listen to or read a model text that demonstrates the function. There are comprehension questions to check that students understand the context and the speakers' roles. Students can work individually or in pairs.
2. **Analyze the text.** Students then analyze the text further and explore the language used. Remember to check and confirm correct answers as a class and deal with any problems.
3. **Practice intonation.** After that, there is usually a focus on intonation. This activity raises students' awareness of correct intonation patterns and provides a model for them to follow. Have the class repeat and practice the intonation.

   In the next stage, students role-play the model text. Students activate the useful phrases they identified and analyzed earlier, as well as use the correct intonation.
4. **Present.** In the final stage, students do some freer spoken practice. In this activity, some of the details and facts in the model text are changed slightly so that students create a different interaction. Have them work in small groups so that everyone will have time to talk, as this is the main spoken outcome of the lesson.

For the general procedure for teaching WRITING, see page xiv.

The WRITING section of the Language and Life lesson allows students to gain practice in a specific real-life task and produce a simple written text related to the FUNCTIONAL LANGUAGE section of the lesson.

5. **Read the text.** Students first read a model text and complete comprehension questions about it. Encourage them to read the text alone, but it may be beneficial to first read the texts as a class or in pairs.
6. **Practice.** The next stage focuses on specific writing skills and mechanics. Students then analyze how the skill or language is used and do a controlled practice activity.
7. **Write and share.** The lesson ends with students producing their own written text using the model text provided and the writing skills or mechanics practiced. This stage includes collaborative work where pairs or small groups work together to edit and improve a text.

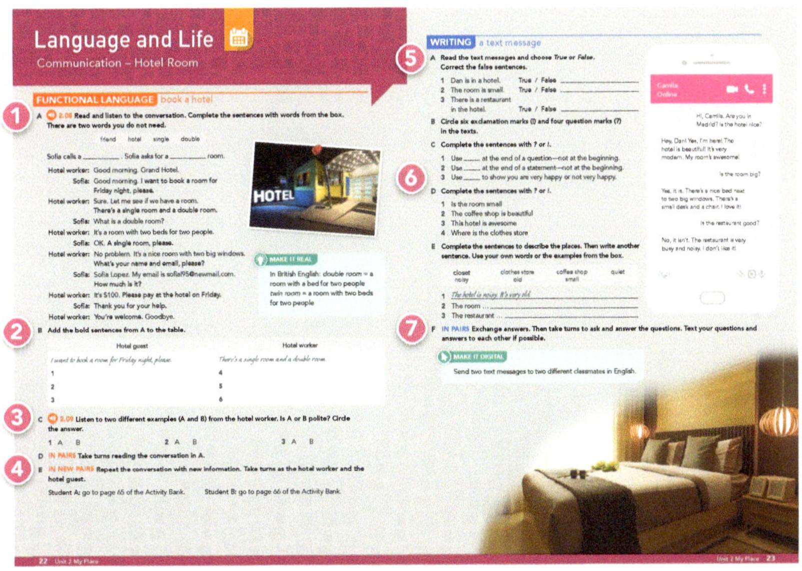

Make It ...

Personalization is an important part of building vocabulary for English language learners. The *Make It ...* features in ***Speak Your Mind*** show students where they should add the words and phrases they need or use for work or study. Students should be encouraged to build a list of words, phrases, or expressions that are meaningful to them.

PROCEDURE: Using the **Make It ...** features in *Speak Your Mind*

Make It Yours. *Make It Yours* boxes encourage students to expand their vocabulary by making a list of words that are useful for them personally or by using target vocabulary in a personalized way. Go over the information in the boxes and elcit words from the class, or ask them to do the task suggested in the box for homework.

MAKE IT YOURS

Write more adjectives to describe your home. Use your dictionary to help you.

Make It Real. GRAMMAR and VOCABULARY sections are often accompanied by a *Make It Real* box. The purpose of this feature is to provide students with examples of language that they may not be formally taught but which is commonly used by native speakers. This helps them understand more easily when they listen to a native speaker, and it can help them sound more natural when they speak English.

MAKE IT REAL

People often say *about* for a time that is not exact.
*The waiters finish **about** 11. = The waiters finish at 10:50/10:55/11:05/11:10.*
People do not always say *o'clock*, *a.m.* or *p.m.* after the time.
The waiters start work at six.

Make It Digital. Every unit in ***Speak Your Mind*** includes a suggestion for online work outside of class. The *Make It Digital* box always appears in Lesson 4 because the Language and Life tasks lend themselves to further investigations or to a product that can be posted on a school website. You could have students do the research for homework and then report back to the class.

MAKE IT DIGITAL

Choose a city and search online for activities to do or places to go. Do you like the recommendations? What places are interesting?

Unit Review

Every unit in ***Speak Your Mind*** includes an end-of-unit review of the target grammar and vocabulary from the unit. The exercises are designed as a general review to help students and teachers identify areas of strength and weakness so that the students know what to focus on when studying for their exams.

The ***Speak Your Mind*** **Teacher's Resource Center** contains an exam for each unit, an exam covering the first half of the book, and a final exam to be given at the end of the book. If possible, it is a good idea to have students do the *Review* section a couple of days before a unit exam so that they have plenty of time to study their weak areas before the exam. The *Review* may be assigned as homework or done in class as a practice test.

When you go over the answers to the *Review* section, make sure that students understand their errors and that they know which section of their **Student's Book** to study for each incorrect item. Remind them that they need to study all of the vocabulary items in the three VOCABULARY sections in the unit, not just the items that were included in the *Review* exercises.

PROCEDURE: Teaching the Unit Review in *Speak Your Mind*

1. **Review.** The VOCABULARY and GRAMMAR *Review* sections each have one or two exercises for a total of 5 items per section. The exercises are written in a variety of formats that reflect the different exercise types that students may encounter on an exam.
2. **Score.** There are 5 points per section for a combined total of 10 points for the two sections. Students should write the number of correct answers in the blank in each section and the total number of correct answers in the *Total Score* box. Point out the score interpretations under the *Total Score* box. Remind students that they will be tested on the grammar and vocabulary of the unit, and if they have a low score on the *Review*, they need to go back to the relevant sections in the unit and study the material.
3. **Further review.** Every *Review* section ends with the question WHAT DO YOU KNOW NOW? Students are asked to go back to the vocabulary activity in the Unit Opener and add words that they have learned in the unit. This is useful both as a reflection activity and as a review tool. It raises students' awareness that they are increasing their vocabulary in English. Also, by looking back at the words they listed in the Unit Opener, they are reviewing vocabulary related to the unit topic.
4. **Study Skill / Follow a Pro.** Please see the following pages for explanations of the STUDY SKILLS and FOLLOW A PRO sections on the *Review* page.

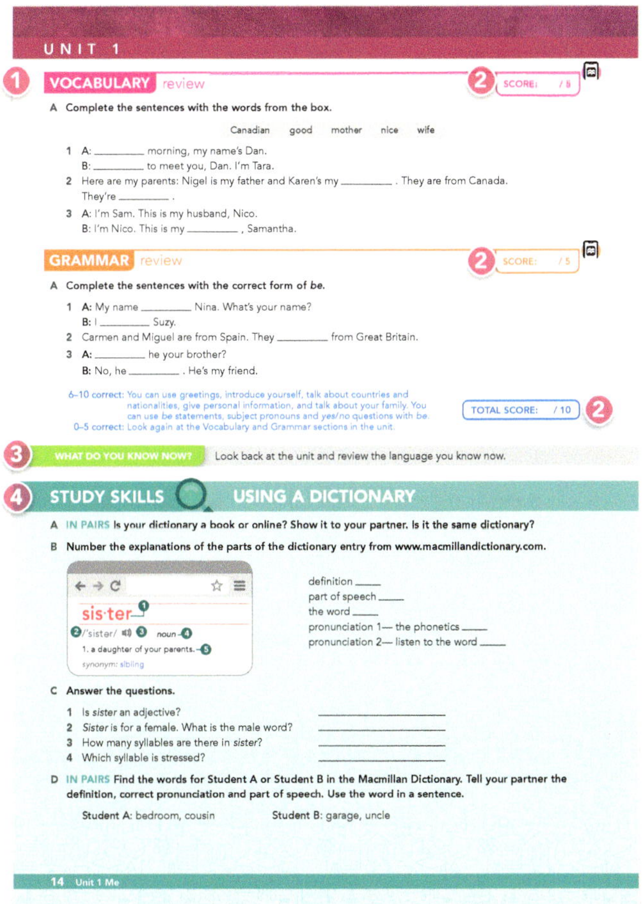

UNIT 1

1 VOCABULARY review — 2 SCORE: / 5

A Complete the sentences with the words from the box.

Canadian good mother nice wife

1 A: ________ morning, my name's Dan.
B: ________ to meet you, Dan. I'm Tara.
2 Here are my parents: Nigel is my father and Karen's my ________ . They are from Canada. They're ________ .
3 A: I'm Sam. This is my husband, Nico.
B: I'm Nico. This is my ________ , Samantha.

GRAMMAR review — 2 SCORE: / 5

A Complete the sentences with the correct form of *be*.

1 A: My name ________ Nina. What's your name?
B: I ________ Suzy.
2 Carmen and Miguel are from Spain. They ________ from Great Britain.
3 A: ________ he your brother?
B: No, he ________ . He's my friend.

6–10 correct: You can use greetings, introduce yourself, talk about countries and nationalities, give personal information, and talk about your family. You can use *be* statements, subject pronouns and *yes/no* questions with *be*.
0–5 correct: Look again at the Vocabulary and Grammar sections in the unit.

TOTAL SCORE: / 10 — 2

3 WHAT DO YOU KNOW NOW? Look back at the unit and review the language you know now.

4 STUDY SKILLS — USING A DICTIONARY

A IN PAIRS Is your dictionary a book or online? Show it to your partner. Is it the same dictionary?

B Number the explanations of the parts of the dictionary entry from www.macmillandictionary.com.

sis·ter 1
2 /ˈsɪstər/ 3 noun 4
1. a daughter of your parents. 5
synonym: sibling

definition ____
part of speech ____
the word ____
pronunciation 1— the phonetics ____
pronunciation 2— listen to the word ____

C Answer the questions.

1 Is *sister* an adjective? ________
2 *Sister* is for a female. What is the male word? ________
3 How many syllables are there in *sister*? ________
4 Which syllable is stressed? ________

D IN PAIRS Find the words for Student A or Student B in the Macmillan Dictionary. Tell your partner the definition, correct pronunciation and part of speech. Use the word in a sentence.

Student A: bedroom, cousin Student B: garage, uncle

14 Unit 1 Me

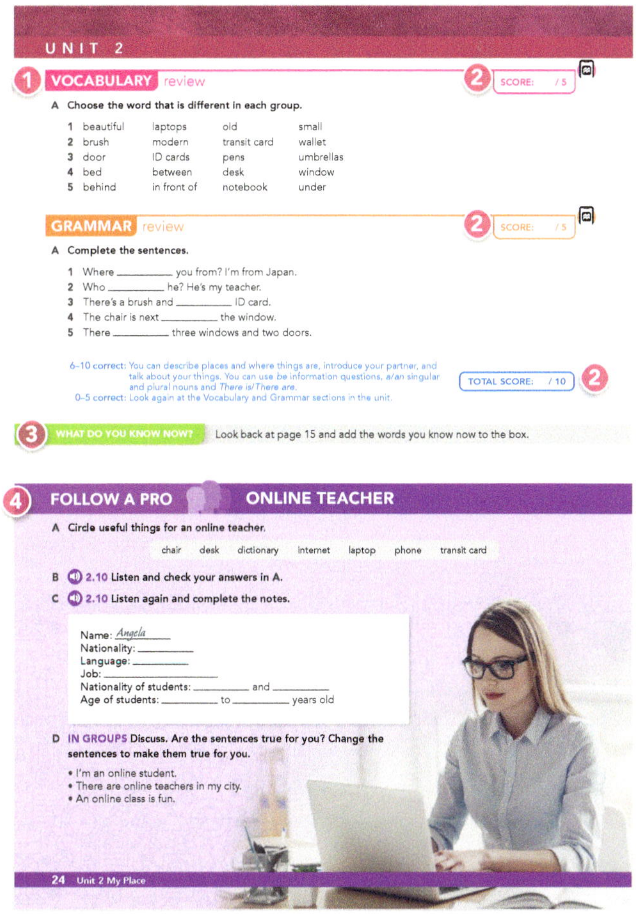

UNIT 2

1 VOCABULARY review — 2 SCORE: / 5

A Choose the word that is different in each group.

1	beautiful	laptops	old	small
2	brush	modern	transit card	wallet
3	door	ID cards	pens	umbrellas
4	bed	between	desk	window
5	behind	in front of	notebook	under

GRAMMAR review — 2 SCORE: / 5

A Complete the sentences.

1 Where ________ you from? I'm from Japan.
2 Who ________ he? He's my teacher.
3 There's a brush and ________ ID card.
4 The chair is next ________ the window.
5 There ________ three windows and two doors.

6–10 correct: You can describe places and where things are, introduce your partner, and talk about your things. You can use *be* information questions, *a/an* singular and plural nouns and *There is/There are*.
0–5 correct: Look again at the Vocabulary and Grammar sections in the unit.

TOTAL SCORE: / 10 — 2

3 WHAT DO YOU KNOW NOW? Look back at page 15 and add the words you know now to the box.

4 FOLLOW A PRO — ONLINE TEACHER

A Circle useful things for an online teacher.

chair desk dictionary internet laptop phone transit card

B 2.10 Listen and check your answers in A.

C 2.10 Listen again and complete the notes.

Name: *Angela*
Nationality: ________
Language: ________
Job: ________
Nationality of students: ________ and ________
Age of students: ________ to ________ years old

D IN GROUPS Discuss. Are the sentences true for you? Change the sentences to make them true for you.

- I'm an online student.
- There are online teachers in my city.
- An online class is fun.

24 Unit 2 My Place

Study Skills

In order to be successful, not only in learning English but also in academics in general, students must develop good study skills, such as using a dictionary and methods for remembering vocabulary. In ***Speak Your Mind***, there is a study skills syllabus that is based on universal needs regardless of the subject but modified when appropriate to focus on skills specific to learning a new language.

In each level of ***Speak Your Mind***, study skills are presented and practiced in every other unit.

PROCEDURE: Teaching **Study Skills** in *Speak Your Mind*

① **Activate previous knowledge.** The STUDY SKILLS sections at the end of the units have activities to help develop useful study skills. In the first activity, students answer questions to create interest and to activate existing knowledge of study skills or study habits.

② **Examine.** The second activity is an exercise that allows students to examine the study skill in more detail through a simple task.

③ **Practice.** The third activity gives students the opportunity to practice using the study skill. Remind students that good study skills will both help their language learning and aid their general academic progress.

④ **Apply the skill.** In the last activity, students apply what they have learned and use the study skill to do an authentic study skills task, compare ideas, or play a language game.

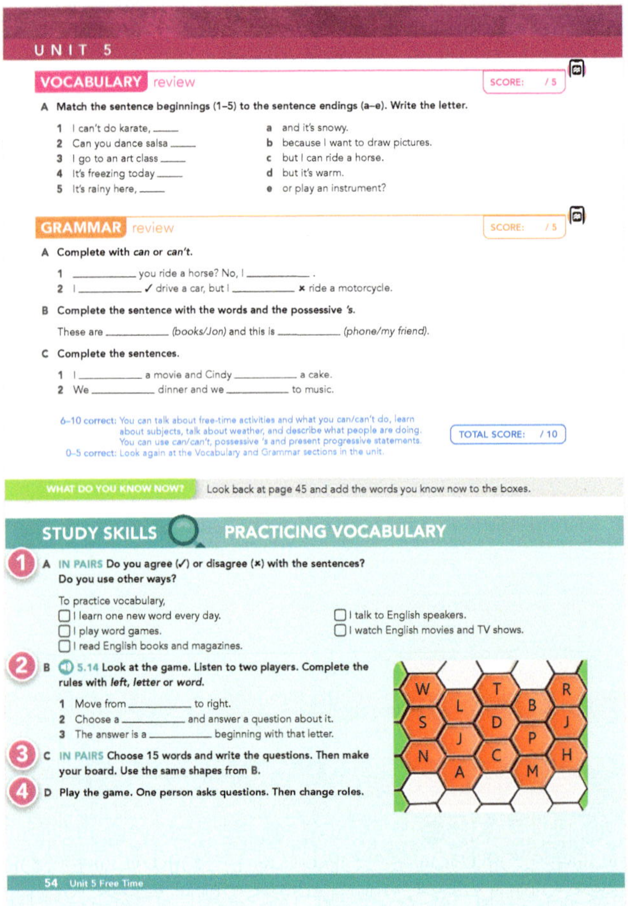

UNIT 5

VOCABULARY review SCORE: / 5

A Match the sentence beginnings (1–5) to the sentence endings (a–e). Write the letter.

1 I can't do karate, ____
2 Can you dance salsa ____
3 I go to an art class ____
4 It's freezing today ____
5 It's rainy here, ____

a and it's snowy.
b because I want to draw pictures.
c but I can ride a horse.
d but it's warm.
e or play an instrument?

GRAMMAR review SCORE: / 5

A Complete with *can* or *can't*.

1 ________ you ride a horse? No, I ________ .
2 I ________ ✓ drive a car, but I ________ ✗ ride a motorcycle.

B Complete the sentence with the words and the possessive *'s*.

These are ________ *(books/Jon)* and this is ________ *(phone/my friend)*.

C Complete the sentences.

1 I ________ a movie and Cindy ________ a cake.
2 We ________ dinner and we ________ to music.

6–10 correct: You can talk about free-time activities and what you can/can't do, learn about subjects, talk about weather, and describe what people are doing. You can use *can/can't*, possessive 's and present progressive statements.
0–5 correct: Look again at the Vocabulary and Grammar sections in the unit.

TOTAL SCORE: / 10

WHAT DO YOU KNOW NOW? Look back at page 45 and add the words you know now to the boxes.

STUDY SKILLS PRACTICING VOCABULARY

1 A IN PAIRS Do you agree (✓) or disagree (✗) with the sentences? Do you use other ways?

To practice vocabulary,
☐ I learn one new word every day.
☐ I play word games.
☐ I read English books and magazines.
☐ I talk to English speakers.
☐ I watch English movies and TV shows.

2 B 5.14 Look at the game. Listen to two players. Complete the rules with *left*, *letter* or *word*.

1 Move from ________ to right.
2 Choose a ________ and answer a question about it.
3 The answer is a ________ beginning with that letter.

3 C IN PAIRS Choose 15 words and write the questions. Then make your board. Use the same shapes from B.

4 D Play the game. One person asks questions. Then change roles.

54 Unit 5 Free Time

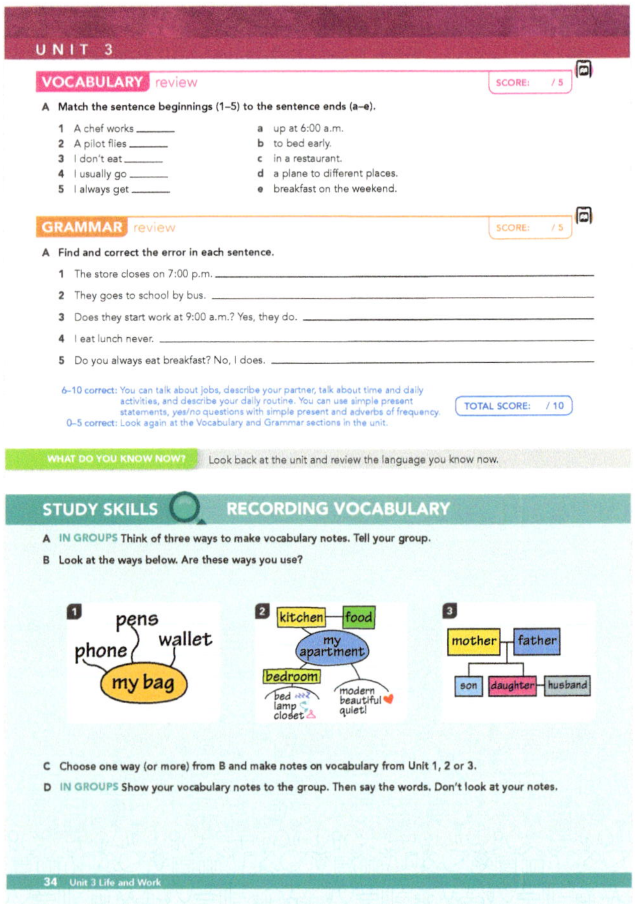

UNIT 3

VOCABULARY review SCORE: / 5

A Match the sentence beginnings (1–5) to the sentence ends (a–e).

1 A chef works ____
2 A pilot flies ____
3 I don't eat ____
4 I usually go ____
5 I always get ____

a up at 6:00 a.m.
b to bed early.
c in a restaurant.
d a plane to different places.
e breakfast on the weekend.

GRAMMAR review SCORE: / 5

A Find and correct the error in each sentence.

1 The store closes on 7:00 p.m. ________
2 They goes to school by bus. ________
3 Does they start work at 9:00 a.m.? Yes, they do. ________
4 I eat lunch never. ________
5 Do you always eat breakfast? No, I does. ________

6–10 correct: You can talk about jobs, describe your partner, talk about time and daily activities, and describe your daily routine. You can use simple present statements, *yes/no* questions with simple present and adverbs of frequency.
0–5 correct: Look again at the Vocabulary and Grammar sections in the unit.

TOTAL SCORE: / 10

WHAT DO YOU KNOW NOW? Look back at the unit and review the language you know now.

STUDY SKILLS RECORDING VOCABULARY

A IN GROUPS Think of three ways to make vocabulary notes. Tell your group.

B Look at the ways below. Are these ways you use?

C Choose one way (or more) from B and make notes on vocabulary from Unit 1, 2 or 3.

D IN GROUPS Show your vocabulary notes to the group. Then say the words. Don't look at your notes.

34 Unit 3 Life and Work

Follow A Pro

Speak Your Mind has a strong emphasis on professional readiness, and in every other unit, a job is highlighted in a section called FOLLOW A PRO.

PROCEDURE: Teaching **Follow A Pro** in *Speak Your Mind*

① **Listen to a profession.** In the first activity, students answer basic questions about a specific profession or listen to or read a text about a person who does a particular job. The job and the topic of the text are related to an aspect of the topic of the unit.

② **Comprehension questions.** In the second activity, students listen to or read the text again and answer some comprehension questions. This helps students learn more about the job and also allows them to practice their reading and listening skills.

③ **Discuss the job.** The last activity is a set of discussion questions related to the job. Students can work in groups, and then the discussion can be opened to the whole class. Encourage all students to participate, and remind students that there are no right or wrong answers; it's an opportunity to express personal opinions. You may wish to focus on fluency for this activity and make fewer (or no) corrections of spoken language errors.

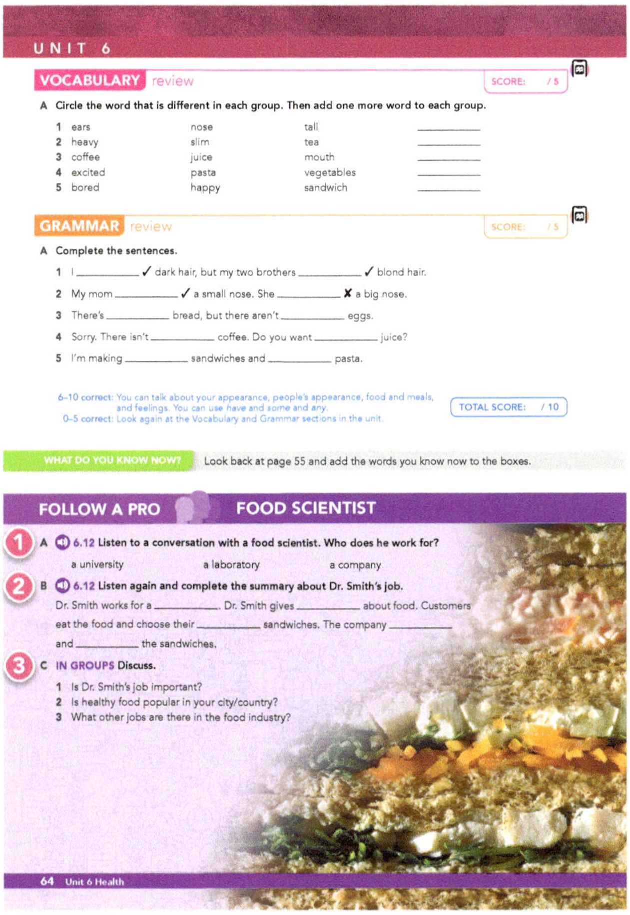
UNIT 6

VOCABULARY review SCORE: / 5

A Circle the word that is different in each group. Then add one more word to each group.

1	ears	nose	tall	______
2	heavy	slim	tea	______
3	coffee	juice	mouth	______
4	excited	pasta	vegetables	______
5	bored	happy	sandwich	______

GRAMMAR review SCORE: / 5

A Complete the sentences.

1 I ______ ✓ dark hair, but my two brothers ______ ✓ blond hair.
2 My mom ______ ✓ a small nose. She ______ ✗ a big nose.
3 There's ______ bread, but there aren't ______ eggs.
4 Sorry. There isn't ______ coffee. Do you want ______ juice?
5 I'm making ______ sandwiches and ______ pasta.

6–10 correct: You can talk about your appearance, people's appearance, food and meals, and feelings. You can use *have* and *some* and *any*.
0–5 correct: Look again at the Vocabulary and Grammar sections in the unit.

TOTAL SCORE: / 10

WHAT DO YOU KNOW NOW? Look back at page 55 and add the words you know now to the boxes.

FOLLOW A PRO FOOD SCIENTIST

① A 6.12 Listen to a conversation with a food scientist. Who does he work for?

a university a laboratory a company

② B 6.12 Listen again and complete the summary about Dr. Smith's job.

Dr. Smith works for a ______. Dr. Smith gives ______ about food. Customers eat the food and choose their ______ sandwiches. The company ______ and ______ the sandwiches.

③ C IN GROUPS Discuss.

1 Is Dr. Smith's job important?
2 Is healthy food popular in your city/country?
3 What other jobs are there in the food industry?

64 Unit 6 Health

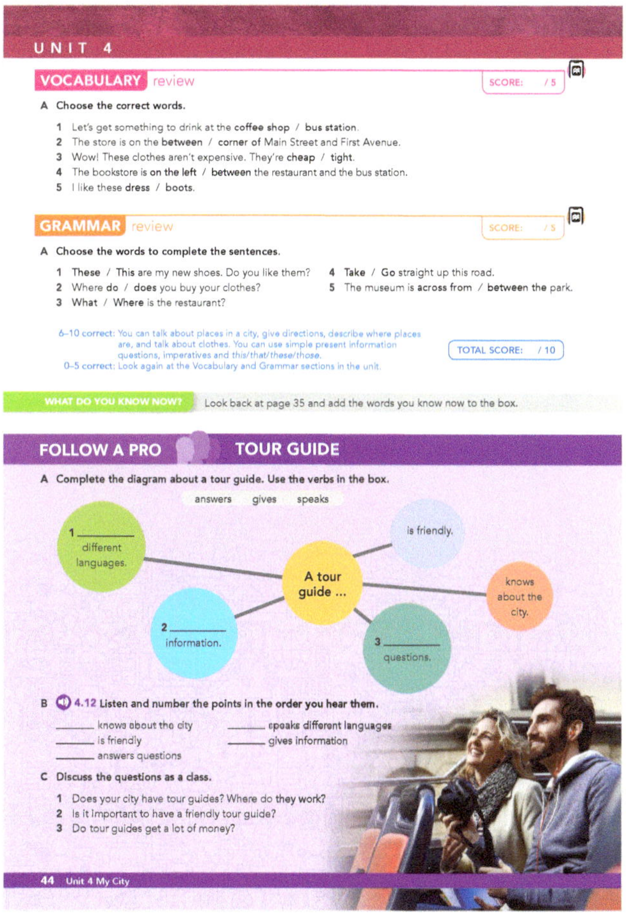
UNIT 4

VOCABULARY review SCORE: / 5

A Choose the correct words.

1 Let's get something to drink at the **coffee shop** / **bus station**.
2 The store is on the **between** / **corner of** Main Street and First Avenue.
3 Wow! These clothes aren't expensive. They're **cheap** / **tight**.
4 The bookstore is **on the left** / **between** the restaurant and the bus station.
5 I like these **dress** / **boots**.

GRAMMAR review SCORE: / 5

A Choose the words to complete the sentences.

1 **These** / **This** are my new shoes. Do you like them?
2 Where **do** / **does** you buy your clothes?
3 **What** / **Where** is the restaurant?
4 **Take** / **Go** straight up this road.
5 The museum is **across from** / **between the** park.

6–10 correct: You can talk about places in a city, give directions, describe where places are, and talk about clothes. You can use simple present information questions, imperatives and *this/that/these/those*.
0–5 correct: Look again at the Vocabulary and Grammar sections in the unit.

TOTAL SCORE: / 10

WHAT DO YOU KNOW NOW? Look back at page 35 and add the words you know now to the box.

FOLLOW A PRO TOUR GUIDE

A Complete the diagram about a tour guide. Use the verbs in the box.

answers gives speaks

A tour guide ...
1 ______ different languages.
2 ______ information.
3 ______ questions.
is friendly.
knows about the city.

B 4.12 Listen and number the points in the order you hear them.

______ knows about the city
______ is friendly
______ answers questions
______ speaks different languages
______ gives information

C Discuss the questions as a class.

1 Does your city have tour guides? Where do they work?
2 Is it important to have a friendly tour guide?
3 Do tour guides get a lot of money?

44 Unit 4 My City

Unit Opener Videos

The Discuss & Share section of the Unit Opener features an optional ***Speak Your Mind*** video. The video provides information and context for the discussion of the question. In each video, two vloggers answer the ***Speak Your Mind*** SYM **question**. One vlogger expresses one point of view, while the other one answers with the opposite point of view. The video ends with the vloggers posing the question to the students. The two opposing answers provide a model for the students' own responses. In most cases, the students' opinions will fall somewhere between the two opposing points of view. You should encourage students to state their opinion and explain where they are on the continuum of the two opposite points of view.

PROCEDURE: Using the **Unit Opener Videos** in *Speak Your Mind*

1. ***Speak Your Mind*** **question.** Make sure students understand the two points of view. You may want to draw a line with the opposing views at either end to show the continuum.

   numbers ____________ words

2. **Before viewing.** The teacher's page provides a question or questions to ask students before they watch the video. Use the question(s) to focus the students' attention on the differing points of view.
3. **Mark the continuum.** After viewing the video, have students mark where they are on the continuum by placing an X on the line between the points of view. Alternatively, ask students to form a line in the classroom, placing themselves between the two ends of the line, according to their opinion.
4. **Discuss & Share.** Ask students to explain why they have placed themselves at their selected point on the continuum. Encourage them to use the words they wrote in the What Do You Already Know? word list.

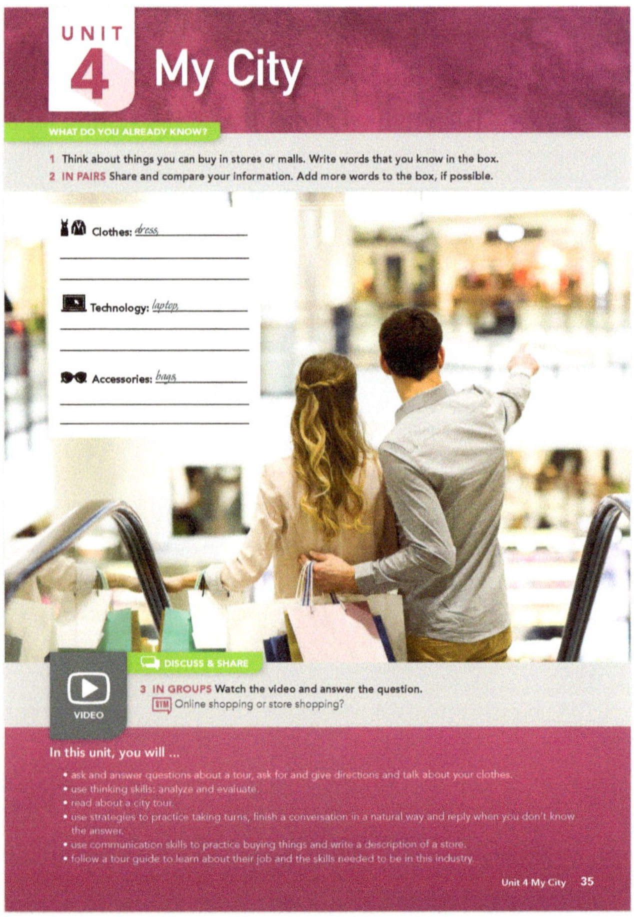

Grammar Reference

At the back of the ***Speak Your Mind* Student's Book**, there is an extensive reference section. The section starts with a page containing a list of common irregular verbs, as well as a pronunciation guide with phonetic symbols and words that represent the different spellings of each sound.

There are 10 pages of *Grammar Reference* material. For each unit, there are explanations, tables, and exercises for the three grammar points taught in the unit. Note that the *Reference* section is in the **Student's Book** only, but the *Answer Key* for the practice exercises in this section is at the back of this **Teacher's Edition**.

(1) Grammar points are labeled clearly with a heading.

(2) The function of the grammar point is explained.

(3) The form of the grammar is shown in a table. The tables in the *Reference* section are different from those in the units, and they are usually expanded to give more examples of the grammar point.

(4) The explanations are followed by written exercises to give students further practice with the grammar point.

(5) Apart from the grammar tables, there are additional notes about the form of the grammar when necessary.

The *Grammar Reference* material can be used in several ways:

- When a new grammar point is introduced in a unit, you may want to refer students to the relevant section in the *Grammar Reference* and go over the explanations of form and function with them, pointing out the examples in the table. You could do this before or after doing the grammar presentation in the unit.
- You may want to do the grammar practice exercise in the unit in class and assign the exercises in the *Grammar Reference* section for homework, along with or instead of the exercises in the **Workbook**.
- The *Grammar Reference* exercises can be used for review before an exam.

Grammar Reference

(1) **UNIT 4 — *this/that/these/those***

(2) Function

We use *this* and *these* to talk about objects that are very near to you. Use *that* and *those* to talk about objects that are not near to you.

(3) Form

(5)

	This/that	Singular Noun
I like	this	jacket.
	that	T-shirt.

	These/those	Plural Noun
Do you like	these	boots?
	those	pants?

A Choose the correct word to complete the sentences.

1 This / These pants are very tight.
2 Look at that / those store across the street!
3 Do you like this / these shirt?
4 Are that / those boots new? They're nice!

B Circle the error. Write the correct word: *this, that, these* or *those*.

(4)
1 I don't like these bag by the window. ___________
2 Look at that red jeans over there! ___________
3 What color are this shoes? Blue or black? ___________
4 Those skirt is beautiful! I want it! ___________

UNIT 5 — *can/can't*

Function

We use *can/can't* to talk about activities that people are and aren't able to do.

Form

Questions			
Can	**Pronoun**	**Infinitive**	
Can	I/you/he/she/it/we/they	play	the piano?

Statements		
Pronoun	***Can/can't***	**Infinitive**
I/You/He/She/It/We/They	can	play football.
	can't	draw.

Short Answers		
Yes/no	**Pronoun**	***Can/can't***
Yes,	I/you/he/she/it/we/they	can.
No,		can't.

Use an apostrophe (') to make the contracted form, e.g., *cannot* = *can't*.

A Complete the statements with *can* or *can't*.

1 I can't speak French, but I ___________ speak Spanish.
2 Liz can ride a horse, but she ___________ ride a motorcycle.
3 They can draw animals, but they ___________ play the piano.
4 He can swim and he ___________ do karate.

B Complete the answers for the *Can* questions.

1 Can they dance salsa? Yes, ___________ .
2 Can Sara bake a cake? No, ___________
3 Can your brother ride a motorcycle? No, ___________ .
4 Can she speak two languages? Yes, ___________ .

76 Grammar Reference

UNIT 5 — possessive *'s*

Function

We use possessive *'s* to say that something belongs to a person.

Form

Name	's	Noun	
Jon	's	motorcycle	is very big.
Andy		books	are on the desk.

Singular Noun	's	Noun	
The teacher	's	jacket	is blue.

Name + 's + Noun
Jon's motorcycle is very big. Andy's books are on the desk.

Singular Noun + 's + Noun
The teacher's jacket is blue.

A Circle the examples of the possessive *'s* in the sentences.

1 Emily's books are in that bag.
2 My teacher's name is Pippa.
3 Jane's major is law.
4 Is that Roberto's laptop?

B Add the possessive *'s* to the sentences.

1 Is that Maria dictionary?
2 My sister bag is on the desk.
3 The teacher classes are interesting.
4 Where is Paola laptop?

UNIT 5 — present progressive statements

Function

We use the present progressive to talk about an activity that is happening now.

Form

Statements		
Pronoun	***To be* (+/-)**	**+ *-ing* (Regular Verbs)**
I	am ('m)	reading a book. watching a movie. eating.
	am ('m) not	
He/She/It	is ('s)	
	is not (isn't)	
You/We/They	are	
	are not (aren't)	

Pronoun	***To be* (+/-)**	**+ *-ing* (Irregular Verbs)**	
		One Vowel and Final Consonant	**Verbs with a Final e**
I	am ('m) am ('m) not	getting coffee. swimming. shopping.	having fun. practicing English. writing.
He/She/It	is ('s) is not (isn't)		
You/ We/They	are are not (aren't)		

Spelling rules for irregular verbs:

- end of verb is consonant, vowel, consonant: double final consonant and add *-ing*
- final *-e*: delete final *-e* and add *-ing*

Grammar Reference 77

The following features are accessible via the ***Speak Your Mind*** Resource Centers.

Student's Resource Center

- **Reading Worksheets**
- **Student's Book** and **Workbook** audio files
- **Student's Book** videos
- **Word Lists**

Teacher's Resource Center

- **Reading Worksheets**
- ***OneStopEnglish*** **Worksheets**
- **Student's Book** and **Workbook** audio files
- **Student's Book** videos
- **Printable Ready-to-Go Tests**
- **CEFR Correlations**
- **Word Lists**

Reading Worksheets

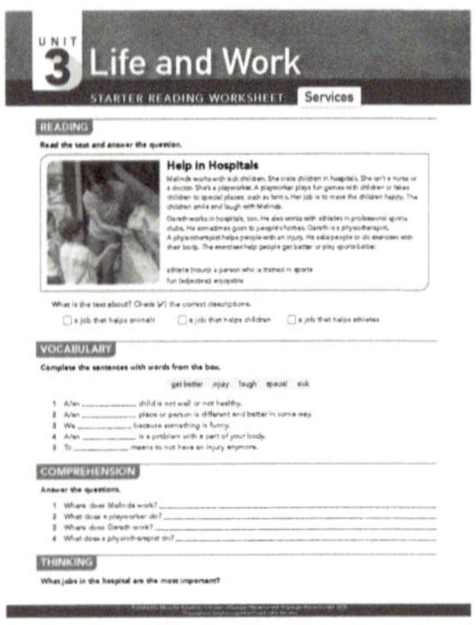

Each unit of ***Speak Your Mind*** has three extensive **Reading Worksheets**, for a total of 36. The topics of the worksheets extend the themes and vocabulary sets of the units in the areas of General English, Business, Science, and Services. They are designed to appeal to students who are studying academic subjects and young adults who are already working in their careers.

The **Reading Worksheets** have a text with a VOCABULARY activity and COMPREHENSION questions. A THINKING question at the end of the worksheet can be used as a departure for discussion in the classroom or a writing assignment for homework.

OneStopEnglish Worksheets

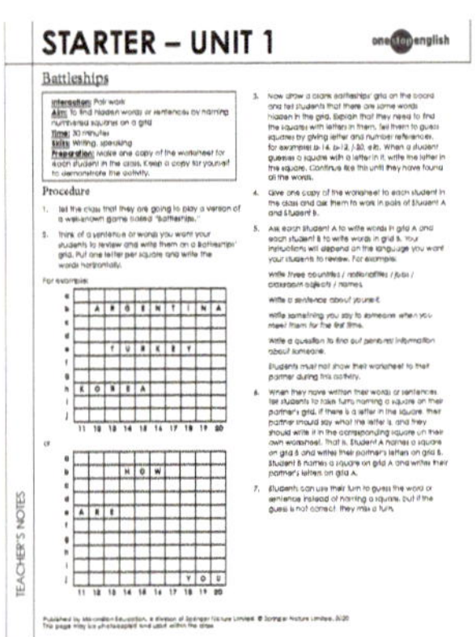

The ***OneStopEnglish*** **Worksheets** give students further speaking practice in a fun and engaging way. Speak Your Mind has chosen select worksheets from the OneStopEnglish website, the world's number one teacher resource site for English Language teachers. The ***OneStopEnglish*** **Worksheets** have been adapted for the course, with one worksheet for each unit. The worksheets consist of one page of teacher's notes, which includes the aim, procedure, and estimated activity time, and one page with the student's activity.

Printable Ready-to-Go Tests

All the tests for ***Speak Your Mind*** can be found in the **Teacher's Resource Center**. This includes a Placement Test, Unit Tests, a Mid-Course Test, and an End-of-Course Test. All tests are available as ready-to-print PDFs. Tests can be customized using the **Test Generator** (see the **How to Use the Digital Components** section, page xxvii).

- The Placement Test places students in a ***Speak Your Mind*** level.
- The Unit Tests include vocabulary, grammar, listening, reading, writing, and speaking items for each unit.
- The Mid-Course Test include vocabulary, grammar, listening, reading, writing, and speaking items for units 1–6.
- The End-of-Course Test includes vocabulary, grammar, listening, reading, writing, and speaking items for units 7–12.

CEFR Correlations

The Common European Framework of Reference for Languages (CEFR) is an international standard that aims

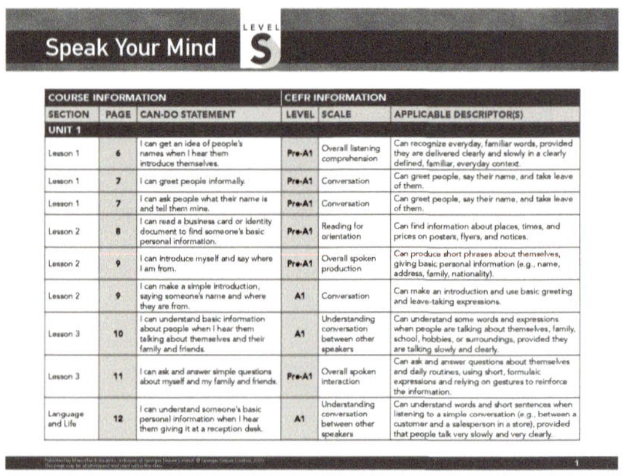

Speak Your Mind LEVEL S

COURSE INFORMATION			CEFR INFORMATION		
SECTION	PAGE	CAN-DO STATEMENT	LEVEL	SCALE	APPLICABLE DESCRIPTOR(S)
UNIT 1					
Lesson 1	6	I can get an idea of people's names when I hear them introduce themselves.	Pre-A1	Overall listening comprehension	Can recognize everyday, familiar words, provided they are delivered clearly and slowly in a clearly defined, familiar, everyday context.
Lesson 1	7	I can greet people informally.	Pre-A1	Conversation	Can greet people, say their name, and take leave of them.
Lesson 1	7	I can ask people what their name is and tell them mine.	Pre-A1	Conversation	Can greet people, say their name, and take leave of them.
Lesson 2	8	I can read a business card or identity document to find someone's basic personal information.	Pre-A1	Reading for orientation	Can find information about places, times, and prices on posters, flyers, and notices.
Lesson 2	9	I can introduce myself and say where I am from.	Pre-A1	Overall spoken production	Can produce short phrases about themselves, giving basic personal information (e.g., name, address, family, nationality).
Lesson 2	9	I can make a simple introduction, saying someone's name and where they are from.	A1	Conversation	Can make an introduction and use basic greeting and leave-taking expressions.
Lesson 3	10	I can understand basic information about people when I hear them talking about themselves and their family and friends.	A1	Understanding conversation between other speakers	Can understand some words and expressions when people are talking about themselves, family, school, hobbies, or surroundings, provided they are talking slowly and clearly.
Lesson 3	11	I can ask and answer simple questions about myself and my family and friends.	Pre-A1	Overall spoken interaction	Can ask and answer questions about themselves and daily routines, using short, formulaic expressions and relying on gestures to reinforce the information.
Language and Life	12	I can understand someone's basic personal information when I hear them giving it at a reception desk.	A1	Understanding conversation between other speakers	Can understand words and short sentences when listening to a simple conversation (e.g., between a customer and a salesperson in a store), provided that people talk very slowly and very clearly.

1

to provide a transparent, coherent, and comprehensive means of describing language ability. It describes what language learners can do in different skills across six broad levels, from A1 to C2, and consists of a set of scales containing descriptors indicating what a learner can do in that context. The **CEFR Correlations** document is a map is organized unit by unit, which allows you to browse the course learning outcomes chronologically. These are mapped to the relevant CEFR descriptors, levels, and scales.

Word Lists

The **Word Lists** are a list of the main vocabulary that appears in ***Speak Your Mind***. These include words that appear in the **Student's Book** and **Student's App** VOCABULARY sections, as well as the glossaries of the **Student's Book** READING sections. The word lists include the word, part of speech, IPA pronunciation, definition, and frequency, as well as an example sentence using the word.

How to Use the Teacher's Edition

The up-to-date, innovative approach to the ***Speak Your Mind* Teacher's Edition** takes into account that teachers have very busy lives and want the class-planning process to be as streamlined as possible. The clear lesson design and the self-explanatory rubrics in the ***Speak Your Mind* Student's Book** make it unnecessary to include lengthy, step-by-step procedures in the **Teacher's Edition**.

The introductory pages of the **Teacher's Edition** are designed to provide general explanations and instructions that are needed in order to teach each section of the units in ***Speak Your Mind***. There are detailed notes on the procedures for teaching each section, as well as explanations of the special features in the units. There are also tips and suggestions for how to get the most from the material. The introductory pages also include information on how to use the **Workbook**, the **Videos**, and the **Digital** material included in the ***Speak Your Mind*** series.

The core pages of the **Teacher's Edition** have reduced **Student's Book** pages with notes that are specific to each lesson. These notes include relevant background information for texts, tips for dealing with specific language issues, common errors to watch out for, cultural information, classroom management ideas, and suggestions for extra or alternative activities. Short answers to exercises are on the reduced **Student's Book** pages, and longer answers are in the margin next to the **Student's Book** pages. The *Answer Key* for the *Grammar Reference* exercises and the *Audio Scripts* for the listening activities in the **Student's Book** and the **Workbook** are at the back of this book.

① ***GO TO.*** Teachers can read the introductory information once for guidelines on how to teach these sections throughout the book. *GO TO* pointers help teachers find the procedure pages they need quickly.

② **Answer Key.** The core pages have the detailed information a teacher needs to teach specific activities. The **Teacher's Edition** has reduced **Student's Book** pages with answers in place or in the margin next to the Student's Book pages.

③ **Specific notes.** Notes below the **Student's Book** reduced page include relevant background information for texts, tips for dealing with specific language issues, common errors to watch out for, cultural information, classroom management ideas, and suggestions for extra or alternative activities.

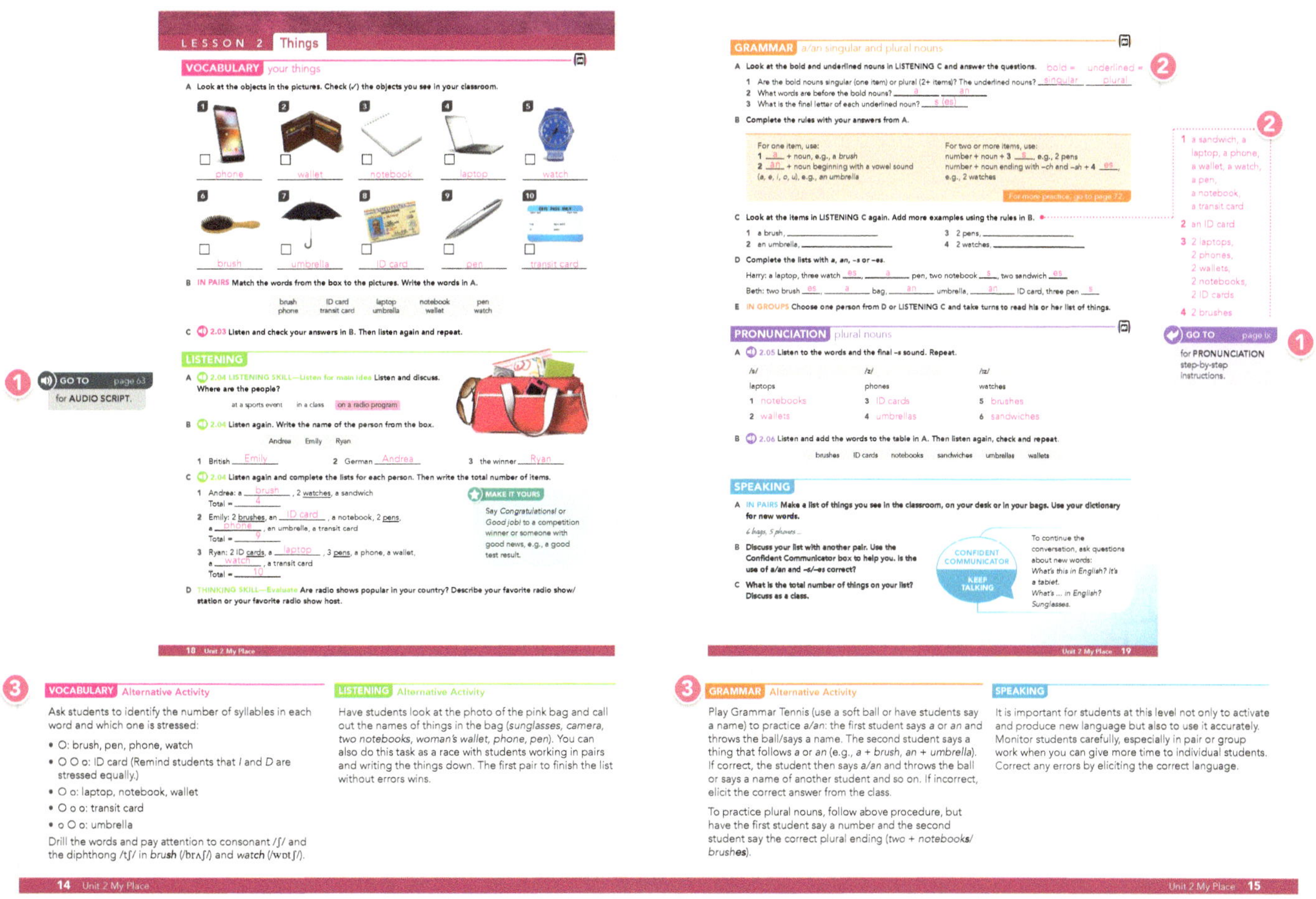

How to Use the Workbook

The ***Speak Your Mind* Workbook** is designed to give students further practice in grammar and vocabulary, as well as the listening, reading, and writing skills taught in the **Student's Book**. The **Workbook** is available in both print and digital form. The digital **Workbook** can be accessed through the **Teacher's** and **Student's Resource Centers**.

The **Workbook** exercises can be used in several different ways:

- As homework or further classroom practice after teaching a section in the **Student's Book.**
- As a review of a whole lesson after finishing the lesson.
- As a review session before a unit exam.

① Skills boxes give explanations of the reading and listening skills taught in the **Student's Book**. You may want to refer students to the explanation in the **Workbook** before asking them to do the skill activity in the **Student's Book**. Following the skill box, there is an exercise to practice the skill.

② There is often a second reading comprehension exercise.

③ There is additional practice of the target vocabulary of the lesson.

④ The grammar of the lesson is practiced in a variety of ways.

⑤ In the WRITING section, there is practice in the mechanics of writing.

⑥ Students also get practice in editing their writing.

Progress Check. Located at the end of the **Workbook**. Students check the areas they feel competent in. If they feel that they need to review a particular point, they are directed to the relevant section in the **Student's Book**.

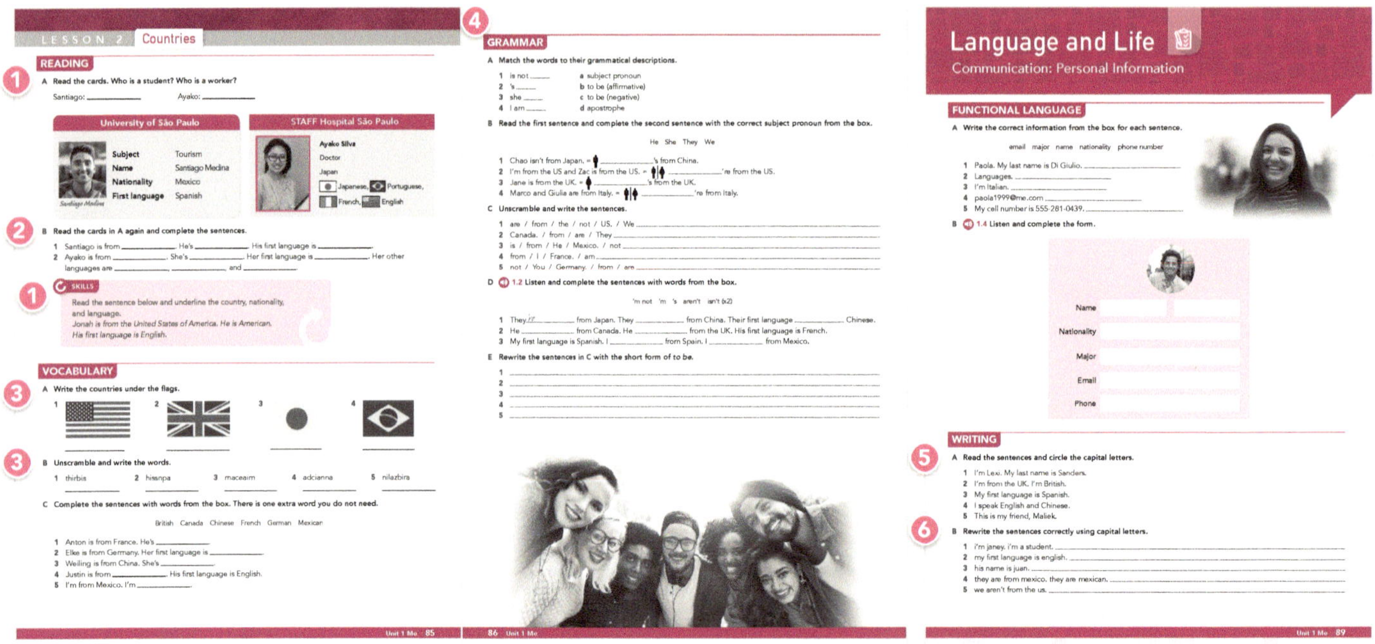

Teacher's App

The ***Speak Your Mind* Teacher's Edition** comes with an innovative **Teacher's App**, which gives access to the **Classroom Presentation Kit**, **Homework Manager**, **Progress Tracker**, **Test Generator**, and **Teacher's Resource Center**.

Classroom Presentation Kit

The **Classroom Presentation Kit** is a page-faithful view of the **Student's Book** and **Workbook**. It is designed to be displayed on an interactive whiteboard (IWB) or using a projector. It is user-friendly for teachers and students, with activities clearly visible for the whole class.

The **Classroom Presentation Kit** allows teachers to play the audio tracks, show the course videos, and present the interactive versions of the book activities from the page. Teachers can zoom in on each activity with one click, then move smoothly through the activities or zoom out to see the whole page. Answer reveal enables teachers to elicit students' responses and check answers one by one or all together.

Embedded tools make it possible to highlight and annotate texts to prompt noticing or self-correction. Teachers also have the option to show scripts when listening to audio or watching video for easy clarification. There is also the option to create a whiteboard area for additional notes.

Homework Manager

Using the practice activities available in the **Student's App**, teachers can assign homework by selecting and publishing content directly to their students' devices. Students will then be alerted by a push notification telling them they have activities to complete. This enables teachers to personalize the amount and kind of practice students have each week and to track their progress using the **Progress Tracker**.

Progress Tracker

The **Progress Tracker** gives teachers an overview of students' progress, allowing teachers to monitor scores and see at a glance that students are performing well or that they may need additional support. Student data is presented in a way that is clear and easy to understand.

Test Generator

Ready-to-Go print tests are available in the **Teacher's Resource Center** for teachers who want to give a test on every skill. If you prefer to customize tests for your students, you can do so through the **Test Generator** in the **Teacher's App**. The **Test Generator** allows you to create tests by selecting only the activities you want from a menu. You can save and print out the tests from the **Test Generator**. You may also use a randomized function to create different tests for the same unit.

Student's App

Each **Student's Book** includes a code for the **Student's App**, which gives access to new **On-the-Go Practice** activities, **Progress Tracker**, **eBook**, **Digital Workbook**, and the **Student's Resource Center**.

On-the-Go Practice

Through the **Student's App**, students will have access to new grammar, vocabulary, and pronunciation activities that have been mapped to the course scope and sequence. These bite-sized activities have been specifically designed for use on smartphones. They include game-like elements to encourage repetition and deeper retention of key language. Questions are shown in random order to increase interest and ensure a thorough understanding of each language point. Students are able to complete activities in a standard practice mode or in a more difficult challenge mode, where they can earn medals based on their performance.

Each **Student's App** unit also contains a new speaking activity that recycles the Unit Opener video, providing an opportunity to review the Unit Opener topic and the language encountered throughout the unit. These activities have been designed to increase students' confidence as they see how their language competence has developed over the course of each unit, while reinforcing what they have learned.

Progress Tracker

The **Student's App** gives a clear overview of students' progress, clearly highlighting areas of strength and areas for improvement. Students have the opportunity to review their weakest activities and repeat them to improve their scores.

eBook

The **eBook** is a digital version of the **Student's Book** with embedded audio and video files, so students can access the book and its media on their desktop, in their classroom, or at home.

Digital Workbook

The **Digital Workbook** is a new, digital version of the students' **Workbook** designed to be accessible on students' devices. The **Digital Workbook** contains digital versions of the **Workbook** activities designed to work across mobile, tablet, and desktop to provide a rich interactive experience. The **Workbook** audio and video files can be accessed from the page so students have everything they need in one place. Built-in answer keys give instant feedback, while students' scores feed to the **Progress Tracker** for easy monitoring.

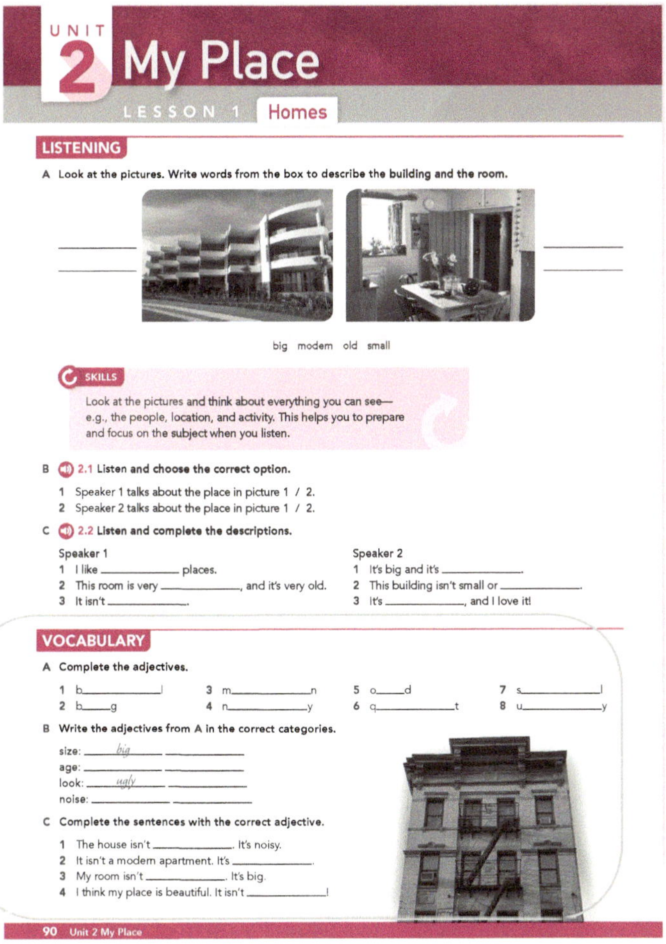
UNIT 2 My Place

LESSON 1 Homes

LISTENING

A Look at the pictures. Write words from the box to describe the building and the room.

big modern old small

SKILLS
Look at the pictures and think about everything you can see—e.g., the people, location, and activity. This helps you to prepare and focus on the subject when you listen.

B 2.1 Listen and choose the correct option.

1 Speaker 1 talks about the place in picture 1 / 2.
2 Speaker 2 talks about the place in picture 1 / 2.

C 2.2 Listen and complete the descriptions.

Speaker 1
1 I like ________ places.
2 This room is very ________, and it's very old.
3 It isn't ________.

Speaker 2
1 It's big and it's ________.
2 This building isn't small or ________.
3 It's ________, and I love it!

VOCABULARY

A Complete the adjectives.

1 b______l 3 m______n 5 o___d 7 s______l
2 b___g 4 n______y 6 q______t 8 u______y

B Write the adjectives from A in the correct categories.

size: ___big___ ________
age: ________ ________
look: ___ugly___ ________
noise: ________ ________

C Complete the sentences with the correct adjective.

1 The house isn't ________. It's noisy.
2 It isn't a modern apartment. It's ________.
3 My room isn't ________. It's big.
4 I think my place is beautiful. It isn't ________!

90 Unit 2 My Place

What is Functional Language?

Tony Prince
Academic Director - NILE - Norwich Institute for Language Education

NILE
PART OF THE INTO GROUP

When we communicate, it is for a purpose. Every time we use language, it is to achieve a particular goal.

We can give these purposes simple descriptive names, such as "introductions and greetings."

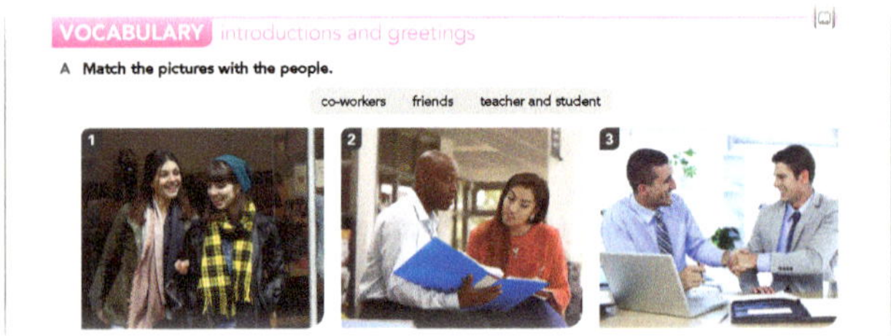

Or we might refer to these functions by more abstract terms, such as "to repair a conversation."

CONFIDENT COMMUNICATOR
REPAIR IT

To repair your conversation after a mistake, say *Excuse me / Sorry.*
He's from Mexico. ***Excuse me.***
She's from Mexico.

There are different areas of functional language because we have many different objectives that we want to achieve when we communicate. In addition, within each area, there are a wide variety of ways in which we can say the same thing, achieving the same purpose. This all provides the teacher with a breadth and depth of resources with which to help the students communicate.

Functional language makes use of fixed expressions or chunks of language.

Introductions and greetings
Good morning. I'm ________. Hi, ________. How are you? I'm fine, thank you. And you?
Repairing a conversation
Can you say that again? Can you repeat that again?

As you can see from these examples, the expressions are often relatively simple, in terms of both the grammar and the vocabulary they use. Frequently, the way in which we can vary an expression is simply by substituting one or two words.

Can you say that ...	again? one more time? once more?
Can you ...	repeat that? go over that again?

This makes it very easy for the teacher to teach and for the learner to learn.

Most importantly, it means that the learner can begin communicating very quickly and can do so in a variety of ways.

Functional language can also be connected together into longer sequences to express multiple purposes.

Apology
I'm sorry.
Excuse me.
Repair
Can you say that again?
Can you repeat that?
Explanation
I didn't hear you.
I don't understand.

In this way, knowing a relatively small number of phrases can take the students a long way in terms of communication. This also allows teachers to extend activities, asking students to add detail to their communication by connecting functions. This can be very useful in teaching mixed-ability or mixed-motivation classes. The teacher can require or encourage those students with more ability or motivation to use more functional language to achieve a variety of communicative purposes. We'll look at this in more detail in the last section of this article, dealing with approaches to teaching functional language.

As you'll have seen from these illustrations, ***Speak Your Mind*** includes a focus on functional language right from the lowest levels of language learning and use. It presents the students and the teacher with expressions that can be used for particular communicative purposes and with activities to help the students.

Why is it Important?

Simplicity and Speed

Most people learning a language do so in order to communicate with others. They want to be able to interact, but most of all, they want to be able to do things: to achieve a goal. Frequently, a major problem with teaching language learners at the lower levels is that they feel there is so much grammar and vocabulary to learn that they lose sight of the purpose of learning. They either feel that they can't communicate or that communication takes too much time and effort.

As we've seen in the first section, functional language is relatively simple to learn and therefore quick to use. This can help learners see that they are achieving something even relatively early in their course.

How are you doing?

Pretty good.

Hi. How are you?

I'm really good, and you?

Real-Life Relevance

Much of functional language is simple because it is so common. Once you have learned a phrase such as "I'm fine, thanks. And you?", you hear it everywhere. So common is functional language that some people pick it up simply by being immersed in the language. They notice that certain phrases are used in certain contexts and understand their purpose.

This is important to students because they want to be able to "function" in real situations. They want to learn language that is "real" and "relevant." The fact that functional language is so common and is used so frequently gives it a lot of validity in the eyes (and ears) of the students. They can hear it being used by native speakers. If they use it, they will be understood.

Finally, much of functional language has a very fundamental purpose. It's the kind of language that we need and that we use in order to survive: to get very basic things done. As such, it's language that students will see and have an immediate use for. We can see an example of this in Unit 2 on the topic of things.

CONFIDENT COMMUNICATOR
KEEP TALKING

To continue the conversation, ask questions about new words:
What's this in English? It's a tablet.
What's ... in English? Sunglasses.

Personalization

In their own language, people have individual ways of saying things. Sometimes this is because they like certain phrases. Other times it is because they want to identify with a certain group or to show that they are definitely not part of that group. The group might be defined by age, by social or economic level, or by region. In this way, language allows people to claim and to shape their identity.

One of the powerful things about functional language is the simple variety that it contains. As seen in the table previously, it is relatively easy to generate different forms of the same functional expression simply by substituting words or chunks of language. In this way, students can choose from a variety of phrases or options, deciding which they like the sound of and which fits them best.

CONFIDENT COMMUNICATOR
START TALKING

To join a conversation, use the following phrases:
Excuse me, can I join you?
Hi there, can I join you?

Contextual Relevance

While people may want to speak in a way that feels true to them, there are contexts and situations in which it is necessary to modify the way in which we speak. Again, functional language can be useful in this regard. As we've seen, there are a variety of ways of saying the same thing and of reaching the same communicative goal. But some of these variations are more suitable in certain contexts. For instance, there are some ways of greeting people or of introducing yourself that are more formal.

Hi, ________. I'm ________.

Pleased to meet you. My name is ________.

How do you do? I don't think we've met. I'm________.

Let me introduce myself: I'm ________.

Providing students with a range of expressions that they can use in a variety of contexts can be a very powerful tool to help them communicate and to feel confident in doing so. Functional language makes the phrases simple and similar enough that they are relatively simple to learn and quick to use.

What Approaches Can You Take to Teaching it?

A General Approach

In general, functional language is something that is "used" more than it is taught. As we've seen in the examples of activities from the **Student's Book**, the language that students are presented with is sometimes only a few words long. Often these words are ones that students will have encountered in general, such as using "OK?" to check comprehension or "How are you?" to greet someone. In general, then, teaching of "functional language" largely consists of presenting students with the phrases and with a context or task in which to use them.

The following methods of presenting language are listed from the least to most time-consuming for the teacher and student:

- Giving students lists of alternative language for achieving the same purpose and letting them choose the expressions they like.
- Providing language within the contexts of conversations and highlighting the phrases.
- Creating a "resource bank" for language in categories (e.g. 'greetings', 'repair') that students can consult and use.
- Creating recordings of semi-authentic dialogues to highlight use of expressions in conversation.
- Curating recordings of authentic dialogues to let students identify examples of functional language.

The focus of functional language, then, is in how students use it. The following sections provide a description of different approaches that can be taken for this.

A Task-Based Approach

Because functional language is based on communicative purposes, it lends itself very easily and clearly to a task-based approach. You'll see from the **Student's Book** that many of the units take this approach in the Confident Communicator box. But you'll also notice that the goal of this type of task is not simply to get the students to do a certain thing (e.g., to introduce themselves) but to achieve a certain kind of function. For example:

CONFIDENT COMMUNICATOR
KEEP TALKING

To check you understand, use *Right?* after a statement.
The bed is next to the door. Right?
No, the bed is next to the window.

Here, the student is being asked to include a simple comprehension check with a description. This is a very simple, yet powerful communication tool. Once students are aware of this function and have practiced it, we can use it in a variety of tasks:

- Checking details about another person (e.g., family members, where they live, hobbies).
- Checking vocabulary or grammar comprehension (e.g., words for classroom objects, grammar forms).
- Checking answers to another task (e.g., a reading or listening task; "You put A for question 1, right?").

We can also extend the language they use to check comprehension:

Degree of Certainty
I'm pretty certain that …
I'm fairly sure that …
I don't know if …
I'm unsure if …
I really don't know if …
Description
the English word for ______ is______…
Check
right?
OK?

In this way, we can introduce new concepts by connecting them to familiar ones, and we can build complex concepts on top of simple ones.

Task-Based Learning

We can also build the task-based approach into one that more closely resembles task-based learning. One form of this has four main stages:

Introductory Stage

Students are given a task to complete:

- This may be open-ended (e.g., you describe five objects found in the classroom to a partner so they can guess what they are).
- This may be project based (e.g., you describe a place you would like to visit to convince another person to join you).
- This may be a role-play (e.g., you are a travel agent wanting to sell a vacation to a customer).
- This may be a case study (e.g., your company has decided to relocate their headquarters; from the descriptions of different locations and the criteria given, decide as a group on which would be best).

Activity Stage and Reflection Stage

Students do the task they have been given, reflecting on what went well, what didn't and what they would change.

Feedback and Follow-Up Stage

This may take a number of forms:

- The teacher may offer feedback on the language that was used by different groups, creating a collective resource bank.
- Students may collectively discuss language they might have used to achieve the communicative goal better.
- The teacher may present a prepared version of the activity, highlighting the language used.

Redoing the Task and Reflecting Stage

The students redo the task, incorporating the language they have identified as useful to the task.

The general intention of this approach is that the language is not imposed on the students but emerges from their need for it. This fits in with the overall ethos of functional language, in that it is "purpose driven"—we are using it because we want to achieve a particular purpose.

Discovery Approach

As we've discussed, functional language is very common in everyday communication. As such, it lends itself very readily to a discovery-based approach where the students are encouraged to "find" or check functional language for themselves. This kind of activity can be particularly useful for students who have already been introduced to the basic phrases and want to find more or for students who are trying to develop their fluency and need exposure to a wide range of language.

If you have access to the internet, then this discovery approach can make use of the wide range of spoken resources available. For instance, websites such as TED (TED.com) not only contain talks on interesting topics, by experts in their field, but also have transcripts of those talks that students can search. The transcripts on TED are also interactive, which means that once you have identified the language you want to find, clicking on it will let you hear that section of the talk.

You can use this method to have students confirm for themselves how often people use different kinds of functional language (e.g., a simple comprehension check such as "Right?" or "OK?"). Alternatively, you can have them use the text to check for collocations (e.g., what words are used together with sure or know to indicate level of certainty).

If you are teaching in a situation where there is little access to speakers of English or the internet, then discovery methods are still possible. One example of this is to simply ask the students to consider what functional phrases they use in their own language (e.g., how do they make requests, offers and suggestions; how do they give advice, say no politely and agree or disagree). They can then be asked to think about how they would translate these into English. This can result in a lot of discussion about cultural differences when compared to the kinds of functional language that English-speaking people would use.

In Closing

Functional language can bring many advantages for the teacher and the student.

For the student:

- It is very easy to learn and can be used very quickly.
- It is relevant to real-life situations and communicative purposes.
- The range of language alternatives lets students personalize their use.
- The range of language alternatives lets students adjust their language for the context (e.g., where more formality is required).

For the teacher:

- Less time is required for presentation and explanation, allowing more time for practice and use.
- Students are motivated by the ease of use and the relevance to real life.
- The range of language alternatives lets teachers vary requirements for multilevel classes.
- The range of language alternatives lets teachers extend and adapt tasks to increase use.

Scope and Sequence

	Outcomes	Vocabulary	Grammar	Speaking
Unit 1 Me pp. 5–13	• Introduce yourself • Talk about your nationality and language • Share information about your family	• Introductions and greetings • Countries and nationalities • Family	• *be* statements • Subject pronouns and *be* statements • *yes/no* questions with *be* Grammar Reference pp. 70–71	• Make introductions • Give personal information • Ask questions about a partner's family
	Language and Life—Communication: Personal Information			
Unit 2 My Place pp. 15–23	• Introduce your partner • Talk about classroom objects • Talk about where things are in a room	• Describing places • Your things • Prepositions of place 1	• *be* information questions • *a/an* singular and plural nouns • *There is / There are* Grammar Reference pp. 71–73	• Describe a person • Talk about your classroom • Describe a room
	Language and Life—Communication: Hotel Room			
Unit 3 Life and Work pp. 25–33	• Share information about people in your class • Ask and answer questions • Talk about how often you do things	• Jobs • Prepositions of time • Daily activities	• Simple present statements • *yes/no* questions with simple present • Adverbs of frequency Grammar Reference pp. 73–74	• Talk about a partner's life • Ask a partner *yes/no* questions • Discuss routines
	Language and Life—Communication: Meet Someone			
Unit 4 My City pp. 35–43	• Ask and answer questions about a tour • Ask for and give directions • Talk about your clothes	• Places in a city • Prepositions of place 2 • Clothes	• Simple present information questions • Imperatives • *this/that/these/those* Grammar Reference pp. 74–76	• Ask and answer questions about a tour • Ask for and give directions • Describe clothes
	Language and Life—Communication: Shop			
Unit 5 Free Time pp. 45–53	• Talk about what you can/can't do • Talk about objects in a classroom • Discuss the weather in different places	• Free-time activities • Subjects • Types of weather	• *can/can't* • Possessive *'s* • Present progressive statements Grammar Reference pp. 76–78	• Find out about free-time activities people in the class can/can't do • Talk about people's possessions • Tell a partner what you are doing / not doing
	Language and Life—Communication: Your City			
Unit 6 Health pp. 55–63	• Describe people's appearance • Talk about food and meals • Ask and answer a quiz	• The face and body • Food • Feelings	• *have* • *some* and *any* • Review Grammar Reference pp. 78–79	• Describe someone to a partner • Plan a meal with a partner • Complete a class quiz
	Language and Life—Communication: Cafe			

Confident Communicator	Pronunciation	Listening/Reading	Thinking Skills	Writing
Start Talking • Join a conversation *Repair It* • Correct yourself *Keep Talking* • Ask questions	• Word stress	Listen to a short conversation with an introduction • Skill—Listen for names Read a selection of ID cards • Skill—Locate information in a text Listen to a short conversation about a family • Skill—Understand key words	• Evaluate • Analyze	An introduction
Unit Review p. 14 **Study Skills**—Using a Dictionary				
Keep Talking • Give extra information *Keep Talking* • Ask questions *Keep Talking* • Check you understand	• Plural nouns	Listen to an interview • Skill—Use visuals to predict content Listen to a radio show • Skill—Listen for main idea Read a college webpage • Skill—Identify the topic	• Analyze • Evaluate • Brainstorm	A text message
Unit Review p. 24 **Follow A Pro**—Online Teacher				
Repair It • Ask questions *Keep Talking* • Check you understand *Keep Talking* • Useful phrases	• Word stress in questions	Read a magazine article about jobs • Skill—Scan for jobs Listen to a job interview • Skill—Listen for names, dates and numbers Read an online article about a hotel • Skill—Recognize different text types	• Evaluate • Analyze	A post
Unit Review p. 34 **Study Skills**—Recording Vocabulary				
Keep Talking • Take turns *Keep Talking* • Finish a conversation *Repair It* • Useful phrases	• Vowel sounds 1	Read an informative text • Skill—Locate information in a text Listen to a short conversation with directions • Skill—Understand key words Listen to people's shopping routines • Skill—Identify information	• Analyze • Evaluate	A description
Unit Review p. 44 **Follow A Pro**—Tour Guide				
Keep Talking • Explain your answer *Keep Talking* • Useful phrases *Keep Talking* • Show understanding	• Stress in *can/can't*	Listen to a college radio show • Skill—Listen for main idea Read a college webpage • Skill—Scan for key words Listen to a group video call • Skill—Listen for reasons	• Analyze • Recall • Brainstorm	A blog
Unit Review p. 54 **Study Skills**—Practicing Vocabulary				
Keep Talking • Think about your answer *Keep Talking* • Useful phrases *Keep Talking* • Ask follow-up questions	• Vowel sounds	Listen to two conversations describing people • Skill—Identify information Read two different types of text • Skill—Recognize different text types Listen to a radio interview • Skill—Identify information in an introduction	• Analyze • Evaluate • Predict	An online review
Unit Review p. 64 **Follow A Pro**—Food Scientist				

Useful Language

The alphabet

0.01 Listen to the letters of the alphabet.

A	B	C	D	E	F	G
H	I	J	K	L	M	N
O	P	Q	R	S	T	U
	V	W	X	Y	Z	

Numbers

0.02 Listen to the numbers 1–20.

1 one	8 eight	15 fifteen
2 two	9 nine	16 sixteen
3 three	10 ten	17 seventeen
4 four	11 eleven	18 eighteen
5 five	12 twelve	19 nineteen
6 six	13 thirteen	20 twenty
7 seven	14 fourteen	21 twenty-one

Months, dates, days

January | February | March | April | May | June
July | August | September | October
November | December

JANUARY

MONDAY	TUESDAY	WEDNESDAY	THURSDAY	FRIDAY	SATURDAY	SUNDAY
1	2	3	4	5	6	7
8	9	10	11	12	13	14
15	16	17	18	19	20	21
22	23	24	25	26	27	28
29	30	31				

January 1, 2020
March 5, 2020
August 22, 2020

Times

six o'clock

six-thirty

a.m.

p.m.

Prices

change

one dollar

five dollars

ten dollars

one hundred dollars

two hundred dollars

Colors

red

yellow

blue

green

orange

purple

black

white

UNIT 1 Me

GO TO page vi
for **UNIT OPENER** step-by-step instructions.

WHAT DO YOU ALREADY KNOW?

1 Think about letters and numbers. Complete the boxes.

2 **IN PAIRS** Share and compare your words. Add your partner's information to the boxes, if possible.

STUDENTS MAY ALREADY KNOW:

- numbers 1–10.
- the alphabet.
- how to say or spell their name.
- how to say a cell number and house number (or house name).

Your name: ____________

Your partner's name: ____________

Your cell number: ____________

Your partner's cell number: ____________

Your house number or name: ____________

Your partner's house number or name: ____________

DISCUSS & SHARE

VIDEO

3 **IN GROUPS** Watch the video and answer the question.

SYM Numbers or words?

GO TO page xx
for **VIDEOS IN SYM** step-by-step instructions.

In this unit, you will ...

- introduce yourself to your group, talk about your nationality and language and share information about your family.
- use thinking skills: evaluate and analyze.
- read a variety of ID cards for information.
- use strategies to start a conversation, use language to repair mistakes while talking and ask extra questions to continue a conversation.
- use communication skills to complete a form and write an introduction.
- learn skills to identify parts of a dictionary definition.

Unit 1 Me 5

WHAT DO YOU ALREADY KNOW?

If you notice students are struggling to understand what to do, you can provide one or two examples to help them get started:

- The alphabet
- Numbers 1–10
- *My name is …*
- *My cell number is …*

VIDEO

Before viewing, ask:

In our daily lifes where can we find numbers? *calendars, money, prices*

In our daily lifes where can we find words? *books, magazines, newspapers*

After viewing, put the continuum on the board.

numbers ———————— words

Have students mark the continuum and explain their preferences.

DISCUSS & SHARE

Ask students how often they use numbers and words every day. Draw a continuum on the board with *numbers* on one side and *words* on the other. Poll students to see where they land on the continuum. Many may land on the "words" side, but if many study or work in mathematics or business, the opposite may be true.

GO TO page vii

for **VOCABULARY** step-by-step instructions.

LESSON 1 **Introductions**

VOCABULARY introductions and greetings

A Match the pictures with the people.

co-workers friends teacher and student

1 

friends

2 

teacher and student

3 

co-workers

B 1.01 Read and listen. Match the conversations (1–3) with the pictures from A. Write the number.

Conversation 1 2
A: Good morning, Sara. How are you?
B: Hi, Mr. Webster. I'm fine, thanks.

Conversation 2 3
A: Good afternoon, I'm Mr. Smith. What's your name?
B: My name's Nick. Nice to meet you, Mr. Smith.
A: Nice to meet you, too.

Conversation 3 1
A: Good night, Lara.
B: Good night. See you, Mia!
A: Goodbye.

C Add the bold phrases from B to the table.

Say hello	Meet friends	Meet new people	Say bye
Hello	How are you?	Nice to meet you.	Goodbye.
Good morning,	3 I'm fine, thanks.	4 Nice to meet you, too.	Good night.
1 Hi			5 See you,
2 Good afternoon,			

MAKE IT REAL

My name's Nicole. = I'm Nicole.

D IN PAIRS Practice the conversations in B.

GO TO page xi

for **LISTENING** step-by-step instructions.

LISTENING

A 1.02 Listen to the conversation. How many people talk: two, three, or four?

B 1.02 LISTENING SKILL—Listen for names Listen again. Write the correct names.

Maria Mr. Taylor Pedro

The man's name is Mr. Taylor .

The woman's name is Maria .

GO TO page 62

for **AUDIO SCRIPT.**

C 1.02 THINKING SKILL—Evaluate Listen again. Are Maria and Peter students or co-workers?

students

VOCABULARY

Write *Good* on the board, and ask students to come to the board and complete the word/phrase (*Good morning*, *Good afternoon*, *Good night*, *Goodbye*). Ask students which expression has one word, not two words (*Goodbye*).

LISTENING OPTIONAL 1.02

This is the first LISTENING activity for your class. If it is difficult for them, allow time to play the audio again (i.e., a fourth time) at the end of the LISTENING section or, allow students to follow with the audio script.

GRAMMAR *be* statements

A Look at the sentences below. The verb *to be* is underlined. Circle the negative (-) sentence.

My name isn't Emma. My name's Eva.

B Complete the table with *isn't* and *'s*.

Possessive Adjectives (Subject)		*To be* Affirmative	*To be* Negative	Object
My				
Your	name	is / 's	is not / isn't	Emma.
His/Her				

C Choose the correct words to complete the rules.

1 The sentence order is subject–verb–object / verb–subject–object.
2 The apostrophe (') substitutes a letter / word, e.g., name is = name's, is not = isn't.

For more practice, go to page 70.

D 1.03 Complete the conversation. Then listen and check your answers.

Rosie: Hello, I'm Rosie. What's your name?
Eva: Hi, Rosie. My *name's* Eva.
Rosie: Nice to meet you, Emma.
Eva: No. My name isn't Emma. My name's Eva. This is my co-worker, Roger.
Rosie: Nice to meet you, Robert.
Eva: No. His name isn't Robert. His name is Roger.

E IN GROUPS Take turns to practice the conversation. Use your own names.

SPEAKING

A IN GROUPS Take turns to say hello and meet your group.

A: Hello, what's your name?
B: I'm Irene. Nice to meet you!

A: Hi, Sophie, how are you?
B: I'm fine, thanks.

B Join another group or work as a class. Say hello and meet everyone in your group/class. Use the Confident Communicator box to help you.

CONFIDENT COMMUNICATOR
START TALKING

To join a conversation, use the following phrases:
Excuse me, can I join you?
Hi there, can I join you?

Unit 1 Me 7

GO TO pages viii–ix for GRAMMAR step-by-step instructions.

GO TO page xii for SPEAKING step-by-step instructions.

GRAMMAR Extra Practice

After students have finished the GRAMMAR section, put students into groups of three. Ask students to practice the conversation in GRAMMAR **D** using names that could be easily changed. Students switch roles so that everyone practices one of the roles. You could ask a more confident group of students to model the activity for the class.

SPEAKING

CONFIDENT COMMUNICATOR

Practice the phrases from the Confident Communicator box as a class and individually. Remember to use polite and interested intonation, and ask students to use this intonation, too.

With a more confident class, you can make this into a game by getting the class to listen to individual students ask one of the questions and decide if it's good. The student then chooses another student or repeats the question with better intonation.

LESSON 2 Countries

GO TO page x
for **READING** step-by-step instructions.

READING

A 1.04 **Read the cards (1–4) and match them to the different types (a–d). Write the number.**

1
Number One Finance
Mike Michelson
762 Fifth Ave, New York, NY USA
Email: mike@numberonefinance.com
Languages: English, German, Japanese

2

Tino Fernandez
Language Teacher
Mexico City
First language: Spanish
Other languages: English, French, Chinese

3
UNIVERSITY
University of Los Angeles
SUBJECT
Law
NAME
Jane Henderson
NATIONALITY
British

4
DRIVER'S PERMIT

Alberto Garcia
Name **Alberto Garcia**
Address **25 Cda. De Topilejo, Molino del Rey, Mexico**
Nationality **Mexican**

a business card __1__
b driver's license __4__
c online profile __2__
d student ID card __3__

B READING SKILL—Locate information in a text **Read the cards in A again and circle the names of countries. Then underline the nationalities and languages.**

Circle:
4 Mexico
Underline:
1 English, German, Japanese
2 Spanish, English, French, Chinese
3 British
4 Mexican

C **Read again. Complete the sentences with countries, nationalities or languages.**

1 Mike is from the __USA__. He's American. His first language is English.
2 Alberto and Tino are from Mexico. They're __Mexican__.
3 Jane is from Great Britain. She's __British__.

D THINKING SKILL—Analyze **What does *first language* mean? What is your first language?**

first language means mother tongue; native language of your home country

VOCABULARY countries and nationalities

A **Complete the table with words from READING A and your dictionary.**

Name	Country	Nationality	Language
Mike	the **1** USA	American	English, German, **7** Japanese
Alberto	Mexico	Mexican	Spanish
Tino	Mexico	Mexican	Spanish, English, **8** French, **9** Chinese
Jane	the UK	**3** British	English, French
	Canada	**4** Canadian	
	Brazil	**5** Brazilian	
	2 China	Chinese	
	Germany	**6** German	

MAKE IT YOURS

IN PAIRS Add more country and nationality words.

READING

Before starting the READING section, show a card of your own (e.g., a business card, driver's license, online profile, or other ID card) and ask the class what it is, giving the wrong information at first. For example, ask *Is this my business card?* And the class should answer *No!* Ask *My driver's license?* The class should answer *Yes!* Then ask groups of students (or the whole class) to do the same. Monitor and provide names of any other cards. Elicit from students what other information could be on an ID card (e.g., job title, course name, cell phone, email, signature, etc.).

CULTURE NOTE

The United Kingdom consists of four countries: England, Scotland, Wales, and Northern Ireland.

Great Britain consists of England, Scotland, and Wales.

The United States of America consists of 50 states and the jurisdictions of Washington, D.C., and Puerto Rico.

Mexico is in North America.

PRONUNCIATION word stress

A 1.05 Listen to the words. Underline the stressed syllable.

1 o O o o A-me-ri-can
2 O o o Me-xi-can
3 o o O Ja-pa-nese
4 O o Spa-nish
5 o O Chi-nese

B 1.06 Listen to the words. Write the number of the correct syllable pattern group from A. Not all groups are used.

1 Brazilian Group 1
2 British Group 4
3 Canadian Group 1
4 English Group 4
5 German Group 4

C 1.07 Listen and check your answers in B. Then listen again and repeat.

GO TO page ix for PRONUNCIATION step-by-step instructions.

GRAMMAR subject pronouns and *be* statements

A Read the texts from READING A and choose the correct answers.

1 Mike is / isn't from China. He's / isn't from the US.
2 Tino and Alberto are / aren't from Mexico. They're / They aren't Mexican.
3 Jane is / isn't from the US. She's / isn't from Britain.

B Complete the table with *'s, isn't, 're* and *aren't*.

Subject Pronouns	*To be* Affirmative	*To be* Negative	Language
I	am / 'm	am not / 'm not	American. / from the US.
You	are / 're	are not / aren't	
He/She	is / 's	is not / isn't	
We/They	are / 're	are not / aren't	

For more practice, go to page 70.

C Complete the sentences with the correct form of *to be*.

1 I'm American. I 'm from New York City.
2 We aren't from China. We're from Brazil.
3 You aren't Canadian. You are / 're from the US.
4 He is / 's German. He isn't from Japan.

SPEAKING

A Complete the ID card to make it true for you.

Name: ____________
Address: ____________
Nationality: ____________
First language: ____________
Other languages: ____________

CONFIDENT COMMUNICATOR
REPAIR IT

To repair your conversation after a mistake, say *Excuse me / Sorry.*
He's from Mexico. Excuse me.
She's from Mexico.

B IN PAIRS Show your ID card. Take turns giving information. Include one negative sentence. Use the Confident Communicator box to help you.

I'm Gabriela Marino. I'm from Mexico. I'm not from Brazil.

C Join another pair. Introduce your partner.

She's Gabriela Marino. She's from Mexico. She isn't from Brazil.

PRONUNCIATION

You can demonstrate the number of syllables in a word by clapping or tapping a desk: the loudest clap or tap is the stressed syllable. Get students to practice this in pairs or small groups. Then ask students to practice this with words from Lesson 1: *morning, afternoon*, and *goodbye*.

GRAMMAR

Ask students what an apostrophe is (') and what it does (*substitutes one or two letters, i.e., makes a contraction*). Ask students to give examples from the previous lesson (*name's, isn't*).

Tell students that the contracted form is common in informal written English and in spoken English.

SPEAKING

Say the words below and ask the class to identify the number of syllables and the stressed syllable:

- O o: address
- o o O o o: nationality
- O o: language
- O o o: languages

LESSON 3 Family

VOCABULARY family

A Look at the pictures. Complete the description with the correct names.

Owen 18, Dan 21, Vicky 15

Joe 48, Nora 42, my parents

Adam 77, Vivian 73, my grandparents

I'm Owen. Dan is my **brother** and Vicky is my **sister**. My parents are Joe and Nora. Joe is my **father** and Nora is my **mother**. They're **husband** and **wife**. My **grandparents** are Adam and Vivian. Adam is my **grandfather** and Vivian is my **grandmother**. They're husband and wife, too.

B Complete the table with words from A.

brother	3 sister	parents
1 father	mother	grandparents
husband	4 wife	
2 grandfather	grandmother	
son	daughter	

MAKE IT REAL

We use short words for our own parents: *father = dad, mother = mom.* In British English, people say *mum.*

C 1.08 **Listen and check your answers to B. Then listen again and repeat.**

LISTENING

friends; reasons: Fiona is asking Ben about his family and co-workers.

A 1.09 THINKING SKILL—Evaluate **Listen to the conversation. Are the speakers friends or family? Decide and give reasons.**

B 1.09 LISTENING SKILL—Understand key words **Listen again. Circle the answer.**

1. Zoe is Ben's (sister) / friend.
2. Max is Ben's (friend) / brother.
3. Hannah and Gavin are Ben's (co-workers) / classmates.
4. Ben's grandparents are over (70) / 80 years old.

GO TO page 62 for AUDIO SCRIPT.

VOCABULARY

Before starting this section, show photos of your family (or a famous family) to the class. Introduce each person. For example, *Alex is my brother. My parents are Juan and Anna. This is my mom. This is my dad.*

After completing this section, ask if any student would like to show photos of their family and say who they are.

LISTENING

For less confident classes, put students into pairs for this section. For more confident classes, ask students to work alone and then check ideas in pairs.

When checking answers in LISTENING **B**, play the audio again and pause it after each part with the answer. This will give students another opportunity to listen intently for individual answers.

GRAMMAR *yes/no* questions with *be*

A Match the questions (1–4) to the answers (a–d) from LISTENING B.

1 Are they your grandparents? __d__
2 Is he your brother? __a__
3 Are they your classmates? __c__
4 Is she your sister? __b__

a No, he isn't.
b Yes, she is.
c No, they aren't.
d Yes, they are.

B Complete the table with the correct verb forms.

Question			Answer		
To be	Pronoun	Object	*Yes/no*	Pronoun	*To be*
1 Is	she	your sister?	Yes,	he/she	3 is
	he	your father?	No,		isn't.
2 Are	they	your grandparents?	Yes,	they	are.
			No,		4 aren't
Are	you	his brother?	Yes,	I	am.
			No,		am (I'm) not.

C Look at the table and complete the rules.

To make a question:
1 Put the verb *to be* at the beginning / end.
2 Put the pronoun before / after the verb *to be*.

To make an answer:
3 Use / Do not use the pronoun from the question.
4 Put the verb *to be* at the beginning / end.

For more practice, go to page 71.

D Choose the correct words.

1 (Is) / Are he your brother? No, he isn't.
2 Are they your parents? Yes, they are / is.
3 Is she your classmate? No, she is / isn't.
4 Are they your co-workers? Yes, he are / they are.
5 Is he / she your friend? Yes, she is.

SPEAKING

A Think of five friends or people in your family. Write their names and their ages.

Sonia 30

B IN GROUPS Ask questions about the people your group member chose in A. Give short answers. Use the Confident Communicator box to help you.

A: Is Sonia your sister? *B: No, she isn't.*
A: Is she your friend? *B: No, she isn't.*
A: Is she your co-worker? *B: Yes, she is!*

CONFIDENT COMMUNICATOR
KEEP TALKING

To continue a conversation, ask extra questions.
Is Pierre French? *No, he isn't.*
OK, is he from Brazil? *Yes, he is.*

C Share information about the people with the class.

Sonia is Ana's co-worker. She's 30.

GRAMMAR

Write an example of a *to be* sentence on the board—for example, *Mike is American*. Ask students to identify the subject (*Mike*), verb (*is*) and object (*American*). Write *S*, *V*, and *O* above the words.

Then write a *yes/no* question with *be* on the board—for example, *Is Mike American*? Ask students to identify the subject (*Mike*), verb (*Is*) and object (*American*). Write *S*, *V*, and *O* above the words.

Encourage students to notice the shift in word order from S–V–O in *to be* statements to V–S–O in *yes/no* questions with *be*.

SPEAKING

Ask the questions in SPEAKING **B** to the class. Use rising (and interested) intonation. Ask students to repeat and practice the intonation as a class and individually.

Monitor during the activity and encourage all students to keep using the rising (and interested) intonation.

GO TO page xv
for **LANGUAGE AND LIFE** step-by-step instructions.

GO TO page 62
for **AUDIO SCRIPT**.

Language and Life

Communication – Personal Information

FUNCTIONAL LANGUAGE complete a form

A 1.10 **Listen to the conversation and choose the correct place.**

1 

Hospital

2 
Hotel

3 
School

B 1.11 **Read and listen to the rest of the conversation. Put the information in the correct order.**

Major 3 Email 4 Name 1 Nationality 2 Phone number 5

Mrs. Jones: So, your name is Rodrigo. What's your last name?
Rodrigo: My last name is Casal.
Mrs. Jones: Sorry. Can you repeat that, please?
Rodrigo: Casal. C-a-s-a-l.
Mrs. Jones: Thanks. Are you from Colombia?
Rodrigo: Yes, I am. I'm from Bogotá. I'm Colombian.
Mrs. Jones: What's your major? Is it English?
Rodrigo: My majors are English and Business.
Mrs. Jones: Great. Thanks. What's your email?
Rodrigo: My email is rodrigo1234@funmail.cg.
Mrs. Jones: And what's your phone number?
Rodrigo: My cell is (555) 555-1058.
Mrs. Jones: Thank you, Rodrigo. Welcome to college!

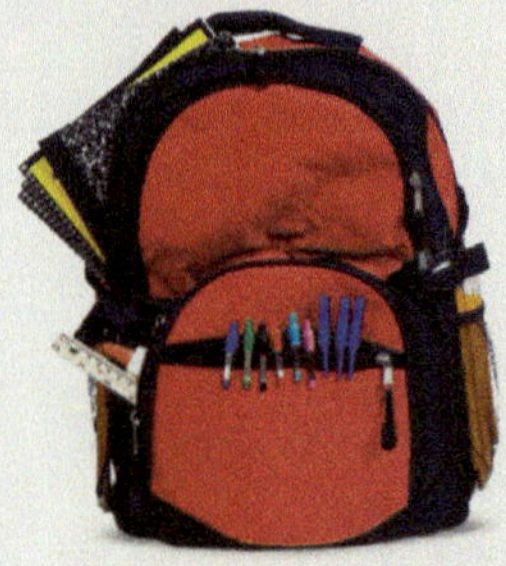

C 1.11 **Listen again and circle the correct answers to complete Rodrigo's form.**

Name	*Rodrigo Casal* / *Rodrigo Casel*
Nationality	*Colombia* / *Colombian*
Major	*English* / *English and Business*
Email	*rodrigoc1234* / *rodrigo1234@funmail.cg*
Phone number	*(216) 555-1058* / *(555) 555-1058*

D IN PAIRS **Practice the conversation in B. Switch roles.**

E IN NEW PAIRS **Take turns to practice the conversation in B again and give answers for you. Make notes on your partner's answers.**

OBJECTIVE

In this lesson, students learn how to complete a form and how to write a short personal introduction. The objective is to help them gain experience in these two real-world tasks. Students will probably have done similar tasks in their first language/culture, but not in a second or foreign language. Having the confidence to do these tasks in English will help them with their studies or in the workplace.

PROCESS OPTIONAL 1.10, 1.11

In FUNCTIONAL LANGUAGE, students listen to a conversation where a new student is completing a registration form at school. Students first identify the location of this conversation and then listen in more detail for important information. Finally, they listen again and correct errors in the details. Students then have the opportunity to practice the conversation and give their own personal details in order to replicate an authentic conversation.

WRITING an introduction

A **Look at the bold letters and circle them.**

capital letter

I'm from Mexico.

B **Circle the capital letters in the introduction.**

Home | Classes | Students | Jobs | Contact us

LEARN **ENGLISH**

LEARN ENGLISH > FORUM > INTRODUCTIONS

Hello! My name is Rodrigo. I'm Mexican. My first language is Spanish. I also speak English and Chinese.

1 day ago

C **Cross out the incorrect writing rule.**

Use a capital letter for the:

- *first letter in a sentence*
- *first letter in someone's name*
- *language*
- *nationality*
- *pronoun I*
- ~~*verb*~~

D **Find and correct the errors in each sentence.**

1 hello, i'm henry. Hello, I'm Henry.
2 i'm from Great Britain. I'm from Great Britain.
3 my first Language is english. My first language is English.

E **Rewrite the sentences in D with your personal information.**

____

____

____

____

____

F **IN PAIRS Exchange sentences. Check that your partner uses capital letters and periods.**

MAKE IT DIGITAL

Find and take a free English class online.

WRITING Alternative Activity

Write the sentences from WRITING **B** on the board. Then do the task as a whole-class activity. Circle the first capital letter and give the marker to a student. The student goes to the board and circles another capital letter before passing the marker to another student and so on.

WRITING Alternative Activity

Write the correct sentences from WRITING **D** on the board. Then ask students to call out the third-person form of the sentences: *Hello, he's Henry. He's from Great Britain. His first language is English.* Ask students to write similar sentences for their partner.

MAKE IT DIGITAL

For a free English class online suggest https://learnamericanenglishonline.com/ for a free English class online.

GO TO page xvii

for **UNIT REVIEW** step-by-step instructions.

UNIT 1

VOCABULARY review

SCORE: / 5

A Complete the sentences with the words from the box.

Canadian good mother nice wife

1 A: Good morning, my name's Dan.
B: Nice to meet you, Dan. I'm Tara.
2 Here are my parents: Nigel is my father and Karen's my mother. They are from Canada. They're Canadian.
3 A: I'm Sam. This is my husband, Nico.
B: I'm Nico. This is my wife, Samantha.

GRAMMAR review

SCORE: / 5

A Complete the sentences with the correct form of *be*.

1 A: My name ________ Nina. What's your name?
B: I ________ Suzy.
2 Carmen and Miguel are from Spain. They ________ from Great Britain.
3 A: ________ he your brother?
B: No, he ________ . He's my friend.

1 **A:** is / 's
B: am / 'm
2 are not / aren't
3 **A:** Is
B: is not / isn't

6–10 correct: You can use greetings, introduce yourself, talk about countries and nationalities, give personal information, and talk about your family. You can use *be* statements, subject pronouns and *yes*/*no* questions with *be*.
0–5 correct: Look again at the Vocabulary and Grammar sections in the unit.

TOTAL SCORE: / 10

WHAT DO YOU KNOW NOW? Look back at the unit and review the language you know now.

GO TO page xviii

for **STUDY SKILLS** step-by-step instructions.

STUDY SKILLS USING A DICTIONARY

A IN PAIRS **Is your dictionary a book or online? Show it to your partner. Is it the same dictionary?**

B Number the explanations of the parts of the dictionary entry from www.macmillandictionary.com.

definition 5
part of speech 4
the word 1
pronunciation 1— the phonetics 2
pronunciation 2— listen to the word 3

C Answer the questions.

1 Is *sister* an adjective? No, it's a noun.
2 *Sister* is for a female. What is the male word? brother
3 How many syllables are there in *sister*? two
4 Which syllable is stressed? first

D IN PAIRS **Find the words for Student A or Student B in the Macmillan Dictionary. Tell your partner the definition, correct pronunciation and part of speech. Use the word in a sentence.**

Student A: bedroom, cousin Student B: garage, uncle

CLASSROOM MANAGEMENT

For this first REVIEW, allow students to work in pairs and monitor and help as necessary. Alternatively, students could work on their own and then check their answers in pairs.

Check and confirm answers as a class. Explain any incorrect answers.

ALTERNATIVE ACTIVITY

If print dictionaries are available, play Dictionary Race. Put students into pairs. Call out words for the class to look up. The first pair to find the correct word and say the part of speech correctly, wins a point. Suggested words: *Canada, daughter, friend, grandparents, license, wife, worker.*

UNIT 2

My Place

WHAT DO YOU ALREADY KNOW?

1 Think about rooms in your home. Write words that you know in the box.

2 IN PAIRS Share and compare your information. Add more words to the box, if possible.

Living room: *sofa,* ____________

Bedroom: *bed,* ____________

Kitchen: *oven,* ____________

DISCUSS & SHARE

VIDEO

3 IN GROUPS Watch the video and answer the question.

SYM City or country?

In this unit, you will ...

- introduce your partner, talk about classroom objects and talk about where items are in a room.
- use thinking skills: analyze, evaluate and brainstorm.
- read about college student rooms.
- use strategies to give extra information and ask about new words to continue a conversation and check understanding.
- use communication skills to book a hotel room and write a text message.
- follow an online teacher to learn about their job and the skills needed to be in this industry.

Unit 2 My Place 15

GO TO page vi
for **UNIT OPENER** step-by-step instructions.

STUDENTS MAY ALREADY KNOW:

- **rooms within a home:** attic, bathroom, bedroom, cellar, family room, dining room, hall(way), kitchen, living room, home office.

GO TO page xx
for **VIDEOS IN SYM** step-by-step instructions.

WHAT DO YOU ALREADY KNOW?

If you notice students are struggling to understand what to do, you can provide one or two examples to help them get started:

- **Living room:** armchair, lamp, rug, TV
- **Bedroom:** closet, desk, drawers, mirror
- **Kitchen:** coffee maker, freezer, refrigerator, table

VIDEO

Before viewing, ask:

How can you describe the country? *quiet, peaceful, there is no traffic*

How can you describe the city? *a lot of activities all day and night*

After viewing, put the continuum on the board.

country ———————— city

Have students mark the continuum and explain why they prefer the country or the city.

DISCUSS & SHARE

Discuss with students the differences between living in a city and living in the country. There are many advantages and disadvantages to both. Consider creating a pro/con chart on the board and have students call out what they think to fill in the chart. Allow students to use their dictionaries.

GO TO page vii
for **VOCABULARY** step-by-step instructions.

Students' own answers

LESSON 1 Homes

VOCABULARY describing places

A IN PAIRS Match the adjectives from the box to the pictures. Which home is your favorite?

beautiful | big | modern | noisy | old | quiet | small | ugly

1

big, noisy, beautiful/ugly, old

2

beautiful/ugly, modern, quiet, small

B Look at the adjectives in A again. Find pairs with opposite meanings.

beautiful–ugly big–small, modern–old, noisy–quiet

C 2.01 Listen and repeat.

D IN PAIRS Answer the question. Which adjectives describe your home?

MAKE IT YOURS

Write more adjectives to describe your home. Use your dictionary to help you.

GO TO page xi
for **LISTENING** step-by-step instructions.

GO TO page 63
for **AUDIO SCRIPT**.

Juno is a student. Nick is on vacation.

in the street

Juno asks Nick questions for his homework.

LISTENING

A LISTENING SKILL—Use visuals to predict content Look at the picture. Who are the people? Where are they? What is the conversation about?

B 2.02 Listen and check your ideas from A.

C 2.02 Listen again. Complete the notes about Nick.

Name	*Nick Smith*
Home	*London—big and* modern *apartment (on vacation with his* friend*)*
Age	24
Email	nick94*@gomail.com*

Suggested answer: No, because he thinks Nick's apartment is beautiful.

D THINKING SKILL—Analyze Juno says his place is *small* and *noisy*. Do you think he likes it or not?

VOCABULARY

Put students in small groups. Write the three categories below on the board and ask groups to look at the two photos. Elicit an example for each category. Ask groups to write more words for the categories. Set a time limit (maximum five minutes). Possible items for categories include:

- **colors:** red, white, yellow, blue, gray, black, brown.
- **furniture:** stereo, desk, computer, bucket, lamp, sofa, door, chair.
- **people:** man, woman, girl, boy, mother, father, son, daughter, baby.

CULTURE NOTE

After checking the answers in LISTENING **C**, write the full email address on the board (*nick94@gomail.com*). Draw a circle around the @ symbol and *.com*. Elicit or teach the correct pronunciation (*at*, *dot com*). Write a short sentence on the board (*Nick lives in London.*) and point out that the punctuation (.) is referred to as a "period" in a sentence and a "dot" for emails.

GRAMMAR *be* information questions

GO TO pages viii–ix for GRAMMAR step-by-step instructions.

A Complete the questions from the conversation.

how how old what ×2 where who

1 What 's your name?
2 How are you?
3 Where are you from?
4 Who is he?
5 How old are you?
6 What 's your phone number?

B Circle the verbs in the questions in A.

C Complete the table with *is* or *are*.

Question Word	*To be*	Subject
How old	1 *are*	your parents?
What	2 is	your email?
Where	3 are	they from?
Who	4 is	she?
How	5 are	you?

D Read the questions in A and C. Match the question words (1–4) to the information in the answer (a–d). Write the letter.

1 How old d
2 What a
3 Where b
4 Who c

a a thing or a number
b a place
c a person or people
d age

For more practice, go to page 71.

E Find and correct the errors in the questions.

1 ~~What~~ How old is your apartment? It's 100 years old.
2 How is his email? It's benji123@yes.co.uk.
3 Where are their names? Sasha and Tina.
4 Who is she from? She's from Canada.
5 What are they? They're my friends.

2 What is his email?
3 What are their names?
4 Where is she from?
5 Who are they?

F IN PAIRS Ask and answer the questions in A so they're true for you.

SPEAKING

GO TO page xii for SPEAKING step-by-step instructions.

A IN PAIRS Role-play. Read the information. Take turns to ask and answer questions. Write the answers in your notebook. Use the Confident Communicator box to help you.

Student A: go to page 65 of the Activity Bank. **Student B:** go to page 66 of the Activity Bank.

B Ask the questions again and answer with true information for you.

C IN GROUPS Tell the group about your partner.

A: His/Her name is …
B: He's/She's from … His/Her apartment/house is …
A: He's/She's … years old.
B: His/Her phone number is …

CONFIDENT COMMUNICATOR
KEEP TALKING

To continue the conversation, give extra information in your answer:
I'm from London.
It's a beautiful city.

GRAMMAR Extra Practice

Ask students to close their books and write the five question words from GRAMMAR **A** as you say them. Quickly check spelling and pronunciation by asking students to say and spell the question words. Put students into pairs and ask them to write their own questions using the question words. Set a time limit of five minutes. Then ask pairs to say their questions. Correct any errors.

SPEAKING Extra Practice

Write the following sentences on the board: *His name is Nick. He's from London.* Circle *His* and *He's*. Ask students if the circled words are subjects or objects (*subjects*). Then ask students which word is a subject pronoun (*He*) and ask for other examples (*I, You, She, We, They*).

For more confident classes, ask students to identify the possessive adjective (*His*) and elicit other examples (*My, Your, Her, Our, Their*).

LESSON 2 Things

VOCABULARY your things

A Look at the objects in the pictures. Check (✓) the objects you see in your classroom.

1  ☐ phone

2  ☐ wallet

3 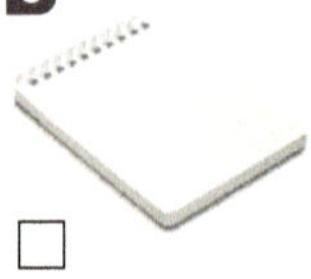 ☐ notebook

4  ☐ laptop

5  ☐ watch

6  ☐ brush

7  ☐ umbrella

8  ☐ ID card

9  ☐ pen

10  ☐ transit card

B IN PAIRS Match the words from the box to the pictures. Write the words in A.

brush	ID card	laptop	notebook	pen
phone	transit card	umbrella	wallet	watch

C 2.03 Listen and check your answers in B. Then listen again and repeat.

LISTENING

GO TO page 63 for AUDIO SCRIPT.

A 2.04 LISTENING SKILL—Listen for main idea Listen and discuss. Where are the people?

at a sports event   in a class   on a radio program

B 2.04 Listen again. Write the name of the person from the box.

Andrea   Emily   Ryan

1 British Emily   2 German Andrea   3 the winner Ryan

C 2.04 Listen again and complete the lists for each person. Then write the total number of items.

1 Andrea: a brush, 2 watches, a sandwich
Total = 4

2 Emily: 2 brushes, an ID card, a notebook, 2 pens, a phone, an umbrella, a transit card
Total = 9

3 Ryan: 2 ID cards, a laptop, 3 pens, a phone, a wallet, a watch, a transit card
Total = 10

MAKE IT YOURS

Say *Congratulations!* or *Good job!* to a competition winner or someone with good news, e.g., a good test result.

D THINKING SKILL—Evaluate Are radio shows popular in your country? Describe your favorite radio show/ station or your favorite radio show host.

VOCABULARY Alternative Activity

Ask students to identify the number of syllables in each word and which one is stressed:

- O: brush, pen, phone, watch
- O O o: ID card (Remind students that *I* and *D* are stressed equally.)
- O o: laptop, notebook, wallet
- O o o: transit card
- o O o: umbrella

Drill the words and pay attention to consonant /ʃ/ and the diphthong /tʃ/ in *brush* (/brʌʃ/) and *watch* (/wɒtʃ/).

LISTENING Alternative Activity

Have students look at the photo of the pink bag and call out the names of things in the bag (*sunglasses, camera, two notebooks, woman's wallet, phone, pen*). You can also do this task as a race with students working in pairs and writing the things down. The first pair to finish the list without errors wins.

GRAMMAR *a/an* singular and plural nouns

A Look at the bold and underlined nouns in LISTENING C and answer the questions. bold = underlined =

1 Are the bold nouns singular (one item) or plural (2+ items)? The underlined nouns? singular plural
2 What words are before the bold nouns? a an
3 What is the final letter of each underlined noun? s (es)

B Complete the rules with your answers from A.

For one item, use:
1 a + noun, e.g., a *brush*
2 an + noun beginning with a vowel sound (*a, e, i, o, u*), e.g., an *umbrella*

For two or more items, use:
number + noun + 3 s, e.g., 2 pens
number + noun ending with *–ch* and *–sh* + 4 es, e.g., 2 watches

For more practice, go to page 72.

C Look at the items in LISTENING C again. Add more examples using the rules in B.

1 a brush, ______
2 an umbrella, ______
3 2 pens, ______
4 2 watches, ______

1 a sandwich, a laptop, a phone, a wallet, a watch, a pen, a notebook, a transit card
2 an ID card
3 2 laptops, 2 phones, 2 wallets, 2 notebooks, 2 ID cards
4 2 brushes

D Complete the lists with *a, an, –s* or *–es*.

Harry: a laptop, three watch es, a pen, two notebook s, two sandwich es

Beth: two brush es, a bag, an umbrella, an ID card, three pen s

E IN GROUPS **Choose one person from D or LISTENING C and take turns to read his or her list of things.**

PRONUNCIATION plural nouns

A 2.05 Listen to the words and the final *–s* sound. Repeat.

/s/	/z/	/ɪz/
laptops	phones	watches
1 notebooks	3 ID cards	5 brushes
2 wallets	4 umbrellas	6 sandwiches

GO TO page ix for **PRONUNCIATION** step-by-step instructions.

B 2.06 Listen and add the words to the table in A. Then listen again, check and repeat.

brushes ID cards notebooks sandwiches umbrellas wallets

SPEAKING

A IN PAIRS **Make a list of things you see in the classroom, on your desk or in your bags. Use your dictionary for new words.**

6 bags, 5 phones ...

B Discuss your list with another pair. Use the Confident Communicator box to help you. Is the use of *a/an* and *–s/–es* correct?

C What is the total number of things on your list? Discuss as a class.

CONFIDENT COMMUNICATOR
KEEP TALKING

To continue the conversation, ask questions about new words:
What's this in English? It's a tablet.
What's ... in English? Sunglasses.

GRAMMAR Alternative Activity

Play Grammar Tennis (use a soft ball or have students say a name) to practice *a/an*: the first student says *a* or *an* and throws the ball/says a name. The second student says a thing that follows *a* or *an* (e.g., *a* + *brush*, *an* + *umbrella*). If correct, the student then says *a/an* and throws the ball or says a name of another student and so on. If incorrect, elicit the correct answer from the class.

To practice plural nouns, follow above procedure, but have the first student say a number and the second student say the correct plural ending (*two* + *notebooks*/ *brushes*).

SPEAKING

It is important for students at this level not only to activate and produce new language but also to use it accurately. Monitor students carefully, especially in pair or group work when you can give more time to individual students. Correct any errors by eliciting the correct language.

LESSON 3 Rooms

VOCABULARY prepositions of place 1

A Look at the pictures. Complete the phrases with the words from the box.

bag bed chair desk door umbrella watch window

1 in the bag
2 behind the chair
3 in front of the umbrella
4 between the door and the window

5 next to the bed
6 on the desk
7 under the watch

B Complete the sentences.

1 The notebook is in the bag.
2 The umbrella is behind the chair.
3 The chair is in front of the umbrella.
4 The bed is between the door and the window.
5 The door is next to the bed.
6 The lamp is on the desk.
7 The dictionary is under the watch.

C IN PAIRS Look at your classroom. Say what's on your desk, next to the door and in front of the window.

GO TO page x

for **READING** step-by-step instructions.

one bed—two beds

one desk—two desks and two chairs

lamp on desk—lamp next to bed and on desk

two doors—one door

READING

A IN PAIRS Look at the pictures on page 65 of the Activity Bank. Find three differences between them.

B 2.07 READING SKILL—Identify the topic Quickly read the webpage and choose a title from the box.

A Place for Teachers | The Rooms at the College | Your Favorite Bedroom

NEW COLLEGE

There are two types of rooms for students.

Single (one student)

There's a bed. There's a window between the door and the bed. There's a desk and a chair in front of the window. There's a small lamp on the desk. There's a small closet next to the bed.

Double (two students)

There are two beds in the room. There's a big window between the two beds. There are two desks and two chairs. They are in front of the window. There's a lamp on each desk. There are two closets behind the door.

VOCABULARY

Use the classroom or your things to replicate a picture from VOCABULARY **A**. Write an incomplete sentence on the board (*The notebook is … the …*) and ask students to complete it. You can use blanks for things (to review vocabulary from Lesson 2), prepositions of place, or both.

READING

READING SKILL—Identify the topic

It is important to identify the topic of a text to verify comprehension. For more confident classes, ask students to work alone and set a short time limit. For less confident classes, read the text out loud yourself first and then allow students to read the text again (alone or in pairs). To identify the topic, ask *Who or what is the text about?*

READING Extra Practice

Put students into pairs. Ask them to read the webpage again and circle the furniture words (*bed, desk, chair, lamp*). Allow students to refer to VOCABULARY **A** for help. Then, ask students to identify a new word that means "a place for clothes" (*closet*).

C **Read the webpage again. Use the words from the box to complete the summary.**

different one same two

There are two types of rooms: single for ___one___ student and double for ___two___ students. There is the ___same___ furniture in each room. The furniture is in a ___different___ place in each room.

D IN PAIRS THINKING SKILL—Brainstorm **Draw a picture of your bedroom. Show your partner.**

GRAMMAR *There is / There are*

A **Complete the sentences from READING B.**

1 There ___'s___ a bed.
2 There ___'s___ a small closet next to the bed.
3 There ___are___ two beds in the room.
4 There ___are___ two closets behind the door.

B **Complete the table with the correct form of *to be*.**

For one thing:	There	**1** 's/is	a	desk.
For two or more things:		**2** are	two	desks.

For more practice, go to page 72.

C **Complete the sentences with *is*, *'s* or *are*.**

1 There ___'s___ a desk. There ___are___ two notebooks on the desk.
2 There ___are___ three laptops on the bed.
3 There ___'s/is___ a small window next to the door.
4 There ___are___ five students in the class. There ___'s/is___ one teacher.

D IN PAIRS **In your notebook, make sentences about your classroom using *There is / There are*.**

SPEAKING

A IN PAIRS **Student A: look at your picture. Do not show it to Student B. Make notes on the items in the room. Then switch roles. Use the Confident Communicator box to help you.**

Student A: go to page 65 of the Activity Bank.
Student A: say what's in your room.
Student B: go to page 66 of the Activity Bank.
Student B: draw a picture of the room that's described.

There's a bed. The bed is next to the window.

CONFIDENT COMMUNICATOR
KEEP TALKING

To check you understand, use *Right?* after a statement.
The bed is next to the door. ***Right?***
No, the bed is next to the window.

MAKE IT DIGITAL

Search online for rooms at colleges or in hotels. Then write a short description of one room from your search.

GRAMMAR

Make sure students are correctly using *There is/are* with *a/an* + singular/plural nouns. This is an example of when students are building on existing grammar knowledge and adding new language, so errors or omissions can easily occur. Correct errors and review *a/an* + nouns, if necessary.

SPEAKING Alternative Activity

Put students into pairs. Ask each student to draw a simple picture of a room, including four or five things or items of furniture. Students then sit back to back and take turns describing the room to their partner. Their partner draws the room but must not show the picture. When finished, students then compare the description and the picture for accuracy and make any corrections.

For less confident classes, ask students to work in pairs to draw a room. Then the pair describes the room to another pair who draws the room and so on.

GO TO page xv
for LANGUAGE AND LIFE step-by-step instructions.

Language and Life

Communication – Hotel Room

FUNCTIONAL LANGUAGE book a hotel

A 2.08 **Read and listen to the conversation. Complete the sentences with words from the box. There are two words you do not need.**

friend hotel single double

Sofia calls a __hotel__. Sofia asks for a __single__ room.

Hotel worker: Good morning. Grand Hotel.
Sofia: Good morning. **I want to book a room for Friday night, please.**
Hotel worker: Sure. Let me see if we have a room. **There's a single room and a double room.**
Sofia: What is a double room?
Hotel worker: It's a room with two beds for two people.
Sofia: OK. **A single room, please.**
Hotel worker: No problem. It's a nice room with two big windows. **What's your name and email, please?**
Sofia: Sofia Lopez. My email is sofial95@newmail.com. **How much is it?**
Hotel worker: It's $100. **Please pay at the hotel on Friday.**
Sofia: **Thank you for your help.**
Hotel worker: **You're welcome.** Goodbye.

MAKE IT REAL

In British English: *double room* = a room with a bed for two people
twin room = a room with two beds for two people

B Add the bold sentences from A to the table.

Hotel guest	Hotel worker
I want to book a room for Friday night, please.	*There's a single room and a double room.*
1 A single room, please.	4 What's your name and email, please?
2 How much is it?	5 Please pay at the hotel on Friday.
3 Thank you for your help.	6 You're welcome.

GO TO page 63
for AUDIO SCRIPT.

C 2.09 **Listen to two different examples (A and B) from the hotel worker. Is A or B polite? Circle the answer.**

1 (A) B 2 A (B) 3 A (B)

D IN PAIRS **Take turns reading the conversation in A.**

E IN NEW PAIRS **Repeat the conversation with new information. Take turns as the hotel worker and the hotel guest.**

Student A: go to page 65 of the Activity Bank. Student B: go to page 66 of the Activity Bank.

OBJECTIVE

In this lesson, students learn how to book a hotel room with the correct vocabulary and write a text message. Students will probably have done similar tasks in their first language/ culture, but not in a second or foreign language. The objective is to help students give some basic personal information and identify formal and informal written and spoken English.

PROCESS OPTIONAL 2.08, 2.09

In FUNCTIONAL LANGUAGE, students listen to a woman call a hotel to make a reservation. Students identify the speakers and the different expressions used by each speaker. Next, students listen for the use of polite intonation by the hotel worker. Finally, students work in pairs to practice and role-play the conversation, with the addition of using different information in the conversation.

ALTERNATIVE ACTIVITY

To practice polite intonation, play the polite examples from Activity **C** again. Ask the whole class to repeat and then ask individual students to repeat. Correct any problems by playing the audio again or by saying the expression yourself. Remind students that polite intonation is an important skill for the tourist industry.

WRITING a text message

A Read the text messages and choose *True* or *False*. Correct the false sentences.

1. Dan is in a hotel. True / **False** Camila is in a hotel.
2. The room is small. True / **False** The room is big.
3. There is a restaurant in the hotel. **True** / False ______

B Circle six exclamation marks (!) and four question marks (?) in the texts.

C Complete the sentences with *?* or *!*.

1. Use ? at the end of a question—not at the beginning.
2. Use ! at the end of a statement—not at the beginning.
3. Use ! to show you are very happy or not very happy.

D Complete the sentences with *?* or *!*.

1. Is the room small?
2. The coffee shop is beautiful!
3. This hotel is awesome!
4. Where is the clothes store!

E Complete the sentences to describe the places. Then write another sentence. Use your own words or the examples from the box.

closet	clothes store	coffee shop	quiet
noisy	old	small	

1. *The hotel is noisy. It's very old.*
2. The room ... is small. There's a closet and a bed. It's quiet.
3. The restaurant ... is big. It's next to a clothes store.

Camila
Online

Hi, Camila. Are you in Madrid? Is the hotel nice?

Hey, Dan! Yes, I'm here! The hotel is beautiful! It's very modern. My room's awesome!

Is the room big?

Yes, it is. There's a nice bed next to two big windows. There's a small desk and a chair. I love it!

Is the restaurant good?

No, it isn't. The restaurant is very busy and noisy. I don't like it!

F IN PAIRS Exchange answers. Then take turns to ask and answer the questions. Text your questions and answers to each other if possible.

MAKE IT DIGITAL

Send two text messages to two different classmates in English.

WRITING Alternative Activity

After WRITING **C**, drill the following questions and statements with the class, using the correct intonation or expression: *Are you in Madrid?* (rising intonation), *Is the hotel nice?* (rising intonation), *My room's awesome!* (very happy), *I love it!* (very happy), *I don't like it!* (very unhappy).

Ask two more confident students to read the text messages as a spoken conversation. Check that students use different and correct intonation for the questions and the statements. Then put students into pairs to practice the conversation.

WRITING Extra Practice

For pairs who finish quickly, ask them to write (or text) questions to each other about the classroom, their home, their place of work, a hotel or coffee shop, and so on. Students can use the questions from the page to help them: *Is the … nice? Is the … big? Is the … good?*

GO TO page xvii
for **UNIT REVIEW** step-by-step instructions.

UNIT 2

VOCABULARY review

SCORE: / 5

A Choose the word that is different in each group.

1	beautiful	laptops	old	small
2	brush	modern	transit card	wallet
3	door	ID cards	pens	umbrellas
4	bed	between	desk	window
5	behind	in front of	notebook	under

GRAMMAR review

SCORE: / 5

A Complete the sentences.

1 Where __are__ you from? I'm from Japan.
2 Who __'s/is__ he? He's my teacher.
3 There's a brush and __an__ ID card.
4 The chair is next __to__ the window.
5 There __are__ three windows and two doors.

6–10 correct: You can describe places and where things are, introduce your partner, and talk about your things. You can use *be* information questions, *a/an* singular and plural nouns and *There is/There are*.
0–5 correct: Look again at the Vocabulary and Grammar sections in the unit.

TOTAL SCORE: / 10

WHAT DO YOU KNOW NOW? Look back at page 15 and add the words you know now to the box.

GO TO page xix
for **FOLLOW A PRO** step-by-step instructions.

GO TO page 63
for **AUDIO SCRIPT**.

FOLLOW A PRO ONLINE TEACHER

A Circle useful things for an online teacher.

chair desk dictionary internet laptop phone transit card

B 2.10 Listen and check your answers in A.

C 2.10 Listen again and complete the notes.

Name: *Angela*
Nationality: __British__
Language: __English__
Job: __English teacher/online teacher__
Nationality of students: __Mexican__ and __Chinese__
Age of students: __15__ to __62__ years old

D IN GROUPS Discuss. Are the sentences true for you? Change the sentences to make them true for you.

- I'm an online student.
- There are online teachers in my city.
- An online class is fun.

24 Unit 2 My Place

CLASSROOM MANAGEMENT

In VOCABULARY **A**, ask more confident students or fast finishers to add another word to each group. Check that word stress and pronunciation are correct.

In GRAMMAR **A**, ask more confident students or fast finishers to write another example sentence for each of the five grammar points. Check and confirm answers as a class.

FURTHER DISCUSSION

Have students discuss in groups their preferences about the following situations, explaining why and giving examples to support their opinions:

- learning a language in a classroom or online with a teacher
- learning a language face-to-face with a teacher or in a class
- learning a language in your country or in a country where it is spoken

UNIT 3

Life and Work

GO TO page vi
for **UNIT OPENER** step-by-step instructions.

WHAT DO YOU ALREADY KNOW?

1 Think about your calendar or planner. Complete the boxes.

2 **IN PAIRS** Share and compare your details. Add your partner's information to the boxes, if possible.

Days: *Monday,* __________

Months: *January,* __________

Your next vacation: __________

Your partner's next vacation: __________

Your birthday: __________

Your partner's birthday: __________

STUDENTS MAY ALREADY KNOW:

- days of the week.
- months of the year.
- some basic ordinal numbers and dates.

VIDEO

DISCUSS & SHARE

3 **IN GROUPS** Watch the video and answer the question.
SYM Birthdays—party or no party?

GO TO page xx
for **VIDEOS IN SYM** step-by-step instructions.

In this unit, you will ...

- share information about people in your class, use the simple present, use adverbs of frequency.
- use thinking skills: evaluate and analyze.
- read about the world of work and a hotel.
- use strategies to ask questions to repair a conversation, ask questions to check understanding and agree with an affirmative statement to continue a conversation.
- use communication skills to plan to meet and write an online post.
- learn skills to record vocabulary.

Unit 3 Life and Work 25

WHAT DO YOU ALREADY KNOW?

Provide one or two examples to help students get started:

- **Days:** Monday, Tuesday, Wednesday, Thursday, Friday, Saturday, Sunday
- **Months:** January, February, March, April, May, June, July, August, September, October, November, December

Practice pronunciation of the words with the class. Ensure students pronounce *Wednesday* (/ˈwenzdeɪ/) correctly.

VIDEO

Before viewing, ask:

Why do they like/not like birthday parties? *they are fun/ they are noisy*

After viewing, put the continuum on the board.

party ———————— no party

Have students mark the continuum and explain why they like parties or not.

DISCUSS & SHARE

Take a poll of students to see how many enjoy celebrating their birthday and how many do not. Of the students who enjoy celebrating, take another poll to see how many prefer to celebrate with a party and how many like to celebrate in a quieter way.

GO TO page vii
for **VOCABULARY** step-by-step instructions.

LESSON 1 Jobs

VOCABULARY jobs

A IN GROUPS **Ask and answer the question *What do you do?***

A: What do you do? *B: I'm a student.*

B **Match the pictures with jobs from the box. Write the words under the pictures.**

chef doctor lawyer manager pilot police officer teacher waiter/waitress

1 
teacher

2 
doctor

3 
police officer

4 
manager

5 
chef

6 
pilot

7 
waiter/waitress

8 
lawyer

C 3.01 **Listen and check your answers to B. Then listen again and repeat.**

MAKE IT YOURS

IN GROUPS Make a list of jobs you know. Use a dictionary to help you.

GO TO page x
for **READING** step-by-step instructions.

READING

A **Look at the pictures. Discuss what jobs you think the people do.**

B 3.02 READING SKILL—Scan for jobs **Read the texts and check your answers. Then answer the question. What other jobs are in the texts?**

Marie: waitress, teacher
Gino: pilot

Hi, I'm Marie. I **live** in the city. I'm a waitress. I **don't work** in a restaurant. I work in a café. I **meet** new people every day. It's fun! I'm also a teacher. I **teach** Chinese in a school. The students are nice. I **like** my jobs.

Hello, I'm Gino. I **don't work**. I'm a student. I **go** to college by bus. My brother is a pilot. He **goes** to work by car. He **speaks** three languages: Italian, French and English. He **doesn't speak** Chinese. He **likes** his job. We **live** in an apartment.

C **Read the texts again. Choose the word to complete the sentences.**

1 Marie **speaks** / doesn't speak Chinese. She **likes** / doesn't like her jobs.
2 Gino works / **doesn't work**. He **goes** / doesn't go to college.
3 Gino's brother speaks / **doesn't speak** Chinese. He **likes** / doesn't like his job.
4 Gino and his brother **live** / don't live in an apartment.

D IN GROUPS THINKING SKILL—Evaluate **Decide which job in the texts you like more. Why?**

VOCABULARY

Write a list of the jobs from VOCABULARY **A** on the board and elicit from students the list after the Make It Yours activity. Review spelling by asking students to spell the jobs. Then ask students to identify the number of syllables and the stressed syllable. Underline the stressed syllable on the board. This will encourage students to keep good vocabulary records.

READING Alternative Activity

After reading the text, put students into pairs: Student A and Student B. Student A reads Marie's text, and Student B reads Gino's text. (Set a time limit appropriate to the level of your class.) Then ask pairs to work together and tell each other the person's job and two more facts. Hold a brief class feedback session to check answers.

GRAMMAR simple present statements

A Complete the table with bold words from READING A.

Subject Pronouns	Verb	
Affirmative		
I	go	to college by bus.
	like	my jobs.
He	speaks	three languages.
	1 goes	to work by car.
	2 likes	his job.
Negative		
I	don't work	in a restaurant.
He	3 doesn't speak	Chinese.

B Look at the table and complete the rules for simple present statements.

1 For affirmative sentences with *He/She/It*:
- add –*s* to regular verbs.
- add ___es___ to irregular verbs ending with –*o*.

2 For negative sentences with *I/You/We/They*, add *don't* before the verb.

3 For negative sentences with *He/She/It*, add ___doesn't___ before the verb.

For more practice, go to page 73.

C 3.03 Choose the word to complete the description. Then listen and check.

I live / lives in Lima. I don't / doesn't work. I'm a student. I go / goes to college by bike. I speak / speaks two languages: English and Spanish. My sister works / doesn't work. She's a doctor. She don't / doesn't live in Lima. She live / lives in New York.

D Write sentences in your notebook using the prompts from the box.

I'm a/an   I live in   I work in   I speak   I don't speak   I go to work/college by

SPEAKING

A IN PAIRS Take turns to say your sentences from GRAMMAR D. Make a note of your partner's answers. Use the Confident Communicator box to help you.

B IN GROUPS Share information about the people in your group/class.

CONFIDENT COMMUNICATOR
REPAIR IT

To repair the conversation, ask questions:
Can you say that again, please? How do you spell engineer?
How do you say that? What does apartment *mean?*

GO TO pages viii–ix
for **GRAMMAR** step-by-step instructions.

GO TO page xii
for **SPEAKING** step-by-step instructions.

GRAMMAR

Write *do not* and *does not* on the board. Tell students that this is the full negative form of the words. Remind students about contractions (i.e., when two words join together to become one word). Ask students to find the contracted forms in the text and to call out the words (*don't*, *doesn't*). Add these words to the board next to the full form and practice the pronunciation.

SPEAKING Alternative Activity

Ask students to stand up, walk around, and take turns saying their sentences. Tell students to speak to three other students or to say each sentence to a different student. Monitor and help as necessary. This will encourage students to practice speaking to new people and gain confidence.

VOCABULARY prepositions of time

A Student A: read the text below. Student B: read the text on page 66 of the Activity Bank.

I go to work by bus in the morning. I start work at 7:00 a.m. I work in an office. I go to college on Wednesday and on Thursday. The class is **1** ___in___ the evening. It starts **2** ___at___ 6:00 p.m. and ends **3** ___at___ 8:00 p.m. I study **4** ___on___ the weekend.

B Take turns to read your text to your partner. (Do not show your partner the text.) Listen to your partner and complete your text.

C Write the correct preposition: *at*, *in* or *on*. Then circle examples from the text.

1 

___at___

2 

___on___

3 

___in___

Who are the people? Anthony: restaurant manager, Mario: wants to be a waiter

Where are they? in Anthony's restaurant

What is the conversation about? job interview for waiter (in the evenings)

LISTENING

GO TO page xi for LISTENING step-by-step instructions.

A IN PAIRS **Look at the picture and discuss the questions: Who are the people? Where are they? What is the conversation about?**

B 3.04 **Listen and check your ideas from A.**

GO TO page 64 for AUDIO SCRIPT.

C 3.04 LISTENING SKILL—Listen for names, dates and numbers **Listen again and complete Anthony's notes.**

Name: Mario

Job: waiter / manager—in the morning / evening

Routine: Mario goes to college in the morning / afternoon and studies in the morning / afternoon. He works in his uncle's shop on Wednesday / the weekend—from 12:00 p.m. to 9:00 p.m.

GO TO page 64 for AUDIO SCRIPT.

D 3.05 **Listen to the next part. Complete Mario's questions.**

1 Does the restaurant open on ___Sundays___ ?
2 Do the waiters speak ___English___ ?

E THINKING SKILL—Analyze **Do you think Mario gets the job? Why?**

Suggested answers: Yes, he is free to work as a waiter on Thursdays and on Fridays.

MAKE IT REAL

People often say *about* for a time that is not exact.
*The waiters finish **about** 11. = The waiters finish at 10:50/10:55/11:05/11:10.*
People do not always say *o'clock*, *a.m.* or *p.m.* after the time.
The waiters start work at six.

CLASSROOM MANAGEMENT

For pair dictation activities similar to VOCABULARY **A**, make sure students sit back to back or do not show their text to their partner. Tell students it is important to develop natural listening skills, and this activity allows students to practice listening intently for detail.

VOCABULARY

Write the three prepositions from VOCABULARY **C** on the board (*at*, *in*, *on*). Ask students to call out the answers again and write these next to the correct preposition. Then ask students to give other examples, or say a word and ask students to choose a preposition (e.g., *Saturday – On*).

LISTENING Extra Practice

You may consider using the Audio Script (page 66) for further practice. Put students into pairs to role-play the conversation: one student is Mario, and one is Anthony. Alternatively, play the audio again and allow students to follow the script while listening. Elicit any new vocabulary words.

GRAMMAR *yes/no* questions with simple present

A Match the phrases to make questions and answers from LISTENING B.

1 Do you	open on Sunday?	Yes, they do.
2 Does the restaurant	speak English?	No, it doesn't.
3 Do the waiters	go to college every day?	No, I don't.

1 Do you go to college every day? No, I don't.
2 Does the restaurant open on Sunday? No, it doesn't.
3 Do the waiters speak English? Yes, they do.

B Complete the table with *Do, Does, don't* and *doesn't*. Then add the example questions from A.

Simple Present Questions			
1 Do	you/we/they	+ infinitive ...?	e.g., **3**
2 Does	he/she/it	+ infinitive ...?	e.g., **4**
Short Answers			
Yes,	I/you/we/they	**5** do	
	he/she/it	does.	
No,	I/you/we/they	**6** don't	
	he/she/it	**7** doesn't	

For more practice, go to page 73.

Do: Do you go to college every day? Do the waiters speak English?

Does: Does the restaurant open on Sundays?

C Find and correct one error in each question. Then complete the short answers.

1 Do your brother study in the afternoon? — Yes, he does.
2 Does she goes to college on Wednesday? — No, she doesn't.
3 Does you work on Saturday? — Yes, I do.
4 Do they starts work at 7:00 p.m.? — No, they don't.

1 Does
2 go
3 Do
4 start

D IN PAIRS Take turns to ask and answer the questions in C. Use different short answers. Change the subject (*your brother–you; she–they*).

PRONUNCIATION word stress in questions

A 3.06 Listen to the conversations and underline the stressed words.

Conversation 1	Conversation 2
Do they speak English?	Does it open in the mornings?
Yes, they do. / No, they don't.	Yes, it does. / No, it doesn't.

B 3.06 Listen again and repeat.

GO TO page ix for PRONUNCIATION step-by-step instructions.

SPEAKING

A Write five simple present *yes/no* questions in your notebook.

B IN GROUPS Take turns to ask and answer your questions. Use the Confident Communicator box to help you.

CONFIDENT COMMUNICATOR
KEEP TALKING

To continue the conversation and check you understand, ask questions:
Is that right? *Is that OK?*

Unit 3 Life and Work 29

GRAMMAR

A common error associated with *yes/no* questions and the simple present is the incorrect pronoun use or omission of the pronoun. When checking answers and when monitoring spoken work, pay close attention to correct use of the pronouns, as well as correct use of the main grammar point. Quickly review pronouns if necessary.

PRONUNCIATION

After PRONUNCIATION **B**, ask students to underline the stressed words in GRAMMAR **C**. Check and confirm answers (questions: main verb, nouns; answers: *Yes/ No, don't/doesn't*) with the class. Then put students into pairs to take turns saying the questions and answers. Monitor and correct any pronunciation errors.

SPEAKING

When doing speaking activities, you may wish to focus on either fluency or accuracy. Fluency practice will allow students to develop greater confidence in speaking for an extended period of time. Accuracy practice will allow students to produce and use more correct language, thus avoiding producing errors in the future.

LESSON 3 Routines

VOCABULARY daily activities

A **Write the activities from the box under the correct picture.**

drink coffee | eat breakfast | get up at 6 a.m. | go to bed | take a shower

1 
take a shower

2 
get up at 6 a.m.

3 
eat breakfast

4 
drink coffee

5 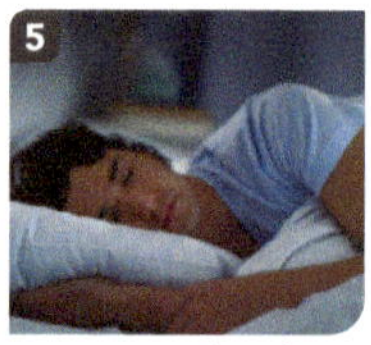
go to bed

B 3.07 **Listen, check and repeat.**

C **Match the verbs (1–5) to the words (a–e) to make phrases.**

1 drink c
2 eat e
3 get up a
4 go to d
5 take b

a at 8:00 a.m.
b a bath
c tea
d college
e lunch

D IN PAIRS **Write five sentences describing your routine. Then talk about your routine.**

I get up at 7:30 a.m. I take a shower.

READING

A 3.08 READING SKILL—Recognize different text types **Quickly read the text. What type of text is it?**

job advertisement | online article (highlighted) | message

The **24-365** Hotel

11:24

Welcome! I'm Michael Olson and I'm the manager. The hotel is 150 years old. It has 200 rooms, two restaurants and a café. About 400 people work here. It's a big hotel.
We are **always** busy. The hotel is **never** closed. It is open 24 hours a day for 365 days a year. There are **always** guests at the hotel. Guests **usually** stay for one week or two weeks. Families **often** stay here in July and August.

Tourists **often** visit the hotel to eat lunch or dinner. The restaurants are very popular on weekends. There is **rarely** a free table!
Our chefs are excellent. They make excellent food. The waiters and waitresses speak different languages. One waiter speaks five languages! People **sometimes** visit the hotel for work meetings. They drink coffee and talk about work. Visitors love the hotel.

VOCABULARY Alternative Activity

Put students into pairs. Put two pairs together and have them take turns saying their sentences from VOCABULARY **D**. Pairs should listen carefully and take notes. Then pairs write a minimum of five sentences describing the other pair's routine. For example, *Paola gets up at 7 a.m. She doesn't eat breakfast*. Monitor and correct errors with vocabulary or grammar.

READING Extra Practice

After READING **C**, direct students back to the text for extra reading practice and vocabulary work. Write the four categories below on the board and ask students to find as many examples as they can in the text. Set a time limit appropriate to your class. Examples can include the following words:

- **adjectives:** big, busy, popular, free, excellent, different
- **singular nouns:** manager, hotel, café, year, week, lunch
- **plural nouns:** rooms, restaurants, hours, days, guests, weeks
- **verbs:** be, have, work, stay, visit, make

B **Read the text again. Write the numbers from the text next to the descriptions below.**

1 age of the hotel 150
2 rooms and restaurants 200, 2
3 people who work there about 400
4 days the hotel is open 365
5 languages one waiter speaks five

C THINKING SKILL—Analyze **Discuss as a class. Look at the phrases in VOCABULARY A. What do you think Michael's routine is? Describe his day.**

I think Michael goes to work at 6 a.m. He has breakfast at the hotel. He ...

Suggested answers:
1 Michael goes to work at 6 a.m.
2 He has breakfast at the hotel.
3 He is always busy.
4 He drinks a lot of coffee.
5 He takes a shower in the evening, after work.

GRAMMAR adverbs of frequency

A **Add the bold adverbs from the reading text to the diagram.**

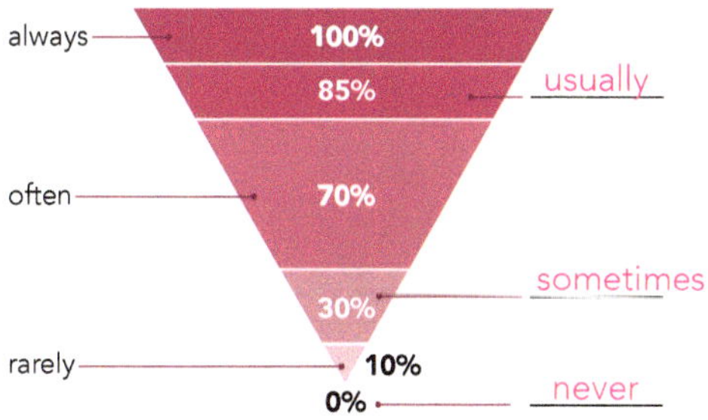

B **Look at the sentences below and underline the two verbs. Then complete the rules.**

1 We are always busy. The hotel never closes.
2 Put the adverb (e.g., *always*):
- before / after the verb *to be*.
- before / after other verbs.

For more practice, go to page 74.

C **Complete the sentences with the correct adverb.**

1 I often (70%) go to work by car, but I sometimes (30%) go by bus.
2 I don't like baths. I always (100%) take a shower.
3 I never (0%) eat breakfast. I eat a big lunch.
4 I usually (85%) study every day, but today I'm at work.
5 I rarely (10%) drink coffee. I prefer tea.

D IN PAIRS **Change the sentences in C to be true for you.**

SPEAKING

A **Complete the sentences with the correct adverb and time for your routine.**

- I ________ take a shower________ .
- I ________ get up before ________ .
- I ________ eat breakfast at ________ .
- I ________ drink coffee ________ .
- I ________ go to bed after ________ .

B IN GROUPS **Take turns to say your sentences and then discuss the question. Use the Confident Communicator box to help you. Are your routines the same or different?**

CONFIDENT COMMUNICATOR
KEEP TALKING

To continue the conversation, you can agree with an affirmative statement:
I always drink coffee. = *Me, too!* (*I always drink coffee.*)
or agree with a negative statement:
I rarely/never drink coffee. = *Me neither!* (*I rarely/never drink coffee.*)

GRAMMAR Extra Practice

Write the two sentences in item 1 of GRAMMAR **B** on the board. Ask students to identify the verbs (*are*, *closes*). Ask students which verb is *to be* (*are*) and quickly review other forms (*am*, *is*). Ask students for a verb with the opposite meaning to *close* (*open*) and an example from the READING text (*It is open 24 hours ...*).

Then ask students to identify the adverb in each sentence (*always*, *never*). Explain that these are opposites in meaning. Ask if the adverb is before or after the verb.

SPEAKING

CONFIDENT COMMUNICATOR

Me, too! and *Me neither!* are examples of common and natural expressions used in real life. Using these expressions will help students develop conversations. It is important to use suitable intonation—enthusiastic for affirmative statements, and not enthusiastic for negative statements. Practice the two expressions with the whole class and individually.

GO TO page xv
for LANGUAGE AND LIFE step-by-step instructions.

Yes

GO TO page 64
for AUDIO SCRIPT.

Language and Life

Communication – Meet Someone

FUNCTIONAL LANGUAGE plan to meet

A 3.09 **Listen to the conversation. Are the speakers friends?**

B 3.09 **Listen again. Circle the correct option to complete Sofia's notes.**

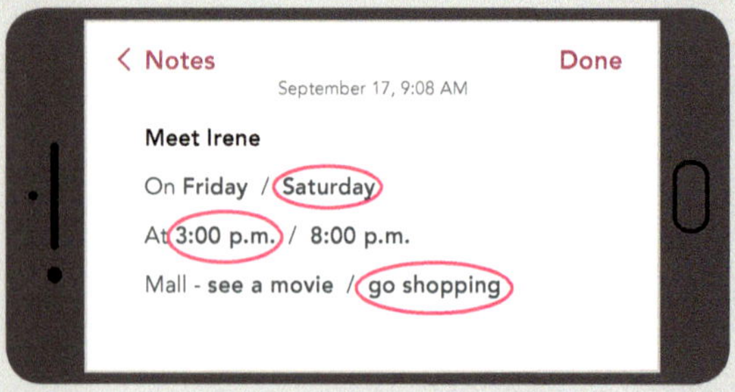

C 3.09 **Listen again. Add three examples of *Let's* and *How about* to the table.**

Let's (= Let us)	+ infinitive.	*Let's go to the mall.* 1 Let's see a movie. 2 Let's go shopping.
How about	+ time? + day?	*How about Saturday?* 3 How about 3:00 p.m.?

D Look at the table again. Then circle to complete the sentences.

1 Use the phrases with friends / people you do not know.
2 *Let's* ... is a sentence / question.
3 *Let's* is a contraction of *Let* + us / is.
4 *How about* is a sentence / question.
5 Use / Do not use a preposition of time after *How about.*

E 3.10 **Listen and underline the stressed words. Then listen again and repeat.**

Let's go to the mall.
Let's see a movie.

F IN PAIRS Complete the conversation with your own words. Then practice the conversation.

A: Hi. Are you free on Thursday? Let's ______________ .
B: Sorry. I work on Thursdays. I study in the evening. How about ______________ ? I'm free in the morning.
A: Me, too. How about ______________ ?
B: OK. Let's ______________ .
A: No. Let's ______________ .

OBJECTIVE

In this lesson, students learn how to make arrangements for meeting a friend. Students are provided with examples by listening to a conversation and reading an online post. The objective is to demonstrate how people develop relationships and to allow students to practice this. This will enable them to use English in the real world and to communicate with other English speakers.

PROCESS OPTIONAL 3.09, 3.10

In FUNCTIONAL LANGUAGE, students listen to a conversation where two friends are chatting on the phone. Students first complete the notes to recognize informal language. Then, students identify and repeat the stressed words in sentences. Finally, students complete the conversation using their own words. Students then have the opportunity to practice the conversation and give their own personal details, in order to replicate an authentic conversation.

CLASSROOM MANAGEMENT

Before students open their books, write the heading *Meet Irene* on the board and *On, At,* and *Mall* in three columns.

Ask students who you are meeting (*Irene*) and ask what type of information goes with *on* (*days*) and *at* (*time*). Ask for examples of days and times. Then ask students to suggest ideas for activities at the mall. Finally, tell students they will listen to a conversation about this situation and then start the lesson.

WRITING a post

A Read the posts and answer the questions. Who is a teacher? Who are students?

Teacher: Roger
Students: Mia and Paola

English **101**

Welcome to your English class! I'm Roger. I'm your teacher. Nice to meet you! There are 95 students in this online language course. Let's say hello!

Hi, Roger! Hi, everyone! I'm Mia. I'm from Salvador. I'm a student. I always go to classes in the mornings. **I usually go by bus, but sometimes I walk.** Do you live in my city? Let's start a study group! **I'm free in the evenings but not in the afternoons.**

Hello Mia! My name's Paola and I'm a police officer. How about Monday? I'm free at 7:00 p.m. Let's meet at the coffee shop across from the train station. **It's quiet and the coffee is great.**
1 day ago

B Look at the bold sentences. Which word ...

1. joins two affirmative phrases or clauses? and
2. joins an affirmative and a negative phrase or clause? but
3. comes after a comma? but

C Complete the sentences with *and* or *but*.

1. I'm a student and I'm a manager.
2. I rarely work in the evening, but sometimes I work on the weekend.
3. I like my city, but I don't like my apartment.
4. I go to bed at 11:00 p.m. and I get up at 7:00 a.m.

D Prepare a reply for Roger's post.

1. Write sentences with:
   - your name ______
   - where you live ______
   - where and when you work/study ______
2. Join two sentences with *and*. Join two sentences with *but*. ______
3. Arrange to meet your classmates. ______

E IN PAIRS Exchange your sentences. Check that your partner includes all the points in D.

F Read your sentences again and make any changes. Then write your reply in a paragraph.

MAKE IT DIGITAL

Go online and search for online courses. What courses are there? Is there a course you like?

WRITING Alternative Activity

After WRITING **A**, ask three students to read one of the three posts out loud. Then put students into groups of three and ask them to repeat the activity. Monitor and correct any errors. If the class needs more support, read Roger's post out loud and then ask each student to read one sentence until the other two posts have been read out loud.

WRITING Alternative Activity

After WRITING **F**, put students into new pairs and ask them to swap their paragraphs. Ask students to review their partner's work and check that the points in **D** have been included. Then ask a few students to read their posts out loud to the class. Remind students that reading out loud helps improve sound and letter recognition, as well as providing good pronunciation practice.

GO TO page xvii
for UNIT REVIEW step-by-step instructions.

VOCABULARY review

SCORE: / 5

A Match the sentence beginnings (1–5) to the sentence ends (a–e).

1 A chef works __c__
2 A pilot flies __d__
3 I don't eat __e__
4 I usually go __b__
5 I always get __a__

a up at 6:00 a.m.
b to bed early.
c in a restaurant.
d a plane to different places.
e breakfast on the weekend.

GRAMMAR review

SCORE: / 5

A Find and correct the error in each sentence.

1 The store closes on 7:00 p.m. __The store closes at 7:00 p.m.__
2 They goes to school by bus. __They go to school by bus.__
3 Does they start work at 9:00 a.m.? Yes, they do. __Do they start work at 9:00 a.m.? Yes, they do.__
4 I eat lunch never. __I never eat lunch.__
5 Do you always eat breakfast? No, I does. __Do you always eat breakfast? No, I don't.__

6–10 correct: You can talk about jobs, describe your partner, talk about time and daily activities, and describe your daily routine. You can use simple present statements, *yes/no* questions with simple present and adverbs of frequency.
0–5 correct: Look again at the Vocabulary and Grammar sections in the unit.

TOTAL SCORE: / 10

WHAT DO YOU KNOW NOW? Look back at the unit and review the language you know now.

GO TO page xviii
for STUDY SKILLS step-by-step instructions.

STUDY SKILLS RECORDING VOCABULARY

A IN GROUPS **Think of three ways to make vocabulary notes. Tell your group.**

B Look at the ways below. Are these ways you use?

1
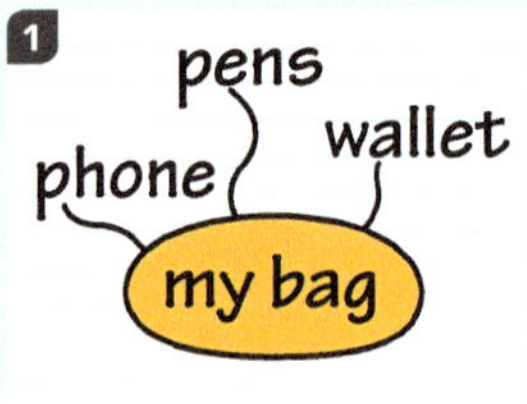

2
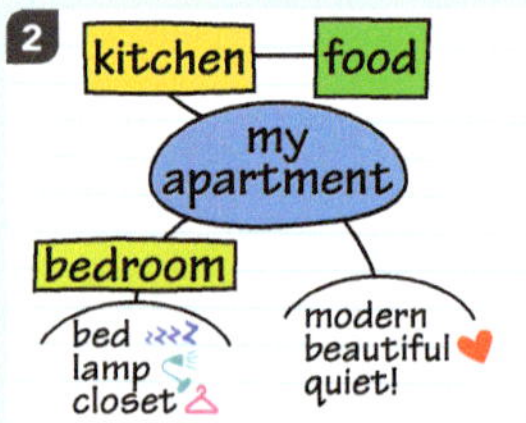

3
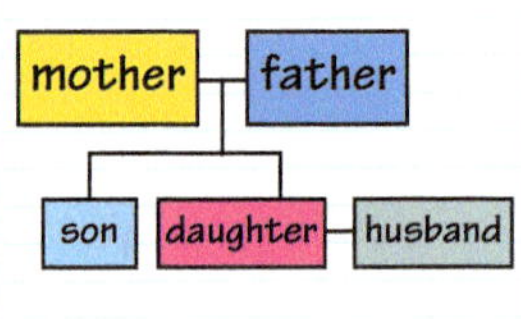

C Choose one way (or more) from B and make notes on vocabulary from Unit 1, 2 or 3.

D IN GROUPS **Show your vocabulary notes to the group. Then say the words. Don't look at your notes.**

CLASSROOM MANAGEMENT

You may wish to introduce a time limit (5–10 minutes) and have students work alone to encourage a more authentic "test" feel to the activity. Allow students to check answers in pairs and make any revisions before confirming answers with the class.

STUDY SKILLS TASK Extra Practice

Ask students to go back and choose one vocabulary topic from Units 1–3. Write the topics on the board and ask students to call out as many words as they can (without referring to their notes).

UNIT 4

My City

GO TO page vi
for UNIT OPENER step-by-step instructions.

WHAT DO YOU ALREADY KNOW?

1 Think about things you can buy in stores or malls. Write words that you know in the box.

2 IN PAIRS Share and compare your information. Add more words to the box, if possible.

Clothes: *dress,* ____________

Technology: *laptop,* ____________

Accessories: *bags,* ____________

STUDENTS MAY ALREADY KNOW:

- basic items of clothing.
- basic items of technology.
- basic accessories.

VIDEO

DISCUSS & SHARE

3 IN GROUPS Watch the video and answer the question.

SYM Online shopping or store shopping?

GO TO page xx
for VIDEOS IN SYM step-by-step instructions.

In this unit, you will ...

- ask and answer questions about a tour, ask for and give directions and talk about your clothes.
- use thinking skills: analyze and evaluate.
- read about a city tour.
- use strategies to practice taking turns, finish a conversation in a natural way and reply when you don't know the answer.
- use communication skills to practice buying things and write a description of a store.
- follow a tour guide to learn about their job and the skills needed to be in this industry.

WHAT DO YOU ALREADY KNOW?

If you notice students are struggling to understand what to do, you can provide one or two examples to help them get started:

- **Clothes:** jacket, jeans, shoes, shirt
- **Technology:** camera, earbuds, e-reader, tablet
- **Accessories:** umbrella, wallet, watch

VIDEO

Before viewing, ask:

Why does he prefer to shop online? *delivery is in two days...*

Why does she like to shop at stores? *she can talk to the sales assistant...*

After viewing, put the continuum on the board.

online —— store

Have students mark the continuum and explain their preferences.

DISCUSS & SHARE

Online shopping is very popular nowadays, but many people still like shopping in stores. Draw a continuum on the board with *online* at one end and *store* at the other. Have students stand in front of the continuum based on how they prefer to shop. Discuss the pros and cons of each style of shopping.

GO TO page vii
for **VOCABULARY** step-by-step instructions.

LESSON 1 Places

VOCABULARY places in a city

A IN PAIRS **Write the correct phrase from the box under the pictures.**

buy a book	buy a drink	eat dinner	get a bus	get a degree
get help	get money	go for a walk	learn about the past	stay on vacation

1 bus station

get a bus

2 park

go for a walk

3 ATM

get money

4 hotel

stay on vacation

5 museum

learn about the past

6 hospital

get help

7 university

get a degree

8 bookstore

buy a book

9 coffee shop

buy a drink

10 restaurant

eat dinner

B 4.01 **Listen, check your answers to A and repeat.**

C IN PAIRS **Think about your hometown and tell your partner about the places in A.**

There's a coffee shop and a park.

MAKE IT YOURS

What other places do you often go to in your hometown? Use your dictionary to find new words.

GO TO page x
for **READING** step-by-step instructions.

READING

A 4.02 **Quickly read the text in B. Choose a description.**

information about a city tour | review of a restaurant | advertisement for a museum

B **Read the text again. What places from VOCABULARY A are in the text?**

bus station
museum
restaurant
hotel

What places does the tour visit?
The tour goes to the important places in the city. For example, there are two museums in the city. There's the history museum and the science museum. The museums are free on Tuesdays. Tourists always love the history museum.

Where does the tour start and finish?
Everywhere! Tourists get on the bus at the bus station or at a bus stop in the city. People get off the bus and go to a museum or have lunch in a restaurant. Then people get on the bus again later. It's very easy!

When does the first tour start?
The first tour leaves the bus station at 7:00 a.m. The last tour is at 9:00 p.m. There is a new tour every hour.

Where do I buy tickets?
We sell tickets at the bus station, online and on the bus. Hotels also sell tickets.

How much do the tickets cost?
The tickets cost $20 for adults and $10 for children or students.

VOCABULARY Alternative Activity

Play the audio from VOCABULARY **B** again and ask students to listen for the number of syllables and the word stress. If necessary, do a few examples:

- O o o: bus station, coffee shop (Explain that the stress falls on the first noun in compound nouns, and give other examples: **train** station, **town** hall, hospital, restaurant.)
- O: park
- O O O: ATM (Explain that letters in an acronym have equal stress. Tell students that *ATM* is an acronym for *automated teller machine*.)

READING

Before starting the READING activities, read the five questions in the text out loud. Ask students to call out ideas or answers. Encourage all ideas. For larger classes, divide the class into five groups. Give one question to each group and ask them to brainstorm answers. Set a time limit of two minutes before checking ideas as a class.

C READING SKILL—Locate information in a text **Read the text again. Choose *True* or *False*. Correct the false sentences.**

1 The museums are free on one day. True / False
2 People have lunch on the bus. True / False
3 The last tour is at 7:00 p.m. True / False
4 People buy tickets online. True / False

D THINKING SKILL—Analyze **Do you like bus tours? Explain why or why not.**

2 People have lunch in a restaurant.
3 The last tour is at 9 p.m.

GRAMMAR simple present information questions

GO TO pages viii–ix for GRAMMAR step-by-step instructions.

A Complete the questions from the text.

1 Where does the tour start and finish?
2 What does the tour visit?
3 When does the first tour start?
4 How much do the tickets cost?

B Match the question words (1–4) to the information (a–d).

1 how much
2 what
3 when
4 where

a place
b time
c general information
d price

1 d
2 c
3 b
4 a

C Complete the table with *do* or *does*.

Question Word	*do/does*	Subject	Verb
Where	1 does	the tour	start and finish?
What	2 does	the tour	visit?
When	3 does	the first tour	start?
Where	4 do	I	buy tickets?
How much	5 do	the tickets	cost?

For more practice, go to page 74.

D Complete the questions.

1 *Where* do you go on the weekend?
2 What do tourists visit in your town?
3 When does your favorite coffee shop open?
4 How much does a bus ticket cost in your town?

E IN PAIRS **Answer the questions in D. Discuss.**

SPEAKING

GO TO page xii for SPEAKING step-by-step instructions.

A IN PAIRS **Read the information about a tour. Take turns to ask and answer questions from GRAMMAR A.**

Student A: look at the information on page 65 of the Activity Bank.
Student B: look at the information on page 67 of the Activity Bank.

B IN GROUPS **Compare and discuss the two tours in the Activity Bank and the tour in READING A. Choose your favorite. Use the Confident Communicator box to help you.**

CONFIDENT COMMUNICATOR
KEEP TALKING

To take turns with your partner, ask and answer:
Is it my turn?
Yes, it's your turn.
No, it's my turn.

GRAMMAR Extra Practice

Ask students to write one simple present information question for each of the four question words in GRAMMAR **B**. Monitor and help as necessary. Then put them into small groups (or do a class mingle) to take turns asking and answering questions. Remind students that they can make up answers. You may not wish to correct errors in answers because the target language is simple present information questions.

SPEAKING Alternative Activity

For less confident classes, divide the class into an even number of small groups and name the groups A and B. Group As read the information on page 65 and Group Bs read page 67. Monitor and help. Then put students into pairs: one from a Group A and one from a Group B. Pairs take turns asking and answering questions.

LESSON 2 Directions

GO TO page xi
for **LISTENING** step-by-step instructions.

GO TO page 65
for **AUDIO SCRIPT**.

LISTENING

A 4.03 **Listen and match the conversations (1–3) to the places (a–c).**

1 Conversation 1 — a hotel
2 Conversation 2 — b museum
3 Conversation 3 — c train station

1 b
2 c
3 a

B 4.03 LISTENING SKILL—Understand key words **Listen again and number the directions in the correct order.**

Conversation 1
4 it's on the left
1 go straight
3 take the second right
2 turn left

Conversation 2
3 take the #5 bus—about 10 minutes
2 bus station
1 go straight

Conversation 3
3 bookstore on left
4 between coffee shop and bookstore
2 take the first left
1 turn right

C IN GROUPS THINKING SKILL—Evaluate **Discuss and compare the ways you remember directions or information. Do you repeat information? Do you write notes or take pictures?**

MAKE IT REAL

Use *Excuse me* before you ask questions to people you don't know.
Excuse me, *is the park near here?*

VOCABULARY prepositions of place 2

A Write a phrase from the box under each picture.

across from | between | next to | on | on the corner of | on the left/right

1 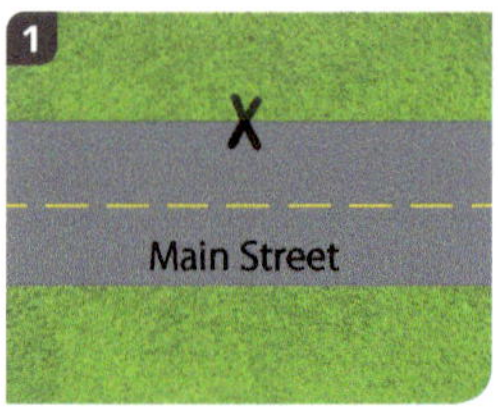

on

2 

on the corner of

3 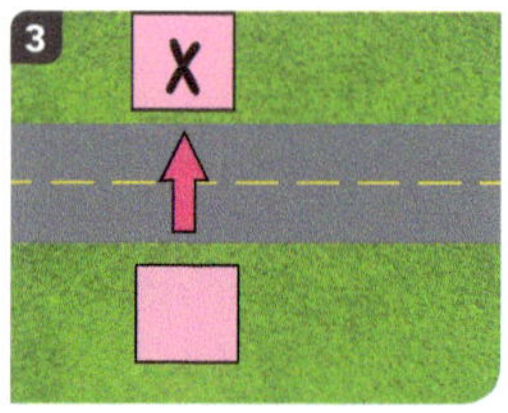

across from

4 

next to

5 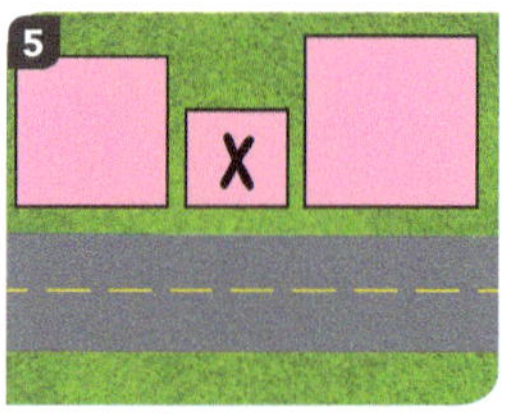

between

6 

on the left, on the right

B 4.04 **Listen and check your answers to A. Then listen and repeat.**

C IN PAIRS **Complete the activity. Then switch roles.**

Student A: close your book.
Student B: say a preposition of place.
Student A: draw a picture that represents the preposition.

LISTENING

LISTENING SKILL—Understand key words

Tell students that understanding key words is an important skill in listening (and reading). It will help them understand the general situation or topic, and it will help them focus on the important details in a conversation. Remind students that learning new vocabulary and increasing their lexicon will support the development of this skill.

VOCABULARY

Ask students to close their books and draw picture 1 on the board. Ask students what the name of the school's street is and write it in the picture. Say *We are on Main Street.* Then draw picture 2 on the board and elicit a place name for the *X* (e.g., *museum*) and write this in the picture. Ask students to say two street names and add these to the picture. Say *The museum is on the corner of [street name] and [street name].* Repeat this for the other pictures.

GRAMMAR imperatives

A Add the sentences to the table.

Is the train station near here? It's across from the park. It's between the park and the school. Take the second right. Turn left.

Ask for Directions	Give Directions	Finish Directions
Where's the museum?	*Go straight up this road.*	*The science museum is on the left.*
1	2	4
	3	5

1 Is the train station near here?
2 Take the second right. OR Turn left.
3 Turn left. OR Take the second right.
4 It's across from the park. OR It's between the park and the school.
5 It's between the park and the school. OR It's across from the park.

B Underline the verbs in the table in A.

C Choose the correct words to complete the rules.

To give directions:
1 Start / Do not start the sentence with a verb.
2 Use / Do not use a subject in the sentence.
To finish directions:
3 Use / Do not use a subject in the sentence.

For more practice, go to page 75.

D 4.05 Put the words in the correct order. Listen and check your answers.

1 where / the hospital? / me, / Excuse / is *Excuse me, where is the hospital?*
2 this / straight / Go / road. / up Go straight up this road.
3 to / bookstore / The / is / the hotel. / next The bookstore is next to the hotel.
4 It's / the / corner of / 1st / and Main. / on It's on the corner of 1st and Main.
5 take / Turn left / first / right. / the / and Turn left and take the first right.

E IN PAIRS Write directions for the questions in D. Use your own ideas or give real directions.

SPEAKING

A IN PAIRS Complete the activity. Choose other places and ask for directions. Use the Confident Communicator box to help you.

Student A and Student B: look at the map on page 66 of the Activity Bank.
Student A: ask for directions to the library. **Student B:** ask for directions to the train station.

CONFIDENT COMMUNICATOR
KEEP TALKING

To finish a conversation in a natural way, it is polite to say *Thanks* or *Thank you* and to reply *No problem* or *You're welcome.*

GRAMMAR Extra Practice

For additional practice asking for and giving directions, have students work in pairs or groups to add to each column of the table. Students could ask for and give directions to known places near the school. To further students' understanding, suggest that they follow these directions after class to see if the directions were correct.

SPEAKING

Ask students to practice using other maps (print or online). Students work in pairs and each choose one place on their map to ask for directions. Students then trade maps and take turns asking for and giving directions using the maps. Monitor and help as necessary. Invite pairs to perform their conversation for the class.

LESSON 3 Clothes

VOCABULARY clothes

A Write one word from each pair in the box under the pictures (1–5).

dress/skirt   jacket/suit   pants/jeans   shirt/T-shirt   shoes/boots

1  skirt

2  jacket

3  pants

4  shirt

5  boots

1 loose, tight
2 dressy, casual
3 long, short
4 cheap, expensive

B 4.06 Go to page 67 of the Activity Bank.

C IN GROUPS Make a list of your clothes in your notebook. Add more information, e.g., style or color.

dressy jacket, new jeans, pink T-shirt

GO TO page ix

for **PRONUNCIATION** step-by-step instructions.

PRONUNCIATION vowel sounds 1

A 4.07 Listen to the vowel sound and the words. Then listen again and repeat.

æ	ɛ	ɜ˞	iː	uː
jacket	dress	skirt	jeans	shoes

B 4.08 Listen and match the words (1–4) to the correct vowel sound (a–d).

1 boots   2 pants   3 shirt   4 T-shirt

a æ   b ɜ˞   c iː   d uː

1 d
2 a
3 b
4 c

LISTENING

A Look at the pictures. Which people are in a store?

2

a 

b 

MAKE IT REAL

Stores use numbers, letters or words for sizes.
Numbers: *4, 6, 8, 10, 12, 14, 16, 18, 20*
Letter and words: *XS* (extra small), *S* (small), *M* (medium), *L* (large), *XL* (extra large)

GO TO page 65

for **AUDIO SCRIPT**.

B 4.09 Listen and check. Match the conversations to the pictures in A.

Conversation 1: a   Conversation 2: b

C 4.09 LISTENING SKILL—Identify information Listen again and complete each sentence.

Conversation 1
1 The clothes are under **$30** / $20.
2 The dress is / **isn't** the correct size.
3 They **like** / don't like the shoes.

Conversation 2
4 The red T-shirt is **$55** / $15.
5 The blue T-shirt **is** / isn't the correct size.
6 The sister **likes** / doesn't like the bags.

D THINKING SKILL—Evaluate Do you buy clothes in a store or online? Why?

VOCABULARY

Ask students to identify the four plural nouns (*pants, jeans, shoes, boots*). Tell students *pants* and *jeans* are always plural. Students can remember this by remembering we have two (plural) legs, not one (singular), like *shoes* and *boots* for two feet.

PRONUNCIATION

Refer students to the five vowel sounds in PRONUNCIATION **A** and practice them again. Then, ask students to match these words (from Lessons 1 and 2) to the correct vowel sound: /æ/: *adult*, /e/: *left*, /ɜː/: *university*, /ɪː/: *between*, and /uː/: *museum*.

MAKE IT REAL

For less-confident classes, quickly review the alphabet and numbers by having each student say the next number/letter in the sequence.

Write *My shoe size is 5.5.* on the board and say the sentence. Elicit *point* for the period and ask a few students what their shoe size is.

GRAMMAR *this/that/these/those*

A Complete the sentences from LISTENING B (1–4) with the correct word from the box.

that these this those ×2

1 Do you like ___this___ blue T-shirt?
2 Look at ___these___ T-shirts!
3 Look at ___that___ jacket over there!
4 It's between ___those___ shoes and ___those___ bags.

B Read the sentences in A and complete the rules.

1 Use ___this___ and ___that___ for singular nouns, e.g., *T-shirt*.
2 Use ___these___ and ___those___ for plural nouns, e.g., *T-shirts*.

C Go to page 69 of the Activity Bank.

D Match the sentence halves.

1 Use *this* and *these* for objects	a not very near to you.
2 Use *that* and *those* for objects	b very near to you.

For more practice, go to page 76.

1 this
2 that
3 these
4 those

1 b
2 a

E Complete the sentences with *this*, *that*, *these* or *those*.

1 ___*This*___ is my favorite shirt and ___these___ are my favorite jeans.
2 Look at ___that___ dress in the window over there! It's beautiful. ___Those___ shoes are pretty, too.
3 I like ___those___ jeans over there. They're next to ___that___ yellow bag.
4 ___These___ skirts over here are expensive. ___Those___ skirts by the door are cheap.

F IN PAIRS Write sentences describing:

1 your clothes using *this* or *these*.
2 your partner's clothes using *that* or *those*.

This shirt is new. These shoes are size 8. That long skirt is nice. Those jeans are loose.

SPEAKING

A IN PAIRS Role-play. Then switch roles and repeat. Use the Confident Communicator box to help you.

Student A: close your book.
Student B: point to clothes on the page (or your clothes) and ask *What's this/these?*
Student A: answer with *That's ... / Those are ...*

CONFIDENT COMMUNICATOR
REPAIR IT

To help you reply when you don't know the answer, say:
✓ *I think so.* ? *I'm not sure. / I don't know.*
× *I don't think so.*

GRAMMAR

Introduce the consonant sound /ð/ for *this*, *that*, *these*, and *those*. Model the sound yourself and ask students to repeat. Listen carefully for any incorrect /d/ or /t/ sounds and correct these. Then refer students to GRAMMAR **A** and read the completed sentences to the class. Ask a few students to repeat, and then put students into pairs to take turns saying the sentences. Monitor and correct any pronunciation errors.

SPEAKING

Remind students that *this* and *these* are used for things near us (i.e., things we can reach) and *that* and *those* are used for things not near us (i.e., things we can't reach).

Additional Activity

Put students into two groups. Each student describes their own clothes (with *this/these*). Then the group works together to describe the other group's clothes (with *that/those*).

CULTURE NOTE

Elicit the different places people can buy things in their own country (e.g., markets, supermarket, Internet, stores, etc.) and ask which places students prefer and why.

Tell students that a *garage sale* (or *yard sale*, *tag sale*) is an informal event where people sell things from their homes they no longer use, need, or like for a very low price. The seller puts everything in the garage (or in the yard) for people to buy.

GO TO page xv

for **LANGUAGE AND LIFE** step-by-step instructions.

Language and Life

Communication – Shop

FUNCTIONAL LANGUAGE buy things

3, 5

A **Look at the pictures and quickly read the conversation. What things (1–6) do the people not talk about?**

1 

2 

3 

4 

5 

6 

Ally: Excuse me. How much is this laptop?
Bob: It's $ __50__ . It isn't new. It's old and slow.
Ally: Oh, OK. No, thank you.
Cate: **How much are these black boots?**
Bob: **They're $ __30__ .**
Cate: **Oh, that's expensive.**
Bob: Do you like these brown boots? These are only $15.
Cate: Oh, yes. Could I take those, please?
Bob: Sure. That's $ __15__ , please.
Cate: Here you go.
Bob: Thanks.
Ally: How much are the books in this box?
Bob: They're $ __1__ each.
Ally: **Could I take these two books, please?**
Bob: **No problem. That's $ __2__ , please.**
Ally: Here you go.
Bob: Thank you. Have a great day!

B 4.10 **Read and listen to the conversation. Complete the prices in A.**

FIRST QUESTION AND ANSWER
Buyer: How much are the books in this box?
Seller: They're are $1 each.
DECISION
Yes: Could I take these two books, please?
No: Oh, that's expensive.
PAYING
Seller: No problem. That's $ 2, please.

C **Look at the diagram. Add more bold examples from the conversation in your notebook.**

FIRST QUESTION AND ANSWER	**Buyer** Excuse me. How much is this laptop? →	**Seller** It's $50.
DECISION	**Yes** Could I take those, please?	**No** No, thank you.
PAYING	**Seller** Sure. That's $15, please. →	**Buyer** Here you go.

OBJECTIVE

In this lesson, students learn how to sell and buy different objects. They will practice different prices and the polite form to ask for information. Also, students will read and write some descriptions. The objective is to help students get familiar with vocabulary when they are buying or selling something.

PROCESS OPTIONAL 4.10, 4.11

In FUNCTIONAL LANGUAGE, students listen to a conversation where two buyers are looking at things for sale and asking the seller questions. Students then identify useful expressions. Finally, students practice the conversation and role-play buying things.

D **Put the conversation in the correct order.**

3 Oh, that's expensive. How much are these small notebooks?
7 Here you go.
2 It's $10.
6 Sure. That's $6, please.
1 Excuse me, how much is this big notebook?
5 OK. Could I take two small notebooks, please?
4 They're $3 each.

E 4.11 **Listen and check. Then listen again and repeat.**

GO TO page 65 for AUDIO SCRIPT.

F IN PAIRS **Take turns to be the seller and the buyer. Choose something to buy from the box. Repeat the conversation in C with the new object and price.**

jeans $40 laptop $200 notebook $4 pens $2 shoes $25 skirt $20

WRITING a description

A **Read the description and answer the questions in your notebook.**

Ellie 12. June 2019

My favorite store is Alfred's. It's a small store on Park Street. It's next to a modern hotel. The store sells old clothes, computers, jewelry and books. It's an interesting store. The things are usually cheap.

1 What is the store's name?
2 Where is the store?
3 What does the store sell?
4 How much are things in the store?

1 Alfred's
2 Park Street; next to a modern hotel
3 old clothes, computers, jewelry, and books
4 cheap

B **Choose the correct word to complete the sentence.**

A noun / verb follows the bold adjectives in **A**.

C **Add the adjectives to the sentences in your notebook.**

1 This is an website. (*interesting*)
2 Those are the books. (*cheap*)
3 It's a store. (*busy*)
4 My sister buys shoes. (*expensive*)

1 This is an interesting website.
2 Those are the cheap books.
3 It's a busy store.
4 My sister buys expensive shoes.

D **Prepare a description of your favorite store. Write answers to the questions in A. Include adjectives.**

E IN PAIRS **Exchange your descriptions in D. Check that your partner answers the questions in A and uses adjectives correctly.**

F **Write your description in a paragraph.**

MAKE IT DIGITAL

Search online for descriptions of stores in your city. Do you agree with the descriptions (of stores you know)? Are there new stores in your city?

WRITING Alternative Activity

After WRITING **E**, put students into new pairs and ask them to swap their descriptions. Ask them to read their new partner's description and answer the questions in WRITING **A**. (Students can underline the answers in the description or make a separate note.) Then join two pairs together to make groups of four, and ask students to take turns telling the group about their partner's store.

FURTHER DISCUSSION

Ask the class if they or anyone they know works in a store. Ask them to describe the store by asking the questions from WRITING **A**. Ask further questions:

- What time does the store open?
- Is it a big store?
- Do you like the store?
- What places are near the store?

Elicit simple sentences from the answers and write these on the board (e.g., *The store opens at …*).

GO TO page xvii for UNIT REVIEW step-by-step instructions.

UNIT 4

VOCABULARY review

SCORE: / 5

A Choose the correct words.

1. Let's get something to drink at the coffee shop / bus station.
2. The store is on the between / corner of Main Street and First Avenue.
3. Wow! These clothes aren't expensive. They're cheap / tight.
4. The bookstore is on the left / between the restaurant and the bus station.
5. I like these dress / boots.

GRAMMAR review

SCORE: / 5

A Choose the words to complete the sentences.

1. These / This are my new shoes. Do you like them?
2. Where do / does you buy your clothes?
3. What / Where is the restaurant?
4. Take / Go straight up this road.
5. The museum is across from / between the park.

6–10 correct: You can talk about places in a city, give directions, describe where places are, and talk about clothes. You can use simple present information questions, imperatives and *this/that/these/those*.
0–5 correct: Look again at the Vocabulary and Grammar sections in the unit.

TOTAL SCORE: / 10

WHAT DO YOU KNOW NOW? Look back at page 35 and add the words you know now to the box.

GO TO page xix for FOLLOW A PRO step-by-step instructions.

FOLLOW A PRO — TOUR GUIDE

A Complete the diagram about a tour guide. Use the verbs in the box.

answers gives speaks

A tour guide …
1 speaks different languages.
2 gives information.
3 answers questions.
is friendly.
knows about the city.

GO TO page 66 for AUDIO SCRIPT.

B 4.12 Listen and number the points in the order you hear them.

2 knows about the city
4 is friendly
5 answers questions
3 speaks different languages
1 gives information

C Discuss the questions as a class.

1. Does your city have tour guides? Where do they work?
2. Is it important to have a friendly tour guide?
3. Do tour guides get a lot of money?

44 Unit 4 My City

CLASSROOM MANAGEMENT

You can do these review activities as a class dictation activity. Students should close their books and use their notebooks and pens. Read some sentences with blanks and have students write a suitable word or phrase to complete each one. Check ideas as a class and accept all grammatically correct ideas. Clarify any doubts.

CAREER NOTE

Before starting the FOLLOW A PRO section, practice the pronunciation of *tour guide* (/ˈtʊr ˈgaɪd/) with the class. Put students into small groups or do this as a whole-class activity. Ask them to quickly brainstorm information about a tour guide. Check ideas as a class. Explain that using and activating their real-life knowledge of the world will help them with topics like this.

GO TO page vi
for **UNIT OPENER** step-by-step instructions.

UNIT 5 Free Time

WHAT DO YOU ALREADY KNOW?

1 Think about the activities people enjoy in different types of weather. Write words that you know in the boxes.

2 IN PAIRS Share and compare your information. Add more words to the boxes, if possible.

Activities in hot weather: *surfing,* ________

Activities in cool weather: *skiing,* ________

STUDENTS MAY ALREADY KNOW:

- basic free-time activities, sports, or hobbies.
- the seasons of the year.
- basic weather vocabulary.

VIDEO

DISCUSS & SHARE

3 IN GROUPS Watch the video and answer the question.

SYM Hot weather or cool weather?

GO TO page xx
for **VIDEOS IN SYM** step-by-step instructions.

In this unit, you will ...

- talk about what you can/can't do, talk about different people's objects and discuss activities people are doing.
- use thinking skills: analyze, recall and brainstorm.
- read an online advertisement for college courses.
- use strategies to add explanations or extra information to continue a conversation, respond to others when playing a game and use expressions to show you understand.
- use communication skills to make recommendations and write a blog post.
- learn skills to practice vocabulary.

WHAT DO YOU ALREADY KNOW?

If you notice students are struggling to understand what to do, you can provide one or two examples to help them get started:

- **Activities in hot weather:** hiking, horseback riding, swimming
- **Activities in cool weather:** baking a cake, going shopping, watching movies

VIDEO

Before viewing, ask:

What activities can you do in hot/cool weather? *swimming, surfing ... / skating, skiing ...*

After viewing, put this continuum on the board.

hot weather ——— cold weather

Have students mark the continuum and explain why they like hot or cold weather.

DISCUSS & SHARE

Have students consider what some of their favorite hobbies and activities are and whether these are done in warmer weather or cooler weather. Ask students what they like and dislike most about each type of weather. List answers on the board.

LESSON 1 Activities

GO TO page vii
for **VOCABULARY** step-by-step instructions.

VOCABULARY free-time activities

A 5.01 **Listen and look at the pictures. Write the numbers of the activities you do not hear.**

2, 3, 4, 5

1 ride a horse

2 draw pictures

3 bake a cake

4 do karate

5 drive a car

6 dance salsa

7 swim 1,500 m

8 play an instrument

B **Write the activities from the box under the pictures in A.**

bake a cake	dance salsa	do karate	draw pictures
drive a car	play an instrument	ride a horse	swim 1,500 m

MAKE IT YOURS

Write other activities that you or your friends do in your notebook. Use your dictionary to help you.

C 5.02 **Listen, check and repeat.**

GO TO page xi
for **LISTENING** step-by-step instructions.

GO TO page 66
for **AUDIO SCRIPT**.

LISTENING

A 5.03 LISTENING SKILL—Listen for main idea **Listen and choose the correct descriptions.**

1 The conversation is on a radio show / in a classroom.
2 The people are new students at a college / friends at a sports event.

B 5.03 **Listen again. What activities from VOCABULARY A do you hear?**

draw, swim, do karate, ride a horse, drive a car, dance salsa, play an instrument

C 5.03 **Listen again and complete the table.**

Name	Can ✓	Can't ✗
Francesca	draw	swim
	do karate	
Javier	drive a car	ride a horse
		dance salsa
		play the piano

D THINKING SKILL—Analyze **Categorize the activities from VOCABULARY A so they are true for you.**

Cheap	Expensive	Easy	Hard

VOCABULARY Alternative Activity

Put students into pairs and ask them to find two nouns that have two syllables (*salsa*, *pictures*) and two nouns that have three syllables (*karate*, *instrument*).

Then ask pairs to find words with these vowel sounds: /eɪ/: *bake*, *cake*, *play*; /ɔː/: *draw*, *horse*; /aɪ/: *drive*, *ride*.

You can give just the vowel sounds to more confident classes or give the vowel sound and one example to less confident classes.

LISTENING OPTIONAL 5.03

LISTENING SKILL—Listen for main idea

Remind students that listening for the main idea will help them recognize the general situation and context or topic. When listening to a new conversation, they should listen for where the speakers are (e.g., at home, at work), what their relationship is (e.g., friends, colleagues), and what's the context (e.g., an informal conversation, a job interview). Once students have identified the main idea, it is easier to understand details.

GRAMMAR *can/can't*

A 5.04 Complete the sentences from LISTENING A with *can* or *can't*. Listen and check.

1 __Can__ you draw? Yes, I __can__.
2 __Can__ you swim? No, I __can't__. I __can't__ swim, I __can__ do karate.
3 __Can__ you ride a horse? No, I __can't__. I __can__ drive a car.

B Look at the questions and answers in A. Match to complete the rules.

1	To make *Can* questions, use	a	*yes/no* + pronoun + *can/can't*.
2	To give short answers, use	b	pronoun + *can/can't* + infinitive.
3	To make *can* statements, use	c	*can* + pronoun + infinitive.

For more practice, go to page 76.

1 c
2 a
3 b

C Complete the sentences.

1 A: __*Can you*__ do karate? B: __No__, I can't.
2 A: __Can__ you play the piano? B: Yes, I __can__.
3 A: Can he swim? B: No, he __can't__.
4 A: Can they bake a cake? B: __Yes__, they can.
5 I can dance salsa, but I __can't__ play an instrument.
6 I can ride a horse and I __can__ drive a car.

D IN PAIRS Ask and answer the questions in A. Answer the questions for you.

GO TO pages viii–ix for GRAMMAR step-by-step instructions.

PRONUNCIATION stress in *can/can't*

A 5.05 Listen and underline the stressed words.

1 Can you <u>bake</u> a <u>cake</u>?
2 <u>Yes</u>, I can <u>bake</u> a <u>cake</u>.
3 <u>No</u>, I <u>can't</u> <u>bake</u> a <u>cake</u>.

B 5.05 Listen again and repeat.

GO TO page ix for PRONUNCIATION step-by-step instructions.

SPEAKING

A Look at the pictures in VOCABULARY A. Put a check (✓) next to the activities you can do and an X (✗) next to the activities you can't do.

B IN GROUPS Take turns to ask and answer what you can/can't do. Use the Confident Communicator box to help you.

Find out:
- How many people can do each activity?
- How many people can't do each activity?
- Who can do an activity very well?

I can swim. I swim in a club. I swim in sports competitions.

CONFIDENT COMMUNICATOR – KEEP TALKING

To continue the conversation, add an explanation or extra information:
Can you ride a horse? No, I can't. ***I don't like big animals.***
Can you play the piano? Yes, I can. ***I'm very good.***

GO TO page xii for SPEAKING step-by-step instructions.

GRAMMAR

Tell students we use *can* to talk about our ability to do something. *Can* means we are able to do an activity and that we are good at it. The activity can be relatively simple (e.g., *I can make a sandwich.*) or difficult (e.g., *I can speak 10 languages.*).

Tell students we also use *can* for requests, such as ordering food and drinks (*Can I have a green salad, please?*).

SPEAKING

Encourage students to aim for fluency in this activity: to communicate what they can or can't do and find out more about their partner. This will give them the opportunity to have an authentic conversation within the supportive environment of the classroom. Encourage all ideas for extra information, and help less-confident students with this by asking them questions (e.g., *Do you like music?*) or offering ideas (e.g., *I don't like cooking.*).

LESSON 2 Studying

VOCABULARY subjects

A IN PAIRS **Answer the questions. Do you take other language classes or study other subjects? What are they?**

B **Match the pictures to the classes. Write the class under the picture.**

art Chinese creative writing dance math music science

1 
science

2 
art

3 
math

4 
Chinese

5 
dance

6 
creative writing

7 
music

C 5.06 **Listen and check your answers to B. Then listen again and repeat.**

1 dance class
2 Chinese
3 art
4 music
5 writing
6 science
7 math

D IN PAIRS **Student A: go to page 67 of the Activity Bank. Read the names of the classroom items. Student B: try to match each item to a subject.**

E IN PAIRS **Discuss. What classes in A do students usually study in high school in your country?**

GO TO page x

for **READING** step-by-step instructions.

READING

A **Quickly read the webpage. What type of text is it?**

an advertisement for courses a letter to students a story about a family

Students | Classes

Want to study a subject or learn a new hobby?
Green Park has the course for you.

Click here to meet our students.

Can you guess what they study?

This is Brad.

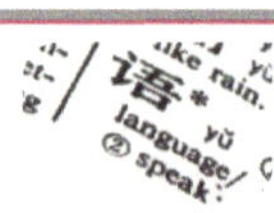

This is Brad's dictionary and these are Brad's shoes.

Brad's mother, Linda, is also a student.

This is Linda's notebook and these are Linda's paint brushes.

B 5.07 READING SKILL—Scan for key words **Read the Classes webpage on page 49. Add the classes from the box to the text.**

art Chinese dance math science writing

VOCABULARY

Remind students that one way of recording and remembering new vocabulary is to draw simple pictures for new words and phrases. Categories like school subjects, food, or clothes are very suitable for this technique. Tell students that the pictures do not need to be very good quality or detailed; they just need to remind students of the word and the meaning.

Extra Practice

Put students into groups and have them play a picture drawing game. A student chooses a word and draws a picture to represent the word. The group then guesses the word.

READING

READING SKILL—Scan for key words

Scanning means to read a text quickly in order to find key words. Key words will help you find specific information without reading the whole text. In order to find key words, you have to understand the text and know how it is structured.

Alternative Activity

Ask students to go online (or use a printed pamphlet or leaflet) to find out about other courses available in their city. Encourage them to find out extra information (e.g., the cost, time, and date). Ask students to learn 10 new words and tell the class about the courses.

science	math	Chinese
What do you know about science? This class is an introduction to biology, chemistry and physics. Our teachers use videos and real-life examples in the classes.	Are numbers hard for you? Our excellent teachers explain how to understand numbers. This is a popular class for young and old people.	Nĭ hăo! Join this class and say hello in a new language! Learn how to write and speak Chinese with our friendly Chinese teachers.
art	**dance**	**writing**
Can you draw? Everyone can learn to draw! The lessons are at the college, but students often visit places in the city.	Tango? Salsa? This course is for beginners. Learn about different dances and practice with our teachers.	Do you want to write a story? Students practice different ways of writing and share their stories with the class.

C IN PAIRS THINKING SKILL—Recall **List the classes Brad and Linda go to in your notebook.**

Brad: Chinese, salsa
Linda: writing, art

D **Read the text again. Find words that mean:**

1 an activity you enjoy (not a job) hobby
2 something that lots of people like popular
3 smiles at people and helps people friendly
4 people who start something new beginners

GRAMMAR possessive 's

A **Circle the five bold possessive 's in the text about Brad and his mother.**

B **Read the sentence and choose the correct meaning:**
This is Brad's dictionary and these are Brad's shoes.

Brad: This is my dictionary and these are my shoes. / This isn't my dictionary and these aren't my shoes.

C **Choose the word to complete the rule.**

1 Add 's before / after a name or noun.

For more practice, go to page 77.

D **Correct the sentences.**

1 Are these Brads books? *Are these Brad's books?*
2 Is this Linda notebook? Is this Linda's notebook?
3 This is the teacher dictionary. This is the teacher's dictionary.
4 These are my pen's. These are my pens.

SPEAKING

A **Work in groups of three. Go to page 69 of the Activity Bank and follow the instructions. Use the Confident Communicator box to help you.**

B **Switch roles and repeat.**

CONFIDENT COMMUNICATOR
KEEP TALKING

To continue the game after your partner gives his or her answer, say: *Yes, that's the correct answer! Good job! No, sorry. That's not the right answer. Try again.*

GRAMMAR

Elicit what a contraction is (two words that become one word with an apostrophe) and ask for examples (e.g., *I'm, don't*). Ask students for examples of apostrophes in the webpage in READING **A** (*Brad's mother, Linda's notebook*). Tell students these are *not* contractions. These apostrophes show possession or a relationship between two people or things.

Extra Practice

Put students into pairs. Ask them to write three sentences about their partner using the possessive 's. Monitor and help as necessary. Check for correct apostrophe use.

SPEAKING Alternative Activity

You could do this as a class activity: you call out one item (e.g., *apartment*) and students (or pairs or groups) call out the answer (*It's Amanda's apartment!*). You can ask students to close their books and use their memories, or for less-confident classes, students can refer to the page.

LESSON 3 Weather

VOCABULARY types of weather

A IN PAIRS **Order the weather from 1 (your favorite) to 5 (not your favorite).**

It's **sunny**. ____ It's **windy**. ____ It's **snowy**. ____ It's **rainy**. ____ It's **cloudy**. ____

B 5.08 **Listen and underline the stressed syllable in the bold words in A. Listen again and repeat.**

C **Add the words from the box to the thermometer.**

cool freezing hot

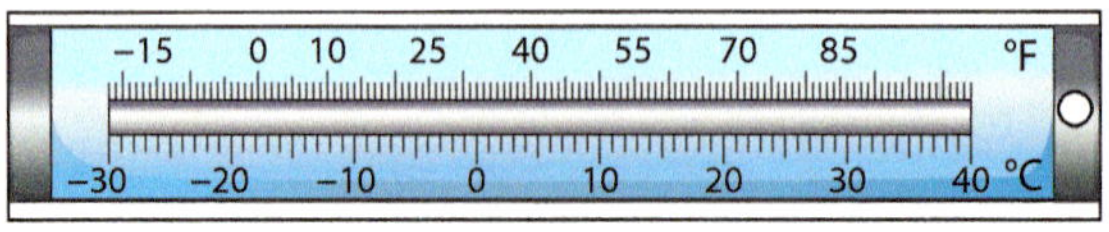

freezing ____ cool ____ hot ____

D 5.09 **Listen and check. Listen again and repeat.**

LISTENING

A IN GROUPS **Answer the question. How do you talk to friends in different places? Circle all the ways you use.**

email	social media
letter	text message
phone call	video call

GO TO page 66 for AUDIO SCRIPT.

B **Look at the picture. Which way from A are the friends using to communicate?**

video call

C 5.10 **Listen to the conversation and choose the correct option.**

The friends live in the same / different places and they are doing the same / different activities.

D 5.10 LISTENING SKILL—Listen for reasons **Listen again and match the sentence beginnings (1–3) to the sentence endings (a–c).**

1 Charlie and his family are at the beach
2 Barney is watching a movie and eating dinner
3 Jessica and her friend are buying food for a barbecue

a because it's very sunny.
b because it's warm.
c because the weather's bad.

1 a
2 c
3 b

E THINKING SKILL—Brainstorm **What other activities can you do in warm or cold weather?**

Suggested answers:
Warm weather: have a picnic, go on a hike, watch the sunset or sunrise

Cold weather: bake cookies, visit a museum, go ice skating

MAKE IT REAL

Use questions with *like* to ask for a short description.
What's the weather like? It's sunny.
What's the restaurant like? It's nice.

VOCABULARY Alternative Activity

Read the sentences in VOCABULARY **A**. Elicit what type of word the words are (*adjectives*). Ask students to write the noun form for each adjective (*sun, wind, snow, rain, cloud*). Check answers as a class by asking pairs to call out the word and the spelling. Drill the pronunciation of each noun. Tell students that word building improves vocabulary and makes reading and listening easier.

LISTENING Alternative Activity

After LISTENING **D**, ask students to listen again and make notes on the time and weather each speaker mentions. For less confident classes, give examples or write the times and weather on the board for students to match to the speaker.

- Charlie: [morning] hot, 86 degrees, sunny
- Barney: 8 p.m., rainy, windy, cold
- Jessica: 3 p.m., warm

CULTURE NOTE

Remind students that in the United States the temperature is measured in Fahrenheit. Other countries measure temperature in Celsius. Celsius is a scale that assigns the freezing point of water to be 0 degrees and the boiling point of water to be 100 degrees. Fahrenheit assigns the freezing point of water to be 32 degrees and the boiling point to be 212 degrees (i.e., 32° Fahrenheit = 0° Celsius).

GRAMMAR present progressive statements

A Read the summary of the conversation and underline seven examples of the present progressive. Then answer the questions (1–3).

Andy is swimming in the ocean. Charlie's mom isn't reading a book. She's sleeping. Charlie's dad is practicing Spanish. Barney is watching a movie and eating dinner. Jessica is shopping. Jessica and her friend are getting food for a barbecue. Charlie is having fun.

1 Are the activities in the past? no
2 Are the activities in the present? yes
3 Are the activities happening now? yes

B Add the verbs from the box to the table.

eat practice shop sleep

Pronoun	*To be* (+/–)	+ *–ing* Regular Spelling	Irregular Spelling	
I	'm 'm not	reading. watching TV. 1 eating 2 sleeping	getting coffee. swimming. 3 shopping	having fun. 4 practicing (Spanish)
He/She/It	's isn't			
You/ We/They	are aren't			

C Write the verbs from the table next to the spelling rule.

1 end of verb is consonant, vowel, consonant: double the final consonant and add *–ing* getting, swimming, shopping
2 a final *–e*: delete the final *e* and add *–ing* having, practicing

For more practice, go to page 77.

D 5.11 Complete the conversations. Then listen and check.

Conversation 1

A: *Are* you *studying*? (study) B: Yes. We 're practicing English. (practice)

Conversation 2

A: Are you eating lunch? (eat)

B: No, I 'm not eating lunch. I 'm having coffee with my sister. (eat, have)

E IN PAIRS Take turns to practice the conversations in D. Then write different answers to the questions.

SPEAKING

A IN GROUPS Role-play. What activities are you doing? What are you not doing?

Student A: go to page 69 of the Activity Bank. **Student B:** go to page 65 of the Activity Bank.
Student C: go to page 67 of the Activity Bank. **Student D:** go to page 68 of the Activity Bank.

B Ask and answer questions. Use the Confident Communicator box to help you.

CONFIDENT COMMUNICATOR
KEEP TALKING

To continue the conversation, use an expression to show you understand:

It's beautiful here. Look at the beach. *Wow!*
It's rainy. It's windy. It's very cold. *Oh, no!*

GRAMMAR

Ask students to find the sentence in GRAMMAR **A** where the verb *to be* is purposely omitted (*Barney is watching a movie and [no verb] eating dinner.*). Tell students that there is no need to repeat *is* for the second activity because it has been used for the first activity. Tell students that this is common practice in spoken and written English; it would be unnatural to repeat the verb.

SPEAKING Alternative Activity

Ask students to add one more activity, weather, and location. Students can go back and review the vocabulary from the lesson. Students should then include these words in the role-play. After the role-play, keep students in their groups of four. Ask Students B, C, and D to try to remember the activities and weather mentioned by Student A. Student A should confirm if their ideas are correct. Then repeat for Students B, C, and D.

GO TO page xv
for LANGUAGE AND LIFE step-by-step instructions.

Language and Life

Communication – Your City

FUNCTIONAL LANGUAGE make recommendations

A IN PAIRS **Discuss. What do tourists usually do in your city?**

B 5.12 **Read the blog and guess the missing words. Then listen and check.**

One Day in My City

530 Followers

Morning

Visit the museum and learn about the city's history. **Go** early because it's free before 10 a.m. **Don't go** on Monday because it's closed!

Afternoon

Go to the beach. **Swim** in the ocean or **take** a boat trip. **Get** a coffee at the beach café or at the hotel's coffee shop.

Evening

Eat dinner at Gino's pizzeria. **Reserve** a table because it's always busy. Then **go** to the park and **watch** a movie at the outdoor movie theater.

follow

C 5.13 **Listen and discuss. Why are the bold verbs stressed?**

Because the bold words have the important information/ message and tell the listener/reader to do something or not to do something.

Note: For negative imperatives, the negative auxiliary (e.g. *Don't*) is stressed, but the main verb is unstressed.

1. Visit the museum.
2. Don't go on Monday.
3. Go to the beach.
4. Swim in the ocean.
5. Get a coffee.
6. Eat dinner at Gino's.
7. Reserve a table.

D 5.13 **Listen again and repeat.**

E **Think about recommendations for your city. Use the verbs to help you.**

Don't ...	Go to ...	Visit ...
Eat ...	Look at ...	Walk ...

F IN PAIRS **Share your recommendations about your city.**

52 Unit 5 Free Time

OBJECTIVE

In this lesson, students learn how to make recommendations about their city. The objective is to provide students with an example of how to make recommendations (through a blog that students read and analyze) and then to guide students through the stages of drafting and writing their own short blog.

PROCESS OPTIONAL 5.12, 5.13

In FUNCTIONAL LANGUAGE, student pairs discuss what tourists usually do in their city. Then, students individually read a blog and complete the gapped sentences. To check answers, they listen to the audio. After that, students listen to a list of recommendations. Point out that the verbs in bold are the imperative form and they are used to make recommendations. Finally, students have the opportunity to make recommendations about their own city.

WRITING a blog

A Complete the sentences from the blog in FUNCTIONAL LANGUAGE B. Then find four more sentences that use the missing words.

1. Visit the museum ___and___ learn about the city's history.
2. Go early ___because___ it's free before 10:00 a.m.
3. Swim in the ocean ___or___ take a boat trip.

Don't go on Monday because it's closed!

Get a coffee at the beach café or at the hotel's coffee shop.

Reserve a table because it's always busy.

Then go to the park and watch a movie at the outdoor movie theater.

B Complete the rules with your answers from A.

1. Use ___because___ to give a reason.
2. Use ___and___ to join two affirmative or two negative phrases.
3. Use ___or___ to give a different idea.

C Complete the sentences with *and*, *or*, or *because*.

1. I go to two classes at the university: dance ___and___ art. I like dance class ___because___ the other students are fun.
2. Go to the bookstore ___and___ buy a dictionary. Take your student ID card ___because___ students get a 50% discount.
3. Do you like cold ___or___ hot weather? I live near the beach ___because___ I like hot weather.

D Prepare a short blog and make recommendations for things to do in your city.

1. Think about activities to do or places to go in the:
   morning   afternoon   evening
2. Write sentences about your ideas using *and*, *or*, or *because*.
3. IN PAIRS Exchange your sentences and discuss your ideas. Do you like your partner's recommendations?

E Write your short blog: *One Day in My City*.

One Day in My City

BLOG | ABOUT ME | CONTACT ME

____

____

____

____

____

____

MAKE IT DIGITAL

Choose a city and search online for activities to do or places to go. Do you like the recommendations? What places are interesting?

WRITING Alternative Activity

After WRITING **E**, put students into pairs or groups of three. Ask students to work together and create another blog for another city. (Tell students the city can be real or imaginary.) Ask groups to repeat steps 1 and 2 in WRITING **D** and then write the blog together. You can help students by telling them to complete these sentences: *I like my city because …; Tourists go to the beach and …; People eat at the café or ….*

MAKE IT DIGITAL

Tell students that an excellent way to search for activities to do or places to go is to visit a vacation planner site. Suggest students use triphobo or trello or download an app, such as TripIt.

GO TO page xvii
for **UNIT REVIEW** step-by-step instructions.

UNIT 5

VOCABULARY review

SCORE: / 5

A Match the sentence beginnings (1–5) to the sentence endings (a–e). Write the letter.

1 I can't do karate, c
2 Can you dance salsa e
3 I go to an art class b
4 It's freezing today a
5 It's rainy here, d

a and it's snowy.
b because I want to draw pictures.
c but I can ride a horse.
d but it's warm.
e or play an instrument?

GRAMMAR review

SCORE: / 5

A Complete with *can* or *can't*.

1 Can you ride a horse? No, I can't .
2 I can ✓ drive a car, but I can't ✗ ride a motorcycle.

B Complete the sentence with the words and the possessive *'s*.

These are Jon's books (books/Jon) and this is my friend's phone (phone/my friend).

C Complete the sentences.

1 I 'm watching a movie and Cindy 's baking a cake.
2 We 're eating dinner and we 're listening to music.

6–10 correct: You can talk about free-time activities and what you can/can't do, learn about subjects, talk about weather, and describe what people are doing. You can use *can/can't*, possessive *'s* and present progressive statements.
0–5 correct: Look again at the Vocabulary and Grammar sections in the unit.

TOTAL SCORE: / 10

WHAT DO YOU KNOW NOW? Look back at page 45 and add the words you know now to the boxes.

GO TO page xviii
for **STUDY SKILLS** step-by-step instructions.

STUDY SKILLS PRACTICING VOCABULARY

A IN PAIRS Do you agree (✓) or disagree (✗) with the sentences? Do you use other ways?

To practice vocabulary,
☐ I learn one new word every day.
☐ I play word games.
☐ I read English books and magazines.
☐ I talk to English speakers.
☐ I watch English movies and TV shows.

GO TO page 67
for **AUDIO SCRIPT**.

B 5.14 Look at the game. Listen to two players. Complete the rules with *left*, *letter* or *word*.

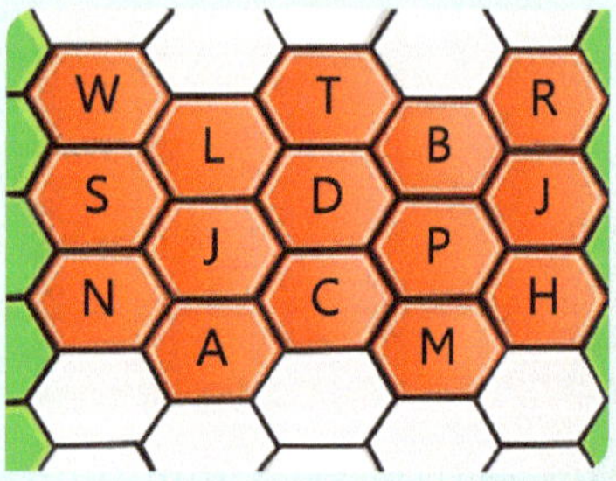

1 Move from left to right.
2 Choose a letter and answer a question about it.
3 The answer is a word beginning with that letter.

C IN PAIRS Choose 15 words and write the questions. Then make your board. Use the same shapes from B.

D Play the game. One person asks questions. Then change roles.

54 Unit 5 Free Time

VOCABULARY Alternative Activity

For more confident classes, write the VOCABULARY **A** sentence beginnings on the board and ask pairs to complete the sentence with a grammatically correct ending. Check answers as a class and correct any incorrect answers. Then proceed with the activity on the page.

CLASSROOM MANAGEMENT

Real-life examples make lessons more memorable. Collect examples of different ways to practice vocabulary (e.g., word searches, crosswords, or newspapers/magazines).

Alternatively, have students watch or listen to an authentic English-language source and listen for vocabulary or grammar they know. Encourage students just to enjoy the experience and not to worry about new words.

UNIT 6

Health

GO TO page vi
for **UNIT OPENER** step-by-step instructions.

WHAT DO YOU ALREADY KNOW?

1 Think about the places where you eat and what you eat there. Write words that you know in the boxes.

2 IN PAIRS Share and compare your information. Add more words to the boxes, if possible.

STUDENTS MAY ALREADY KNOW:

- food and drink items: eggs, fish, fruit, juice, tea

Food you like: ______________________
____
____
____

Food you don't like: ______________________
____
____
____

VIDEO

DISCUSS & SHARE

3 IN GROUPS Watch the video and answer the question.

SYM Eat in or eat out?

GO TO page xx
for **VIDEOS IN SYM** step-by-step instructions.

In this unit, you will ...

- describe people's appearance, talk about food and meals and ask and answer a quiz.
- use thinking skills: analyze, evaluate and predict.
- read two advertisements for food companies.
- use strategies to learn language to use when you need to think about your answer and agree or ask questions to continue a conversation.
- use communication skills to order food and drinks and write an online review.
- follow a food scientist to learn about their job and the skills needed to be in this industry.

WHAT DO YOU ALREADY KNOW?

If you notice students are struggling to understand what to do, you can provide one or two examples to help them get started:

- **Food:** bread, cereal, chips, meat, pasta, pizza, potatoes
- **Drink:** water, soda, coffee, milkshake

VIDEO

Before viewing, ask:

What are some advantages of eating in? *cook healthy food, save money*

What are some advantages of eating out? *it is fun, no dishes to wash*

After viewing, put this continuum on the board.

eat in ——— eat out

Have students mark the continuum and explain the advantages and disadvantages of eating in and out.

DISCUSS & SHARE

Many people's eating habits depend on their lifestyles. Create a continuum on the board with *eat in all the time* on one end and *eat out all the time* on the other. Poll students to see where they land on the continuum. Then discuss the pros and cons of each extreme.

GO TO page vii
for **VOCABULARY** step-by-step instructions.

LESSON 1 Appearance

VOCABULARY the face and body

A IN PAIRS **Label the pictures with the words from your box. Then compare your answers.**

Student A: eyes gray leg mouth nose old short slim

Student B: arm blond dark ears heavy tall teeth young

B 6.01 **Listen and check. Then listen again and repeat.**

C IN PAIRS **Close your books. Point to your face/body and say the words. How many can you remember?**

GO TO page ix
for **PRONUNCIATION** step-by-step instructions.

PRONUNCIATION vowel sounds

A **Match the words that have the same underlined sound.**

arm dark heavy leg nose old

arm, dark
heavy, leg
nose, old

MAKE IT YOURS

Use your dictionary to find more words to describe your face/body.

B 6.02 **Listen and check your answers to A. Then listen again and repeat.**

GO TO page xi
for **LISTENING** step-by-step instructions.

LISTENING

A 6.03 **Listen to the conversations and answer the question. Are the speakers talking about people in the same room or people in pictures?**

Conversation 1: people in the same room
Conversation 2: people in pictures

GO TO page 67
for **AUDIO SCRIPT**.

VOCABULARY

Ask students to look at the pictures. Ask them to call out which picture shows an old man (1st row, right), a young boy (2nd row, left), an old woman (3rd row, left), a woman with blond hair (2nd row, middle), and so on. For more confident students, ask them to cover the word boxes and say as many descriptive words as they can about the people. Set a time limit of two minutes.

LISTENING Extra Practice

Write this sentence with blanks about Alison's mother on the board: *She has ..., ... hair.* Ask students to listen again and find the two missing adjectives (*short*, *brown*). Add these to the sentence and write *1st* and *2nd* above them, respectively. Ask which is about size (*short*) and which is about color (*brown*). Elicit other examples (e.g., *long*, *tall*, *blond*, *gray*). Tell students that the correct adjective order is size and then color.

B 6.03 LISTENING SKILL—Identify information **Listen again and label the people in the pictures with the phrases from the box.**

a Alison's brother	**b** Alison's father	**c** Alison's mother	**d** Alison's mother's sister
e Alison's mother's friend	**f** John	**g** Rosa's grandmother	**h** Rosa's grandmother's brother

Scene 1 (Conversation 1)

1 f
2 a
3 b
4 d
5 c
6 e

Scene 2 (Conversation 2)

1 g
2 h

C IN GROUPS THINKING SKILL—Analyze **Look at your group and answer the questions. Who has similar hair? Who has the same eye color? Who is tall and who is short?**

GRAMMAR *have*

A 6.04 **Listen to the sentences from LISTENING A on page 56 and complete with *has/have* or *don't/doesn't have*.**

1 She has short brown hair.
2 They don't have the same color eyes.
3 We don't have the same nose.
4 I have a big nose.

B Complete the table with your answers from A.

Pronoun	+	–	(Adjective +) Noun
I/We/They	1 have	3 don't have	blond hair. big ears. blue eyes.
He/She	2 has	4 doesn't have	a small nose.

For more practice, go to page 78.

C IN PAIRS **Discuss. Look at the pictures in LISTENING B. Describe the people and say what they have / don't have.**

GO TO pages viii–ix

for **GRAMMAR** step-by-step instructions.

SPEAKING

A IN PAIRS **Guess the person. Use the Confident Communicator box to help you.**

Student A: go to page 69 of the Activity Bank. **Student B:** go to page 68 of the Activity Bank.

CONFIDENT COMMUNICATOR
KEEP TALKING

To think about your answer and continue the conversation, say:
Let me see … Does she have blue eyes?
Let me think … Is her name Lisa?

GO TO page xii

for **SPEAKING** step-by-step instructions.

GRAMMAR Alternative Activity

Have a class dictation. Tell students you will read a description with blanks. (Instead of saying the word *blank*, say the number shown in parentheses.) Students write the numbers and the correct form of *have*. Use both descriptions or the shorter one for less confident classes and the longer for more confident classes.

I (1) ***[have]*** *blond hair, but my sister (2)* ***[has]*** *dark hair. We both (3)* ***[have]*** *green eyes.*

Cindy (4) ***[has]*** *long hair and brown eyes. She (5)* ***[doesn't have]*** *blue eyes. Cindy and her sister (6)* ***[have]*** *small ears. They (7)* ***[don't have]*** *big ears.*

SPEAKING

CONFIDENT COMMUNICATOR

Model the two phrases by saying them slowly and thoughtfully. Tell students it is important to express the meaning or feeling behind a phrase because this will help them sound more natural. Practice the phrases with the class. Monitor for correct use.

LESSON 2 Food

VOCABULARY food

A Write the words under the pictures. Some pictures have more than one word and one word is not used.

cereal chicken coffee ×2 eggs fish juice ×2
pasta salad ×2 sandwiches tea toast ×2 vegetables ×2

1 
cereal, juice, toast, coffee

2 
eggs, coffee, toast

3 
sandwiches, juice, salad

4 
fish, vegetables

5 
pasta, vegetables

6 
chicken, salad

B 6.05 Listen, check your answers to A and repeat.

C IN PAIRS Discuss. Tell your partner what you usually eat and drink for breakfast, lunch and dinner.

GO TO page x

for **READING** step-by-step instructions.

COOK KING
The King of Dinners: advertisement

Time for Breakfast!: blog

READING

A 6.06 READING SKILL—Recognize different text types **Quickly read the texts. Which text is a blog and which is an advertisement?**

COOK KING *The King of Dinners*

Help! I'm busy. I don't have any time to cook! Can you help?
Sure. We cook and bring delicious dinners to your home.

What do you mean? How does Cook King work?
Go to our website and order some meals. We cook your meal. Our driver drives to your house with your meal. You pay the driver.

Are there any vegetarian meals?
Yes! We have meals for everyone. We have some salads, some pasta with vegetables and other vegetable meals.

Do you cook and deliver at any time?
We open at 12:00 p.m. and close at 11:00 p.m.
We do not deliver after 11:00 p.m.

We don't have any cash!
No problem. Pay the driver with your credit card or debit card.

CONTACT COOK KING TODAY!

Time for Breakfast!

By: Michael White Mar. 15, 2019

Breakfast is my favorite meal of the day and it's important for our bodies. It prepares us for the day. Try these two meals for breakfast.

1 Cereal and toast—easy! You need some milk, some cereal and some bread. Don't forget to drink something. Drink a cup of coffee or a glass of orange juice.

2 Pancakes are another quick and easy meal. I like eating pancakes for breakfast, but some people eat them for a snack.

You need an egg, some milk and some flour. Mix everything together. Then cook.

VOCABULARY Alternative Activity

Ask students to look at the words in VOCABULARY **A** and find three plural nouns (*eggs*, *sandwiches*, *vegetables*). Elicit the singular forms (*egg*, *sandwich*, *vegetable*). For more confident classes, ask which nouns could also be used as countable nouns when people are in a café or restaurant (*two coffees, three teas, four salads, five juices*). Tell students that some nouns become countable when ordering food and drinks.

READING

READING SKILL—Recognize different text types

For students to recognize different text types, they should identify the purpose of the text. The purpose of the text can be to persuade, inform, describe, or instruct.

Extra Practice

Ask students to find words that mean:

- to take something to someone's home (*deliver*).
- a small amount of food eaten between meals (*snack*).
- a thing we use for cooking food (*pan*).

B Read the texts in A again. Choose *T* (True) or *F* (False).

1 Cook King is a food business. T / F
2 It sells some vegetarian meals. T / F
3 Michael eats two meals for breakfast. T / F
4 Michael uses some milk for both meals. T / F

C IN GROUPS THINKING SKILL—Evaluate **Do you have food businesses, like Cook King, in your city/town? Do you use them? Compare your answers.**

Are there any vegetarian meals?

Do you cook and deliver at any time?

We don't have any cash!

Go to our website and order some meals.

We have some salads, some pasta with vegetables, and other vegetable meals.

GRAMMAR *some and any*

A **Look at the advertisement in READING A. Find and circle three examples of *any* and three examples of *some*. Then complete the rules.**

1 Use *any* in affirmative sentences / negative sentences and questions.
2 Use *some* in affirmative sentences / negative sentences / questions.

For more practice, go to page 78.

B **Underline examples of *a/an/some* + noun in the texts in READING A. Then complete the sentences below.**

1 Use *a* or *an* for one thing / two or more things.
2 Use *some* to say there are / aren't two or more things.
3 Use *some* to say we do / do not know the exact number.

We have some salads, some pasta with vegetables, and other vegetable meals.

You need some milk, some cereal, and some bread.

Drink a cup of coffee or a glass of orange juice.

... but some people eat them for a snack.

You need an egg, some milk, and some flour.

MAKE IT YOURS

Make a shopping list for some food or write an easy recipe for your favorite meal. Use your dictionary to help you.

C **Complete the conversations with *some* or *any*.**

Conversation 1
A: There isn't ___any___ cereal. There's ___some___ bread.
B: Great. Let's have ___some___ toast.

Conversation 2
A: Are there ___any___ vegetables?
B: No. There aren't ___any___ vegetables. There's ___some___ pasta.

D IN PAIRS **Take turns to read the conversations in C.**

SPEAKING

A IN PAIRS **Read your list of food. Work together to make a meal for breakfast, lunch and dinner.**

Student A	Student B
cake, cereal, coffee, eggs, fish, flour, salad, sandwiches	*honey, juice, milk, pasta, chicken, tea, toast, vegetables*

Student A: Let's make eggs on toast for breakfast. Are there any eggs on our list?
Student B: Yes. Do you have any toast?
Student A: Yes!

CONFIDENT COMMUNICATOR
KEEP TALKING

To continue the conversation, agree with your partner or ask about another meal.
Let's make eggs on toast. *OK! / I don't like eggs. How about cereal?*

GRAMMAR

When teaching this section and monitoring students, pay attention to correct word order and correct use of *There is/are* and *a/an*. Students are now building on previous grammar points and increasing their grammatical range, so listen carefully for any errors and correct them. You could either correct these errors on the spot or make a note and write them on the board to correct as a class.

SPEAKING

CONFIDENT COMMUNICATOR

Remind students of the importance of natural and expressive intonation, and elicit ways in which students can express the phrases in the Confident Communicator box. Ask which phrase is enthusiastic because it's a suggestion (*Let's* = *Let us*), which is enthusiastic because it's agreeing with a suggestion (*OK!*), and which is not enthusiastic because it isn't agreeing (*I don't like ...*). Practice the phrases and monitor for correct use.

Suggested answers:
1 the description of a restaurant, the restaurant history, some anecdotes about the restaurant
2 the restaurant owner, restaurant fans
3 yes, it is a popular book

1 The writer's grandfather's restaurant and the family who works there.
2 Maria Parker/ granddaughter
3 very popular

1 father, parents, brother, mom
2 dark hair, short, heavy, blond hair
3 snowy
4 beautiful, modern, window
5 ride a horse, drive a car

GO TO page 68 for AUDIO SCRIPT.

GO TO page 68 for AUDIO SCRIPT.

VOCABULARY feelings

A Write the words from the box under the pictures (a–f). Then complete the sentences (1–6).

bored excited happy hungry sad tired

a  happy

b  hungry

c  bored

d  tired

e  excited

f  sad

1 I'm happy because it's sunny today.
2 There isn't any food and I'm hungry .
3 I'm bored . This movie is terrible.
4 What a long day! I'm tired .
5 The party is tonight! I'm very excited !
6 Are you OK? You look very sad .

B 6.07 Listen and check your answers to A. Then listen again and repeat.

C Write the adjectives from A in the correct group.

Positive: excited, happy
Negative: bored, hungry, sad, tired

D IN PAIRS Discuss. How do you feel today?

MAKE IT REAL

You may hear people adding *so*, *very* or *really* before adjectives to make them sound stronger.

*I'm **so** excited!* *I'm **very** sad.*
*I'm **really** bored.*

LISTENING

A IN PAIRS THINKING SKILL—Predict Look at the title of a book. Answer the questions.

1 What do you think it's about?
2 Who's the writer?
3 Do you think it's a popular book?

B 6.08 LISTENING SKILL—Identify information in an introduction
Listen to the introduction and check your ideas.

C 6.09 Listen to the complete interview. Choose the correct words.

1 Maria's grandfather is from America / Spain.
2 Her brother is always happy / tired.
3 Her father and grandfather are wearing dress hats / suits.
4 Maria and her brother are bored or hungry / sad.
5 Maria's parents are standing in front of / next to their house.
6 She lives in a beautiful and modern / old apartment.

D 6.09 Listen again and write words related to the topics.

1 family: *grandfather,*
2 appearance: *tall, slim,*
3 weather: *sunny,*
4 the home: *apartment, big,*
5 hobbies: *go for a walk,*

VOCABULARY

Ask students to use their phones to find other emojis or emoticons that express positive and negative feelings similar to those in VOCABULARY **A**. If possible, set up a class messaging group and ask students to send an emoji or a sentence including an emoji (as in **A**) showing how they feel today.

LISTENING Alternative Activity

Ask students to listen again to the complete interview and make notes on the four photos described in it. Encourage students to work alone and then compare answers in pairs.

1. father and grandfather, happy, dress suits, tall and slim, dark hair
2. sister and brother, short and heavy, don't have blond hair, bored or hungry
3. street, sunny, pretty, parents house, next to restaurant
4. restaurant, in December, excited boy, dancing and laughing

GRAMMAR review

A Look at the sentences in the box from LISTENING B. Complete the table.

He's **always** tired.
We **don't have** blond hair.
I **can** drive a car.
I **live** in an apartment.
Their house is **next to** the restaurant.
We **aren't** smiling in the picture.
We **aren't** tall and slim.
~~We're short and heavy.~~

to be (+)	He's from Spain.	*We're short and heavy.*
to be (–)	My grandfather isn't from America.	1 We aren't tall and slim.
simple present	He starts work at 8:00 a.m.	2 I live in an apartment.
adverbs of frequency	He rarely has any free time.	3 He's always tired.
to have (+)	They have dark hair!	
to have (–)		4 We don't have blond hair.
present progressive (+)	He's dancing and laughing.	
present progressive (–)		5 We aren't smiling in the picture.
prepositions of place	They're standing in front of it.	6 Their house is next to the restaurant.
can		7 I can drive a car.

B Match the sentences from the table in A to the correct use. Write the numbers.

describe an ability or skill 10
describe someone's appearance 5 , 6
explain where something is 9
make general statements about your life 3
make very simple statements about yourself 1, 2
say how often you do or don't do an activity 4
say what you are doing now 7, 8

For more practice, go to page 79.

C IN PAIRS Complete the sentences in a quiz.

Student A: go to page 68 of the Activity Bank and complete the questions.
Student B: go to page 68 of the Activity Bank and complete the answers.

D 6.10 Compare and check the quiz. Then listen and check.

Student A
1 What's your name? **2** Where are you from? **3** Do you have a big family? **4** What color hair and eyes do you have? **5** What do you do? **6** Where is your college or workplace? **7** What time do you start and finish work or college? **8** What do you do on the weekend? **9** Can you drive a car or ride a horse? **10** What are you doing now?

Student B
1 My name's Louise Jones. **2** I'm from Argentina. I'm Argentinian. **3** I have three brothers, my parents and my grandfather. He's 78 years old. **4** My hair is brown and I have blue eyes. **5** I'm a lawyer. **6** It's on Main Street. It's across from the park. **7** I get to work at 9 a.m., and I finish work at 5 p.m. I get home at about 6 p.m. **8** I usually meet my friends and watch a movie. **9** I can drive a car, but I can't ride a horse. **10** I'm speaking English, and I'm talking to you!

SPEAKING

A IN PAIRS Write two more questions for the quiz in GRAMMAR C. Then ask and answer the two new questions.

B As a class, use the quiz to ask one question to each student. Use the Confident Communicator box to help you.

C Share the answers with the class.

CONFIDENT COMMUNICATOR
KEEP TALKING

To continue the conversation, ask for more information:
Really? How old is your grandfather?
That's interesting! Tell me more about your job.

GRAMMAR Alternative Activity

Give students a few minutes to go over the GRAMMAR sections in previous units. Ask if there is any grammar that the class finds difficult. If so, set aside 10 minutes of class time for a "grammar workshop." This will allow students to focus specifically on their own needs and take responsibility for their learning. Allow students to revisit the relevant earlier lesson and the *Grammar Reference*. Monitor and answer any questions.

CLASSROOM MANAGEMENT

For larger classes, divide the class into two groups and have students mingle within their own group. This will reduce unnecessary classroom movement and disruption.

SPEAKING

After the quiz in SPEAKING **A**, put students into new groups to talk about their findings. Students should share interesting information about their classmates. Monitor during this stage and choose whether to correct any errors on the spot or to correct them later on the board as a class activity.

GO TO page xv

for **LANGUAGE AND LIFE** step-by-step instructions.

Language and Life

Communication – Cafe

FUNCTIONAL LANGUAGE order food and drinks

a coffee shop

A Quickly read the conversation. Are the people in a coffee shop or a restaurant?

Waiter: Good morning. What can I get you?
Customer: Good morning. Can I get a black coffee, please?
Waiter: Sure. What size: small, medium or large?
Customer: Large, please. I'm very tired today!
Waiter: OK. Any other drinks?
Customer: Yes. An orange juice, please.
Waiter: No problem. One large black coffee and one orange juice. Is that for here or to go?
Customer: Here, please.
Waiter: Can I get you some food? We have some cookies and some cakes. The chocolate cake is delicious!
Customer: No, thanks. That's all.
Waiter: No worries. That's $6.25, please.
Customer: Here you go.
Waiter: Thank you. Here's your change: $0.75.

B Match the conversation with the correct picture. Then write the price.

1

2

Picture: 2
$ 6.25

C Complete the table with the bold questions and answers from the conversation in A.

Waiter	Customer
What can I get you?	Can I get a black coffee, please?
What size: small, medium or large?	Large, please.
Any other drinks?	An orange juice, please.
1 Is that for here or to go?	5 Here, please.
2 Can I get you some food?	6 No, thanks. That's all.
3 That's $6.25, please.	
4 Here's your change.	

D 6.11 Complete the conversation. Then listen and check.

A: Hi, what can I get for you?
B: Can I have a coffee, please?
A: Sure. What size: small, medium or large?
B: Small, please.
A: OK. Is that for here or to go?
B: To go, please.

E IN PAIRS Practice the conversation in D. Change the drink and the size.

62 Unit 6 Health

OBJECTIVE

In this lesson, students learn how to order food and drinks and write an online review. The objective is to help students practice these life skills. Ordering food and drinks allows students to interact with native speakers, and the language can be used in other similar situations. Online reviews are another useful life skill, and writing these allows students to practice expressing their own opinions.

PROCESS OPTIONAL 6.11

In FUNCTIONAL LANGUAGE, students read a conversation and choose whether it is in a coffee shop or a restaurant and write the correct price. Then, they identify and write the questions a customer and a waiter ask. After that, students complete, listen, and check a real conversation. Finally, students have the opportunity to practice the conversation with their own personal details.

WRITING an online review

A Quickly read the posts. Then choose the correct option.

1 The Blue Café is asking customers to visit / vote for the café.
2 There is a competition for cakes / coffee shops.
3 Meg is a customer / waitress at The Blue Café.

The Blue Café
Followers

BC Dear customer,
Thank you for visiting The Blue Café! Do you like our ☕ ? Does our homemade 🍰 make you 🙂 ? Yes? Please vote for us in the city's *Top Coffee Shop* competition! The link is below. ⬇ Please say why you like The Blue Café.
Thank you! ❤

Top Coffee Shop competition

M **Meg** ★★★★★ April 16 2019
The Blue Café is my favorite coffee **❶shop, The ❷Waiters** are always happy **❸but** friendly. The coffee **❹great is.** It has some delicious cakes. There are **❺any** salads and vegetarian meals. It's popular with students **❻becuase** students have a 50% discount on Mondays!

B Look at the bold errors in Meg's post in A. Match each error to an error type.

capital letter = 2 W = w
incorrect words (2) = 3 but =and, 5 any = some
punctuation = 1 shop.
spelling = 6 becuase = because
word order = 4 great is = is great

The Blue Café is my favorite coffee shop. The waiters are always happy and friendly. The coffee is great. It has some delicious cakes. There are some salads and vegetarian meals. It's popular with students because students have a 50% discount on Mondays!

C Prepare a post for the competition.

1 Choose a coffee shop you like.
2 Make notes on:
- the people who work there
- the food and drinks you like
- the meals and food
- who likes the coffee shop and why

3 **IN PAIRS** Exchange your sentences and check for errors.

D Write your post.

MAKE IT DIGITAL

Look on social media for local coffee shops or other places in your city. Do you like their social media page? Send them a message!

WRITING Alternative Activity

After WRITING **B**, put students into pairs and ask them to read the posts: one reads the Blue Café, and one reads Meg's review. Alternatively, you could do this as a class activity and have individual students read one sentence each. Encourage students to try reading new texts out loud to practice pronunciation and intonation.

FURTHER DISCUSSION

After WRITING **C**, put students into small groups and encourage to take notes and then exchange sentences within the group:

- the people who work in the coffee shop.
- the food they like and food served there.
- reasons why they like it.

CULTURE NOTE

Online reviews are very popular in the United States. There are many popular review sites. These sites receive millions of visitors (or a lot of "traffic") each month. According to the blog Vendasta, statistics show that 88% of online shoppers decide what to buy after reading reviews.

GO TO page xvii
for **UNIT REVIEW** step-by-step instructions.

UNIT 6

VOCABULARY review

SCORE: / 5

A Circle the word that is different in each group. Then add one more word to each group.

1	ears	nose	(tall)	eyes, mouth, teeth
2	heavy	slim	(tea)	short, tall
3	coffee	juice	(mouth)	tea
4	(excited)	pasta	vegetables	cereal, chicken, eggs
5	bored	happy	(sandwich)	hungry, sad, tired

GRAMMAR review

SCORE: / 5

A Complete the sentences.

1 I __have__ ✓ dark hair, but my two brothers __have__ ✓ blond hair.

2 My mom __has__ ✓ a small nose. She __doesn't have__ ✗ a big nose.

3 There's __some__ bread, but there aren't __any__ eggs.

4 Sorry. There isn't __any__ coffee. Do you want __some__ juice?

5 I'm making __some__ sandwiches and __some__ pasta.

6–10 correct: You can talk about your appearance, people's appearance, food and meals, and feelings. You can use *have* and *some* and *any*.
0–5 correct: Look again at the Vocabulary and Grammar sections in the unit.

TOTAL SCORE: / 10

WHAT DO YOU KNOW NOW? Look back at page 55 and add the words you know now to the boxes.

GO TO page xix
for **FOLLOW A PRO** step-by-step instructions.

GO TO page 69
for **AUDIO SCRIPT**.

FOLLOW A PRO FOOD SCIENTIST

A 6.12 **Listen to a conversation with a food scientist. Who does he work for?**

a university a laboratory a company

B 6.12 **Listen again and complete the summary about Dr. Smith's job.**

Dr. Smith works for a __food company__. Dr. Smith gives __advice__ about food. Customers eat the food and choose their __favorite__ sandwiches. The company __makes__ and __sells__ the sandwiches.

C IN GROUPS Discuss.

1 Is Dr. Smith's job important?
2 Is healthy food popular in your city/country?
3 What other jobs are there in the food industry?

64 Unit 6 Health

CLASSROOM MANAGEMENT

Ask students for the topic of each group in VOCABULARY **A** (*1 appearance: face, 2 appearance: body, 3 drinks, 4 food, 5 feelings*) and to write one sentence for each.

Ask for five volunteer students to read the sentences in GRAMMAR **A** out loud.

Students should go back to previous reviews and compare scores. For any units with low scores, have students redo these reviews again at home.

FOLLOW A PRO TASKS Alternative Activity

Ask the class what they think a *food scientist* is (someone who does research on food or nutrition). Practice the pronunciation of *scientist* and *laboratory*.

After FOLLOW A PRO **B**, ask students to listen again and list the food (*sandwiches, snacks, fruit, vegetables, bread, salad*).

Ask students to find advertisements for food-related jobs.

Student's Book Grammar Reference Answer Key

Unit 1

be statements

A **1** are **2** aren't **3** is **4** isn't

B **1** is not *or* isn't **2** is *or* 's **3** are not *or* aren't **4** are

subject pronouns and *be* statements

A **1** You're **2** He isn't **3** We're **4** They're

B **1** isn't = are not / aren't **2** are = is / 's **3** aren't = am not / 'm not **4** 's = are / 're

yes/no questions with *be*

A **1** Is **2** they **3** Are **4** he

B **1** isn't **2** aren't **3** are **4** is

Unit 2

be information questions

A **1** is **2** are **3** is **4** are

B **1** is, c His name is Louis. **2** are, d They're from Canada. **3** is, f She's 17. **4** are, e I'm fine, thanks. **Not used:** He's fine, thanks. They're 16.

a/an singular and plural nouns

A **1** b **2** d **3** a/c **4** a/c

B **1 an** ID card **2** three bags **3 a** laptop **4** two watch**es**

There is/There are

A **1** There are five bags. **2** There is a chair. **3** There are two umbrellas. **4** There is one student.

B **1** is/'s **2** are **3** is/'s **4** are

Unit 3

simple present statements

A **1** work **2** lives **3** speaks **4** don't

B **1** don't live **2** goes **3** speak **4** doesn't work

yes/no questions with simple present

A **1** Do **2** Does **3** Do **4** Does

B **1** Does Angela study in the evening? Yes, she **does**. **2** Do they go to college? No, they **don't**. **3** Does the coffee shop open on Sunday? No, it **doesn't**. **4** Do you like your job? Yes, I **do**.

adverbs of frequency

A **1** He sometimes works on Saturday. **2** The college is usually busy. **3** She often eats breakfast at 8 a.m. **4** The waiters are always friendly.

B **1** usually **2** always **3** rarely **4** often

Unit 4

simple present information questions

A **1** do **2** does **3** does **4** do

B **1** Where **2** What **3** How much **4** When

imperatives

A **1** c **2** a **3** d **4** b

B **1** where **2** Turn **3** Go **4** is

this/that/these/those

A **1** These **2** that **3** this **4** those

B **1** these; that **2** that; those **3** this; these **4** Those; This/That

Unit 5

can/can't

A **1** can **2** can't **3** can't **4** can

B **1** they can **2** she can't **3** he can't **4** she can

possessive *'s*

A **1** Emily**'s** **2** My teacher**'s** **3** Jane**'s** **4** Roberto**'s**

B **1** Is that Maria**'s** dictionary? **2** My sister**'s** bag is on the desk. **3** The teacher**'s** classes are interesting. **4** Where is Paola**'s** laptop?

present progressive statements

A **1** practicing **2** having **3** swimming **4** reading

B **1** are not/aren't eating **2** am/'m having **3** are not/aren't shopping **4** is/'s listening

Unit 6

have

A **1** have **2** has **3** have **4** have

B **1** has; have **2** have; has **3** has; have **4** has; have

some and *any*

A **1** d **2** c **3** a **4** b

B **1** any **2** some **3** some **4** an

review

A **1** have **2** are **3** walk **4** always

B **1** do **2** are **3** Can **4** have

Useful Language

Track 01

A B C D E F G H I J K L M N O P Q R S T U V W X Y Z

Track 02

1 2 3 4 5 6 7 8 9 10 11 12 13 14 15 16 17 18 19 20

Unit 1

Track 01

Conversation 1

A: Good morning, Sara. How are you?
B: Hi, Mr. Webster. I'm fine, thanks.

Conversation 2

C: Good afternoon, I'm Mr. Smith. What's your name?
D: My name's Nick. Nice to meet you, Mr. Smith.
C: Nice to meet you, too.

Conversation 3

E: Good night, Lara.
F: Good night. See you, Mia!
E: Goodbye.

Track 02

Mr. Taylor: Good morning! Welcome to class! I'm Mr. Taylor. What's your name?
Maria: Good morning. Nice to meet you, Mr. Taylor. I'm Maria.
Mr. Taylor: Pardon? Can you repeat that?
Maria: Ma-ri-a.
Mr. Taylor: Ah, OK. Nice to meet you, Maria.
Maria: And this is Peter.
Mr. Taylor: Nice to meet you, Pedro.
Maria: No. His name isn't Pedro. His name is Peter.
Mr. Taylor: Peter! Sorry. Nice to meet you!

Track 03

Rosie: Hello, I'm Rosie. What's your name?
Eva: Hi, Rosie. My name's Eva.
Rosie: Nice to meet you, Emma.
Eva: No. My name isn't Emma. My name's Eva. This is my co-worker, Roger.
Rosie: Nice to meet you, Robert.
Eva: No. His name isn't Robert. His name is Roger.

Track 04

1 Number One Finance
Mike Michelson
762 Fifth Ave, New York, NY USA
Email: mike@numberonefinance.com
Languages: English, German, Japanese

2 Tino Fernandez
Language Teacher
Mexico City
First language: Spanish
Other languages: English, French, Chinese

3 University University of Los Angeles
Subject Law
Name Jane Henderson
Nationality British

4 Driver's Permit
Name Alberto Garcia
Address 25 Cda. De Topilejo, Molino del Rey, Mexico
Nationality Mexican

Track 05

1 A-me-ri-can
2 Me-xi-can
3 Ja-pa-nese
4 Spa-nish
5 Chi-nese

Track 06

1 Brazilian
2 British
3 Canadian
4 English
5 German

Track 07

Group 1—American, Canadian, Brazilian
Group 4—Spanish, English, German, British

Track 08

brother
father
husband
grandfather
son
sister
mother
wife
grandmother
daughter
parents
grandparents

Track 09

Ben: Look at this photo!
Fiona: Wow! Who's that, Ben? Is she your sister?
Ben: Yes, she is. Her name's Zoe. She's 22.
Fiona: And who's he? Is he your brother?
Ben: No, he isn't. He's my friend. His name's Max.
Fiona: And who are they, Ben? Are they from your college? Are they your classmates?
Ben: No, they aren't. They're my co-workers from the mall. Their names are Hannah and Gavin.
Fiona: OK. And who's in this picture? It's black and white. It's old.
Ben: Mmm. I'm not sure.
Fiona: Are they your grandparents?
Ben: Yes, they are. My grandfather is 78 and my grandmother is 73.

Track 10

Mrs. Jones: Good morning. What's your name?
Rodrigo: Good morning. My name's Rodrigo. I'm a new student. My major is English and business.
Mrs. Jones: Welcome, Rodrigo! I'm Mrs. Jones. I'm your teacher. Nice to meet you.
Rodrigo: Nice to meet you, too.
Mrs. Jones: Now, let's complete your class registration form.
Rodrigo: OK.

Track 11

Mrs. Jones: So, your name is Rodrigo. What's your last name?
Rodrigo: My last name is Casal.
Mrs. Jones: Sorry. Can you repeat that, please?
Rodrigo: Casal. C–A–S–A–L.
Mrs. Jones: Thanks. Are you from Colombia?
Rodrigo: Yes, I am. I'm from Bogotá. I'm Colombian.
Mrs. Jones: What's your major? Is it English?
Rodrigo: My majors are English and business.
Mrs. Jones: Great. Thanks. What's your email?
Rodrigo: My email is rodrigo1234@funmail.cg.
Mrs. Jones: And what's your phone number?
Rodrigo: My cell is (555) 555-1058.
Mrs. Jones: Thank you, Rodrigo. Welcome to college!

Unit 2

Track 01

beautiful
big
modern
noisy
old
quiet
small
ugly

Track 02

Juno: Excuse me? Good morning! My name's Juno. I'm a student. Is it OK to ask you questions? It's my homework.
Nick: Umm. OK.
Juno: Thank you. What's your name?
Nick: I'm Nick Smith.
Juno: Nice to meet you, Nick! How are you?
Nick: I'm fine, thanks.
Juno: Great! Where are you from?
Nick: I'm from London. I'm British. I'm on vacation with Henry.
Juno: Who is he? Is he your brother?
Nick: No, he isn't. He's my friend.
Juno: OK. Is your home in London?
Nick: Yes, it is. It's a big and modern apartment. It's quiet. I like it! Look at this picture on my phone.
Juno: It's beautiful! My place is small and noisy. So, umm, next question … How old are you, Nick?
Nick: I'm 24.
Juno: Thanks. And the final question: What's your email?
Nick: It's nick—n-i-c-k—94@gomail.com.
Juno: Thank you so much, Nick!
Nick: No problem, Juno. Have a great day!

Track 03

1 phone
2 wallet
3 notebook
4 laptop
5 watch
6 brush
7 umbrella
8 ID card
9 pen
10 transit card

Track 04

Billy: Good morning! I'm Billy, and welcome to the show! How are you today? I'm grrrrrrrreat! And today … Oh, it's the competition! So, the big question is … What's … in ... your … bag?! OK, call me, tell me! Who's first?
Andrea: Hello, I'm Andrea.
Billy: Hi, Andrea! Where are you from?
Andrea: I'm from Germany. My home is Brazil now.
Billy: Grrrrrrreat! So, what's in your bag, Andrea?
Andrea: Umm … a brush, two watches—one is old, one is OK, and a sandwich.
Billy: Urgh! Four things? Four?! Bye-bye, Andrea! Who's next? Hello?
Emily: Good morning. My name's Emily.
Billy: Good morning, Emily. Are you British?
Emily: Yes, I am.
Billy: Great! What's in your bag, Emily?
Emily: Nine things: two brushes, an ID card, a notebook, two pens—one pen is red, and one pen is blue, a phone, an umbrella, and a transit card.
Billy: Nine! OK. Next! Who's this? Is this Ryan?
Ryan: Yeah, hello. I'm Ryan. Umm … two ID cards—one card is for college and one is for work, a laptop, three pens. Oh, and a phone. My beautiful phone. A wallet, a watch, a transit card. Yeah. Ten things?
Billy: Ten! Ryan! You're the winner! Congratulations!

Track 05

/s/ laptops
/z/ phones
/ɪz/ watches

Track 06

brushes
ID cards
notebooks
sandwiches
umbrellas
wallets

Track 07

New College
There are two types of rooms for students.
Single (one student)
There's a bed. There's a window between the door and the bed. There's a desk and a chair in front of the window. There's a small lamp on the desk. There's a small closet next to the bed.
Double (two students)
There are two beds in the room. There's a big window between the two beds. There are two desks and two chairs. They are in front of the window. There's a lamp on each desk. There are two closets behind the door.

Track 08

Hotel worker: Good morning. Grand Hotel.
Sofia: Good morning. I want to book a room for Friday night, please.
Hotel worker: Sure. Let me see if we have a room. There's a single room and a double room.
Sofia: What is a double room?
Hotel worker: It's a room with two beds for two people.
Sofia: OK. A single room, please.
Hotel worker: No problem. It's a nice room with two big windows. What's your name and email, please?
Sofia: Sofia Lopez. My email is sofial95@newmail.com. How much is it?
Hotel worker: It's $100. Please pay at the hotel on Friday.
Sofia: Thank you for your help.
Hotel worker: You're welcome. Goodbye.

Track 09

1
A: What's your name and email, please?
B: What's your name and email, please?
2
A: Please pay at the hotel on Friday.
B: Please pay at the hotel on Friday.
3
A: You're welcome.
B: You're welcome.

Track 10

Host: Good morning. Nice to meet you. What's your name?
Angela: My name's Angela.
Host: Where are you from?
Angela: I'm from Great Britain. I'm British. My first language is English. I'm an English teacher.
Host: Where is your college?
Angela: I'm not at a college. I'm an online teacher. I'm at home.
Host: Where's your classroom?
Angela: My laptop is my classroom! My laptop's on my desk. There are four or five pens and two notebooks next to the laptop. There's a big book about grammar behind the laptop. There's a chair in front of the desk.
Host: Great! Where are your students from?

Angela: Mexico and China. We are in a class together online.
Host: How old are they?
Angela: They are 15 years old to 62 years old.
Host: Thank you.

Unit 3

Track 01

1 teacher
2 doctor
3 police officer
4 manager
5 chef
6 pilot
7 waiter/waitress
8 lawyer

Track 02

Marie: Hi, I'm Marie. I live in the city. I'm a waitress. I don't work in a restaurant. I work in a café. I meet new people every day. It's fun! I'm also a teacher. I teach Chinese in a school. The students are nice. I like my jobs.
Gino: Hello, I'm Gino. I don't work. I'm a student. I go to college by bus. My brother is a pilot. He goes to work by car. He speaks three languages: Italian, French, and English. He doesn't speak Chinese. He likes his job. We live in an apartment.

Track 03

I live in Lima. I don't work. I'm a student. I go to college by bike. I speak two languages: English and Spanish. My sister works. She's a doctor. She doesn't live in Lima. She lives in New York.

Track 04

Anthony: Hello! Are you Mario?
Mario: Yes, I am.
Anthony: Hello, Mario. I'm Anthony. I'm the restaurant manager. Nice to meet you.
Mario: Nice to meet you, too.
Anthony: So, do you have your form? For the job?
Mario: Yes, I do. Here it is.
Anthony: Thanks. So, … it's for a waiter … you want to work in the evening. Is that right?
Mario: Yes. I'm a student. I go to college in the mornings and I study in the afternoons.
Anthony: OK. Do you go to college every day?
Mario: No, I don't. There are no classes on Wednesdays. I work in my uncle's shop on Wednesdays. I start work at 12 p.m., and I finish at 9 p.m.

Track 05

Anthony: So, this job is for a waiter on Thursdays and on Fridays. The waiters start work at 6 in the evening and they finish about 11. Is that OK?
Mario: Yes, that's fine.
Anthony: Great! Any questions?
Mario: Yes. Does the restaurant open on Sundays?
Anthony: No, it doesn't. It is closed.
Mario: Oh, OK. Do the waiters speak English?
Anthony: Yes, they do. They speak two or three languages. They are all very friendly.

Track 06

Conversation 1
Mario: Do they speak English?
Anthony: Yes, they do. / No, they don't.
Conversation 2
Mario: Does it open in the mornings?
Anthony: Yes, it does. / No, it doesn't.

Track 07

1 take a shower
2 get up at 6 a.m.
3 eat breakfast
4 drink coffee
5 go to bed

Track 08

The 24-365 hotel
Welcome! I'm Michael Olson, and I'm the manager. The hotel is 150 years old. It has 200 rooms, two restaurants, and a café. About 400 people work here. It's a big hotel. We are always busy. The hotel is never closed. It is open 24 hours a day for 365 days a year. There are always guests at the hotel. Guests usually stay for one week or two weeks. Families often stay here in July and August.
Tourists often visit the hotel to eat lunch or dinner. The restaurants are very popular on weekends. There is rarely a free table! Our chefs are excellent. They make excellent food. The waiters and waitresses speak different languages. One waiter speaks five languages!
People sometimes visit the hotel for work meetings. They drink coffee and talk about work. Visitors love the hotel.

Track 09

Sofia: Hi, Irene. How are you?
Irene: Hey, Sofia! I'm good. And you?
Sofia: Good. Are you free on Friday? Let's go to the mall.
Irene: Sorry, Sofia. I go to school on Fridays, and I work in the evening. I finish work at 8 p.m. How about Saturday? I'm free in the afternoon.
Sofia: Me, too. How about 3 p.m.?
Irene: 3 p.m. … OK. Let's see a movie.
Sofia: No. Let's go shopping.
Irene: Sure!

Track 10

Let's go to the mall.
Let's see a movie.

Unit 4

Track 01

1 bus station—get a bus
2 park—go for a walk
3 ATM—get money
4 hotel—stay on vacation
5 museum—learn about the past
6 hospital—get help
7 university—get a degree
8 bookstore—buy a book
9 coffee shop—buy a drink
10 restaurant—eat dinner

Track 02

What places does the tour visit?
The tour goes to the important places in the city. For example, there are two museums in the city. There's the history museum and the science museum. The museums are free on Tuesdays. Tourists always love the history museum.
Where does the tour start and finish?
Everywhere! Tourists get on the bus at the bus station or at a bus stop in the city. People get off the bus and go to a museum or have lunch in a restaurant. Then people get on the bus again later. It's very easy!
When does the first tour start?
The first tour leaves the bus station at 7 a.m. The last tour is at 9 p.m. There is a new tour every hour.

Where do I buy tickets?
We sell tickets at the bus station, online, and on the bus. Hotels also sell tickets.

How much do the tickets cost?
The tickets cost $20 for adults and $10 for children or students.

Track 03

Conversation 1

A: Excuse me, where's the museum?
B: The history museum?
A: No, the science museum.
B: Let me think … OK. Go straight up this road. Turn left. Take the second right. The science museum is on the left. It's between the park and the school.
A: Great. Thanks for your help.
B: Sure. The history museum is great, too. It's across from the park.
A: OK. Thanks.
B: No worries. Have a great day!

Conversation 2

C: Excuse me, is the train station near here?
D: The train station … OK. Go straight. The bus station is on the corner of Madison and Berkeley. Take the …
C: Straight. Bus station. On the corner.
D: Yeah. Take the number 5 bus to the train station. It's about 10 minutes.
C: Number 5. 10 minutes. OK. Thank you so much.
D: You're welcome.

Conversation 3

E: Excuse me, where's the Four Seasons Hotel?
F: Umm, let me think. Walk up this road. Turn right. Take the first left. There's a bookstore on your left. The hotel's between the coffee shop and the bookstore. It's on Main Street.
E: Thank you.
F: No problem. See you!

Track 04

1 on
2 on the corner of
3 across from
4 next to
5 between
6 on the left, on the right

Track 05

1 Excuse me, where is the hospital?
2 Go straight up this road.
3 The bookstore is next to the hotel.
4 It's on the corner of 1st and Main.
5 Turn left and take the first right.

Track 06

loose, tight
dressy, casual
long, short
cheap, expensive

Track 07

/æ/ jacket
/ɛ/ dress
/ɝ/ skirt
/iː/ jeans
/uː/ shoes

Track 08

boots pants shirt T-shirt

Track 09

Conversation 1

A: Look at this website! These clothes are great!
B: Let me see. Wow! They're cheap, too. Look—all clothes under $30.
A: Great! Look at this green dress!
B: What's the size?
A: Oh, it's large. It's the wrong size. Hmm … This skirt is nice. Do you like it?
B: No. It's short. I like long skirts.
A: Oh, OK. What about these shoes! They're $20. Wow, they're cheap! Do you like them?
B: Yes, I love them!
A: These boots are great, too. What do you think?
B: Yeah, they're nice. What size are they? I'm a size 7.
A: Me, too. They have sizes 5 to 8. Great! Let's buy them!

Conversation 2

C: It's Mom's birthday next week. Let's buy a present from this store.
D: OK. What do we buy?
C: Well, she loves clothes. There are a lot of great clothes here.
D: Yeah. Look at these T-shirts! They're pretty.
C: Yes, they are. Look! This red T-shirt is nice. It's $55!
D: $55 is expensive!
C: Hmm. You're right. Do you like this blue T-shirt? It's $15. It's cheap. I like it!
D: Me, too. Is it the correct size?
C: Uh, yes, it's medium.
D: Great! And look at that jacket over there! It's very dressy! Mom loves dressy clothes.
C: Uh, jacket? Where?
D: Over there … the black jacket … by the window … between those shoes and those bags.
C: Ah yes! Hmm. I'm not sure. She doesn't like black clothes, but I love those bags!

Track 10

Ally: Excuse me. How much is this laptop?
Bob: It's $50. It isn't new. It's old and slow.
Ally: Oh, OK. No, thank you.
Cate: How much are these black boots?
Bob: They're $30.
Cate: Oh, that's expensive.
Bob: Do you like these brown boots? These are only $15.
Cate: Oh, yes. Could I take those, please?
Bob: Sure. That's $15, please.
Cate: Here you go.
Bob: Thanks.
Ally: How much are the books in this box?
Bob: They're $1 each.
Ally: Could I take these two books, please?
Bob: No problem. That's $2, please.
Ally: Here you go.
Bob: Thank you. Have a great day!

Track 11

A: Excuse me, how much is this big notebook?
B: It's $10.
A: Oh, that's expensive. How much are these small notebooks?
B: They're $3 each.
A: OK. Could I take two small notebooks, please?
B: Sure. That's $6, please.
A: Here you go.

Track 12

I work on a bus tour. We stop at famous places. I give information about the place, for example, how old it is, who lives there, how big it is. I know everything about my city. I live here. I work here. I love it!
I speak four languages. Good morning! Buenos dias! Buongiorno! Guten tag! It's important to speak other languages. Tourists come from all over the world. I talk to everyone on the bus. I'm a friendly man! We don't speak the same language? No problem. I smile. We're friends! People usually ask me questions about the tour or the city. I answer the questions, for example, "Does the park open in the morning?" "Yes, it does. It opens at 9 a.m. It closes at about 6."

Unit 5

Track 01

1 [SFX: solo piano being played well (by amateur rather than professional musician)]
2 [SFX: salsa music excerpt]
3 [SFX: splashing water/breathing of confident swimmer (rather than weaker swimmer)]
4 [SFX: neighing horse and clip-clopping]

Track 02

1 ride a horse
2 draw pictures
3 bake a cake
4 do karate
5 drive a car
6 dance salsa
7 swim 1,500 m
8 play an instrument

Track 03

Ricardo: Hey, everybody! Welcome to Campus Chat, your favorite digital radio station! I'm Ricardo! We're all very excited today because it's the first day of college! It's the first show of the year! How are you, guys? How are the new students? Is this your first day? Call me … and say hello. So, who's this?
Francesca: Hello, I'm Francesca.
Ricardo: Hey, Francesca. Welcome to college! Where are you from?
Francesca: New York.
Ricardo: And what's your major?
Francesca: Art.
Ricardo: Art? Can you draw?
Francesca: Yes, I can.
Ricardo: What can you draw? Can you draw animals?
Francesca: Yes, I can.
Ricardo: OK. Do you like sports, Francesca? Can you swim?
Francesca: No, I can't. I can't swim, but I can do karate.
Ricardo: Wow! Thanks, Francesca. Well, there are over 75 sports clubs at the college. There's a club for every sport! Who's next?
Javier: Meeeeee! It's my first day! I'm Javier.
Ricardo: Hi. Javier! Are you Spanish?
Javier: No, I'm from Costa Rica!
Ricardo: And what's your major?
Javier: Languages. I can speak four languages. My first language is Spanish and I can speak French, English, and Chinese.
Ricardo: Great. What are your hobbies? Can you … ride a horse?
Javier: No, I can't. I can drive a car. I love cars!
Ricardo: Me, too! And I love music. Can you dance salsa?
Javier: Uh. No, I can't.
Ricardo: Can you play the piano?
Javier: No, I can't.
Ricardo: Well, the music center gives lessons. You can learn!

Track 04

1 Can you draw? Yes, I can.
2 Can you swim? No, I can't. I can't swim, but I can do karate.
3 Can you ride a horse? No, I can't. I can drive a car.

Track 05

Can you bake a cake?
Yes, I can bake a cake.
No, I can't bake a cake.

Track 06

1 science
2 art
3 math
4 Chinese
5 dance
6 creative writing
7 music

Track 07

What do you know about science? This class is an introduction to biology, chemistry, and physics. Our teachers use videos and real-life examples in the classes.
Are numbers hard for you? Our excellent teachers explain how to understand numbers. This is a popular class for young and old people.
Nǐ hǎo! Join this class and say hello in a new language! Learn how to write and speak Chinese with our friendly Chinese teachers.
Can you draw? Everyone can learn to draw! The lessons are at the college, but students often visit places in the city.
Tango? Salsa? This course is for beginners. Learn about different dances and practice with our teachers.
Do you want to write a story? Students practice different ways of writing and share their stories with the class.

Track 08

1 It's sunny.
2 It's windy.
3 It's snowy.
4 It's rainy.
5 It's cloudy.

Track 09

It's freezing! It's cool. It's hot!

Track 10

Charlie: Hello, Barney! How are you?
Barney: Hi, Charlie! Where are you? Is that a beach?
Charlie: Yeah. The weather's great. It's very sunny so we're at the beach. It's beautiful here. Look!
Barney: Wow! Yeah! Is it hot?
Charlie: Oh, yes! It's about 86 degrees. It's very sunny. I'm here with my parents and my brother, Andy.
Barney: Oh, how is your brother?
Charlie: He's good. Can you see him? He's swimming in the sea. Hey Andy, say hi to Barney!
Andy: Hi, Barney!
Barney: Where are your parents? Are they swimming?
Charlie: No, they aren't swimming. Mom's over there. She's reading a book. Oh … I think she's

sleeping! Dad's getting coffee for us. He's practicing Spanish with the waiter. So what time is it there? What's the weather like?
Barney: It's 8 p.m. It's rainy … It's windy … It's very cold.
Charlie: Oh, no! So what are you doing?
Barney: I'm not going out because the weather's bad. I'm watching a movie, and I'm eating dinner.
Charlie: Hey, let's call Jessica. What time is it there?
Barney: Uh. She's in New York. So, it's 3 p.m.
Charlie: OK … Hi, Jessica!
Barney: Hey, Jessica!
Jessica: Hey! How are you guys?
Barney: Charlie is having fun at the beach. I'm eating pizza! What are you doing?
Jessica: Well, it's usually cool in March, but it's warm today, so I'm shopping with my friend. We're getting food for a barbecue this evening.
Charlie: Great!
Dad: "Charlie! Charlie!"
Charlie: Oh … Dad's shouting at me. Sorry! Let's talk later. Have fun tonight, Jessica! Enjoy the movie, Barney!
Jessica and Barney: Bye bye!

Track 11

Conversation 1

A: Are you studying?
B: Yes. We're practicing English.

Conversation 2

C: Are you eating lunch?
D: No, I'm not eating lunch. I'm having coffee with my sister.

Track 12

One Day in My City
530 Followers
Morning
Visit the museum and learn about the city's history. Go early because it's free before 10 a.m. Don't go on Monday because it's closed!
Afternoon
Go to the beach. Swim in the ocean, or take a boat trip. Get a coffee at the beach café or at the hotel's coffee shop.
Evening
Eat dinner at Gino's pizzeria. Reserve a table because it's always busy. Then go to the park and watch a movie at the outdoor movie theater.

Track 13

1 Visit the museum.
2 Don't go on Monday.
3 Go to the beach.
4 Swim in the ocean.
5 Get a coffee.
6 Eat dinner at Gino's.
7 Reserve a table.

Track 14

M1: OK. Start on the left. What letter do you want?
F1: S, please!
M1: S. What S is something people wear on their feet?
F1: Shoes!
M1: Yes. Next letter?
F1: L.
M1: L. What L is a type of computer?
F1: Uh, laptop. D, please!
M1: What D is the opposite of son?
F1: Oh, I don't know. Sorry.
M1: Hello! What letter do you want?
M2: N, please!
M1: What N is something you write in?
M2: Notebook.
M1: Notebook! Well done. Next letter?
M2: J, please.
M1: What J is something you wear on your legs?
M2: Jeans. C, please.
M1: What C is a breakfast meal with milk?
M2: C? ... Cheese? ... No. Cereal! P, please.
M1: What P is a big, beautiful instrument?
M2: Err … p … piano! H, please!
M1: What H is the opposite of sad?
M2: Happy! And I'm happy now! Yesss!
M1: Well done! You're the winner!

Unit 6

Track 01

1 eyes
2 ears
3 nose
4 mouth
5 teeth
6 old
7 young
8 blond
9 dark
10 gray
11 short
12 tall
13 leg
14 slim
15 heavy
16 arm

Track 02

nose, old
arm, dark
heavy, leg

Track 03

Conversation 1

Alison: Hi, Jenny! Welcome to my party! Come in. Say hello to John.
Jenny: OK. Who's John? Is he your co-worker?
Alison: Yes, that's right. He's over there with my brother. They are both tall and slim. John has blond hair, but my brother has dark hair.
Jenny: Ah, who is the other man next to John? He's heavy and he has brown hair.
Alison: Oh, that's my father. And there's my mother over there.
Jenny: Is she the tall woman?
Alison: Yes, that's right. She has short brown hair. The short woman on the right is her friend. The tall woman on the left is her sister.
Jenny: Ah, sisters! Yes! They're both tall and they both have brown hair.
Alison: But they don't have the same color eyes. My mom has blue eyes, and her sister has brown eyes. Come and say hello to everyone!

Conversation 2

Peter: I like this picture, Rosa. Who's this woman?
Rosa: I think that's my grandmother. Yes, it is! She's young in this picture! And she has long blond hair and green eyes. She doesn't have blond hair now, of course. She has gray hair. And she has glasses!
Peter: She looks very happy here. She has a beautiful smile. Hmm. I think you have the same smile.
Rosa: Really? Thanks! We don't have the same nose. I have a big nose. She has a small nose.
Peter: You don't have a big nose, Rosa! And who's this man?
Rosa: Hmm, I don't know.
Peter: Is he your grandfather?

Rosa: No, my grandfather is short and he has big ears. This man is tall and he doesn't have big ears. Ah, I think this is my grandmother's little brother.

Track 04

1 She has short brown hair.
2 They don't have the same color eyes.
3 We don't have the same nose.
4 I have a big nose.

Track 05

1 cereal, juice, toast, coffee
2 eggs, coffee, toast
3 sandwiches, juice, salad
4 fish, vegetables
5 pasta, vegetables
6 chicken, salad

Track 06

1 Cook King—The King of Dinners
Help! I'm busy! I don't have any time to cook! Can you help?
Sure. We cook and bring delicious dinners to your home.
What do you mean? How does Cook King work?
Go to our website and order some meals. We cook your meal. Our driver drives to your house with your meal. You pay the driver.
Are there any vegetarian meals?
Yes! We have meals for everyone. We have some salads, some pasta with vegetables, and other vegetable meals.
Do you cook and deliver at any time?
We open at 12 p.m. and close at 11 p.m.
We do not deliver after 11 p.m.
We don't have any cash!
No problem. Pay the driver with your credit card or debit card.

CONTACT COOK KING TODAY!

2 Time for Breakfast!
By Michael White
March 15, 2019
Breakfast is my favorite meal of the day, and it's important for our bodies. It prepares us for the day. Try these two meals for breakfast.

1 Cereal and toast—easy! You need some milk, some cereal, and some bread. Don't forget to drink something. Drink a cup of coffee or a glass of orange juice.
2 Pancakes are another quick and easy meal. I like eating pancakes for breakfast, but some people eat them for a snack.
You need an egg, some milk, and some flour. Mix everything together. Then cook.

Track 07

1 happy
2 hungry
3 bored
4 tired
5 excited
6 sad

Track 08

Bella: Good afternoon. Welcome to Books with Bella. I'm Bella Benson. Today, I'm talking to Maria Parker about her book, Our Restaurant. It's a very popular book. Let's find out more. Good afternoon, Maria. Nice to meet you.
Maria: Nice to meet you, too. It's great to be here.
Bella: Tell us about the book.
Maria: Sure. It's about my grandfather's restaurant and my family. My grandfather isn't from America. He's from Spain. My family all works in the restaurant. I'm the manager. My parents are chefs. My brother is a waiter. He starts work at 8 a.m. and finishes about 11 p.m. He rarely has any free time. He's always tired.

Track 09

Bella: Good afternoon. Welcome to Books with Bella. I'm Bella Benson. Today, I'm talking to Maria about her book, Our Restaurant. It's a very popular book. Let's find out more. Good afternoon, Maria. Nice to meet you.
Maria: Nice to meet you, too. It's great to be here.
Bella: Tell us about the book.
Maria: Sure. It's about my grandfather's restaurant and my family. My grandfather isn't from America. He's from Spain. My family all works in the restaurant. I'm the manager. My parents are chefs. My brother is a waiter. He starts work at 8 a.m. and finishes about 11 p.m. He rarely has any free time. He's always tired.
Bella: Let's talk about some pictures from the book. I like this picture of your father and your grandfather in the kitchen. They're tall and slim. They have dark hair. They look very happy. They're wearing dress suits.
Maria: Yeah. Look at this old picture of me and my brother. We aren't tall and slim. We're short and heavy. We don't have blond hair! We aren't smiling in the photo. I think we're bored or hungry. And this is a picture of our street. It's sunny and pretty. That's my parents' house. They're standing in front of it. Their house is next to the restaurant.
Bella: Where do you live?
Maria: I live in an apartment across from the restaurant. It isn't big, but it's beautiful and modern. Oh, and here's a picture of the restaurant in December.
Bella: Who's the boy in the window? He looks excited.
Maria: That's my brother. He's young in this picture! He's dancing and laughing because he loves snowy weather.
Bella: Do you or your family have any free time? What do you do?
Maria: Well, I don't have any free time. My mom has some free time. She rides her horse …
Bella: Wow! Can you ride?
Maria: No, I can't! I can drive a car!
Bella: That's great! Let's take a break and …

Track 10

1 A: What's your name?
B: My name's Louise Jones.
2 A: Where are you from?
B: I'm from Argentina. I'm Argentinian.
3 A: Do you have a big family?
B: I have three brothers, my parents, and my grandfather. He's 78 years old.
4 A: What color hair and eyes do you have?
B: My hair is brown and I have blue eyes.
5 A: What do you do?
B: I'm a lawyer.
6 A: Where is your college or workplace?
B: It's on Main Street. It's across from the park.

7 **A:** What time do you start and finish work or college?
B: I get to work at 9 a.m., and I finish work at 5 p.m. I get home at about 6 p.m.

8 **A:** What do you do on the weekend?
B: I usually meet my friends and watch a movie.

9 **A:** Can you drive a car or ride a horse?
B: I can drive a car, but I can't ride a horse.

10 **A:** What are you doing now?
B: I'm speaking English, and I'm talking to you!

Track 11

A: Hi, what can I get you?
B: Can I have a coffee, please?
A: Sure. What size: small, medium, or large?
B: Small, please.
A: OK. Is that for here or to go?
B: To go, please.

Track 12

Zac: Good morning, Dr. Smith. I'm Zac. Nice to meet you!
Dr. Smith: Nice to meet you, Zac.
Zac: Dr. Smith, it says here you're a scientist. But we're not in a science lab. Can you explain?
Dr. Smith: Sure. I'm a food scientist. I work for a food company. The company sells sandwiches and other healthy snacks. I give advice about food—how to make it, and what food is good or bad for the body. I also eat the different foods. It's a great job!
Zac: Ah, I understand. So, is this your office?
Dr. Smith: Yes, it is. There's food everywhere! We have fruit, vegetables, different types of bread over there, salad, and …
Zac: And what are these people doing? Are they eating lunch?
Dr. Smith: Yes and no! These are our customers, but they're working for us today! They're eating the new sandwiches. Then they choose their favorite sandwiches, we make their favorite sandwiches—and we sell the sandwiches. The customers are happy. We're happy!
Zac: Wow! That's great.
Dr. Smith: Come on. Let's try a sandwich …

UNIT 1

Lesson 1

LISTENING A students

LISTENING B ♂ Max ♀ Francesca Mrs. Wood

LISTENING C **2** I'm Francesca. Nice to meet you, Max. **6** Good evening! Welcome to the first English class! I'm your teacher. My name's Mrs. Wood. **3** Pardon? Can you repeat that? **5** Francesca. Nice to meet you, too. Ah, here's the teacher. **1** Hello, I'm Max. I'm here for the English class. What's your name? **4** Francesca. Fran-ces-ca.

VOCABULARY A **1** Good morning. **2** Good afternoon. **3** Good evening.

VOCABULARY B **1** A: Hello, Amelia. How are you? B: I'm fine, thanks. **2** A: See you, Lenny! B: Goodbye! **3** A: I'm Lorenzo. Nice to meet you. B: I'm Josh. Nice to meet you, too.

GRAMMAR A **1** b is subject—verb—object. **2** c before a noun. **3** a with an apostrophe.

GRAMMAR B **1** I**'m** Mr. Cooper. **2** My name**'s** Andreas. **3** Her name **is** Irene. **4** Your name **isn't** Harry. **5** I**'m** fine, thanks.

GRAMMAR C **1** My name is Dora. **2** Her name is not Charlotte. **3** This is my co-worker. **4** His name isn't Tony. **5** Your name is Mr. Banks.

GRAMMAR D **1** I **am** Emily. = I'm Emily. **2** His name is Tom. = His name's Tom. **3** Her name is not Karina. = Her name isn't Karina. **4** Your name **is** Tilda. = Your name's Tilda. **5** My name is not Gina. = My name isn't Gina.

GRAMMAR E **Tommy:** Good afternoon. My name's Tommy. What's your name? **Luis:** I'm Luis. Nice to meet you, Timmy. **Tommy:** My name is / name's Tommy. My name isn't Timmy. **Luis:** Sorry! Your name is / name's Tommy. Nice to meet you. **Tommy:** Nice to meet you, too. This is my co-worker. His name is / name's Sebastian. **Luis:** Nice to meet you, Sebastian.

Lesson 2

READING A **Student:** Santiago **Worker:** Ayako

READING B **1** Santiago is from Mexico. He's Mexican. His first language is Spanish. **2** Ayako is from Japan. She's Japanese. Her first language is Japanese. Her other languages are Portuguese, French, and English.

VOCABULARY A **1** The US **2** The UK **3** Mexico **4** Brazil

VOCABULARY B **1** British **2** Spanish **3** American **4** Canadian **5** Brazilian

VOCABULARY C **1** Anton is from France. He's French. **2** Elke is from Germany. Her first language is German. **3** Weiling is from China. She's Chinese. **4** Justin is from Canada. His first language is English. **5** I'm from Mexico. I'm Mexican.

GRAMMAR A **1** c **2** d **3** a **4** b

GRAMMAR B **1** He's from China. **2** We're from the US. **3** She's from the UK. **4** They're from Italy.

GRAMMAR C **1** We are not from the US. **2** They are from Canada. **3** He is not from Mexico. **4** I am from France. **5** You are not from Germany.

GRAMMAR D **1** They're from Japan. They aren't from China. Their first language isn't Chinese. **2** He's from Canada. He isn't from the UK. His first language is French. **3** My first language is Spanish. I'm not from Spain. I'm from Mexico.

GRAMMAR E **1** We aren't from the US. **2** They're from Canada. **3** He isn't from Mexico. **4** I'm from France. **5** You aren't from Germany.

Lesson 3

LISTENING A **picture 1**—father Seth, mother Nancy, grandfather Bill; **picture 2**—friend Benji, sister Tonya, brother Jake, Jake's wife Jenny

LISTENING B Seth and Nancy are Jeff's parents. Jeff's father is 54. Benji is Jeff's friend. Tonya is Jeff's sister. Jake is 25. Jenny is Jake's wife.

VOCABULARY A **1** daughter **2** wife **3** mother **4** grandmother **5** sister

VOCABULARY B **2** husband **3** father **4** grandfather **5** brother

VOCABULARY C **1** This is my mom and dad. They are my parents. **2** This is my grandmother and my grandfather. They are my grandparents. **3** My father's wife is my mother. **4** My mom's dad is my grandfather. **5** Mr. and Mrs. Black are husband and wife.

GRAMMAR A **1** Verb—pronoun—object **2** *Yes/No*—pronoun—verb

GRAMMAR B **1** Are they your friends? **2** Is he your co-worker? **3** Is she your sister? **4** Are you his mom?

GRAMMAR C **1** Yes, I am. **2** Yes, he is. **3** No, they aren't. **4** No, she isn't.

GRAMMAR D **1** Are they your friends? **a** No, they aren't. **2** Is he your co-worker? **b** Yes, he is. **3** Is she your sister? **c** No, she isn't. **4** Are you his mom? **d** Yes, I am.

GRAMMAR E **Tammy:** Are Henry and Elsa your grandparents? **Lara:** No, they aren't. They're my parents. **Tammy:** Oh, OK. Is Stacey your sister? **Lara:** Yes, she is. She's my sister and my best friend. She's great! **Tammy:** My sister is great, too. Is Phil your brother? **Lara:** No, he isn't. Phil is my co-worker. Felix is my brother. **Tammy:** Are Darlene and

Emma your friends? **Lara:** Yes, they are. They're my friends from college.

Language and Life

FUNCTIONAL LANGUAGE A **1** name **2** major **3** nationality **4** email **5** phone number

FUNCTIONAL LANGUAGE B **Name:** Mark Peterson **Nationality:** American **Major:** English **Email:** markp21@me.com **Phone:** 315-716-4300

WRITING A **1** I'm Lexi. My last name is Sanders. **2** I'm from the UK. I'm British. **3** My first language is Spanish. **4** I speak English and Chinese. **5** This is my friend, Maliek.

WRITING B **1** I'm Janey. I'm a student. **2** My first language is English. **3** His name is Juan. **4** They are from Mexico. They are Mexican. **5** We aren't from the US.

UNIT 2

Lesson 1

LISTENING A **Picture 1:** big, modern **Picture 2:** old, small

LISTENING B **1** picture 2 **2** picture 1

LISTENING C Speaker 1: **1** big **2** small **3** modern Speaker 2: **1** modern **2** old **3** beautiful

VOCABULARY A **1** beautiful **2** big **3** modern **4** noisy **5** old **6** quiet **7** small **8** ugly

VOCABULARY B **size:** *big*, small **age:** old, modern **look:** *ugly*, beautiful **noise:** quiet, noisy

VOCABULARY C **1** quiet **2** old **3** small **4** ugly

GRAMMAR A **1** Question word—*to be*—subject **2** a different **3** use

GRAMMAR B **1** c What are their names? **2** e Where is she from? **3** d Who is he? **4** b How are you? **5** a How old are your grandparents?

GRAMMAR C **1** are **2** is **3** is **4** are **5** are

GRAMMAR D **1** 're/are, 5 **2** 's/is, **3** 3 'm/am, 1 **4** 're/are, 4 **5** 's/is, 2

GRAMMAR E **1** how **2** 'm **3** Who **4** How old **5** 's **6** Where **7** 's **8** What **9** 's

Lesson 2

LISTENING A **1** family **2** school, home **3** bag

LISTENING B **1** *laptop 1* **2** notebooks 5 **3** pens 3 **4** phone 7 **5** sandwiches 4 **6** transit card 8 **7** umbrella 2 **8** wallet 6

LISTENING C **1** True **2** False. The laptop is in Nathan's bag. **3** False. Three or four pens are in Nathan's bag. Two notebooks are in Nathan's bag. **4** True **5** False. Nathan's transit card isn't in the bag.

VOCABULARY A **1** ID card **2** wallet **3** phone **4** laptop **5** pen **6** watch **7** notebook **8** umbrella **9** brush **10** transit card

VOCABULARY B **One:** phone, watch, brush, pen **Two:** wallet, notebook, laptop **Three:** umbrella, transit card, ID card

VOCABULARY C **1** phone, laptop **2** brush **3** transit card **4** watch, laptop, phone **5** wallet **6** pen

GRAMMAR A **1** c for singular nouns. **2** d for singular nouns beginning with a vowel sound. **3** b + *s* for plural nouns. **4** a + *es* for plural nouns ending with *ch* and *sh*.

GRAMMAR B **Singular nouns:** wallet, brush, pen, transit card, notebook **Plural nouns:** phones, laptops, watches, umbrellas, ID cards

GRAMMAR C **1** a notebook **2** an umbrella **3** a wallet **4** an ID card **5** a phone **6** a brush **7** a laptop **8** a transit card **9** a pen **10** a watch

GRAMMAR D **1** three brushes **2** two umbrellas **3** two or three pens **4** five notebooks **5** two wallets **6** four phones **7** ten watches **8** six laptops **9** five or six ID cards **10** four transit cards

GRAMMAR E **Remember to buy:** five new pens, two black pens and three blue pens, two or three notebooks, an ID card for college, a transit card for seven days **My wish list:** two brushes for my sister, a phone, two watches—a watch for sports and a watch for going out, an umbrella for my vacation

Lesson 3

VOCABULARY A **1** False. The chair is next to the desk. **2** True **3** False. The bag is on the chair. **4** True **5** False. The book is between the umbrella and the desk.

VOCABULARY B **1** bed **2** in front of **3** window **4** under **5** books **6** next to

READING A a room in a person's home

READING B GAP 1 pens GAP 2 laptop GAP 3 cell phone GAP 4 2 bags GAP 5 umbrella

GRAMMAR A **1** is **2** are **3** is

GRAMMAR B **1** is **2** are **3** is **4** are **5** is

GRAMMAR C **1** are **2** an **3** are **4** is **5** a

GRAMMAR D There are two bedrooms in the apartment. The big bedroom is beautiful. There are three big windows. There's a bed. There's a desk. There are two chairs. The small bedroom isn't beautiful. There is a window. There's a bed behind the door. There's a small desk next to the bed.

GRAMMAR E There are two rooms in the apartment. The small room is my favorite. There is a window. There's a bed behind the door. There's a desk next to the bed. There are two bags under the bed.

Language and Life

FUNCIONAL LANGUAGE A **1** book **2** Saturday **3** much **4** Kellie Black **5** help

FUNCTIONAL LANGUAGE B **1** Not polite **2** Polite **3** Not polite **4** Polite

WRITING A **Question marks:** What's your email? Where is the hotel? **Exclamation marks:** The room is awesome! My city is beautiful!

WRITING B **1** How much is it? **2** No problem! **3** Thank you! **4** Where is the coffee shop?

UNIT 3

Lesson 1

VOCABULARY A One syllable: chef Two syllables: doctor, lawyer, pilot, teacher, waiter, waitress Three syllables: manager

VOCABULARY B **1** A police officer helps people with problems. **2** A lawyer understands the law and rules. **3** A waiter/waitress carries food to people. **4** A manager controls a store, a restaurant, etc. **5** A chef makes food for people. **6** A pilot flies to different countries. **7** A teacher teaches a subject to students. **8** A doctor gives medicine to sick people.

READING A police officer

READING B student, teacher, police officer, lawyer, chef

READING C **1** Gabriel, Caroline **2** student **3** Caroline, law **4** France **5** police officer **6** chef

GRAMMAR A **1** make a general statement **2** the same **3** don't **4** doesn't

GRAMMAR B **1** He goes to college by car. **2** She doesn't speak four languages. **3** He works in a restaurant. **4** I don't work in a school. **5** She lives in an apartment.

GRAMMAR C **1** My brother walks to college. **2** I love the city. **3** She doesn't go by bus. **4** She doesn't speak two languages. **5** We work in a store.

GRAMMAR D **1** teaches **2** doesn't work / does not work **3** lives **4** goes **5** speaks

GRAMMAR E Sara's a student. She studies languages. She speaks English, French, and Spanish. She doesn't speak Chinese. She doesn't have a job. She lives in Lima. She lives with her parents and her grandfather. Her brother doesn't live in Lima. He works in the UK.

Lesson 2

VOCABULARY A **at** 10:00 a.m., 2:00 p.m., the weekend; **in** the morning, the evening, the afternoon; **on** Monday, Thursday, the weekend

VOCABULARY B 1 in 2 on 3 at 4 in 5 on

LISTENING A photo 1

LISTENING B **1** friends **2** work **3** student

LISTENING C Linda is a student and a waitress. She works in the coffee shop on **Thursday**. She works at the store on **Tuesday**. Her last class finishes at **5:00 p.m.** She goes to work by bus. She finishes work at about **10:00 p.m.**

GRAMMAR A **1** a **2** b

GRAMMAR B **1** Do you work on Friday? **2** Does the store open in the evening? **3** Does he go to college on Wednesday? **4** Does she start work at 8:00 a.m.? **5** Do they drive to the office?

GRAMMAR C **1** a Do **2** b Does **3** b Does **4** a Do **5** b Does

GRAMMAR D **a** Question 4 No, she doesn't. **b** Question 3 No, he doesn't. **c** Question 1 Yes, I do. **d** Question 5 Yes, they do. **e** Question 2 Yes, it does.

GRAMMAR E **1** Does **2** doesn't **3** Do **4** do **5** Does **6** does

Lesson 3

VOCABULARY A **1** breakfast **2** table **3** bed **4** a shower **5** tea

VOCABULARY B **1** take **2** goes to **3** eat **4** drinks **5** get up

READING A **1** job advertisement **2** email

READING B **1** False. Jay's is a very big restaurant. **2** True **3** False. Jay's usually closes at 11:30 p.m. **4** True **5** False. Number Ten is a small coffee shop. **6** False. Suzie usually eats lunch at work.

GRAMMAR A **1** how often **2** after **3** before

GRAMMAR B 0% never 10% rarely 30% sometimes 70% often 85% usually 100% always

GRAMMAR C **1** I always go to bed early. **2** The coffee shop never opens on Sundays. **3** Do you usually go to bed early? **4** They rarely eat at home. **5** There are sometimes problems with the food. **6** We often go to college by bus.

GRAMMAR D **1** always **2** never **3** often **4** sometimes **5** usually **6** rarely

GRAMMAR E **1** usually eats **2** rarely drinks **3** never goes **4** sometimes drives **5** often works

Language and Life

FUNCTIONAL LANGUAGE A **1** good **2** Saturday **3** weekend **4** Friday **5** afternoon. **6** 2:00 p.m.

FUNCTIONAL LANGUAGE B Let's go to the park. Let's go on Friday.

WRITING A **1** c He works on Saturday, but he doesn't work on Sunday. **2** d I study law, and I work in a coffee shop. **3** b She works in the afternoon but not in the evening. **4** a I usually get up at 7:00 a.m. and eat breakfast.

WRITING B **1** Incorrect. They eat lunch at 12:30 p.m., but they sometimes eat lunch at 2:00 p.m. **2** Correct **3** Correct **4** Incorrect. They study in the evening and on the weekend.

UNIT 4

Lesson 1

READING A advertisement

READING B **1** What do visitors do in the museum? **2** When does the museum open? **3** Where does the museum tour start? **4** How much do tickets cost?

READING C **1** restaurant **2** store **3** 6:00 p.m. **4** Sunday **5** $20 **6** students **7** free **8** $15

VOCABULARY A **1** bookstore **2** hotel **3** ATM **4** park **5** museum **6** hospital **7** restaurant **8** bus station **9** coffee shop **10** university

VOCABULARY B **1** get – 8, 10, 6, 3 **2** buy – 1, 9 **3** eat – 7 **4** learn – 5

GRAMMAR A **1** always **2** always **3** question word—*do/does*—subject—verb

GRAMMAR B **1** How much **2** When **3** Where **4** What

GRAMMAR C **1** d Where do you go in the evening? **2** e What do students learn at college? **3** b How much does a course cost? **4** a When do you get to work? **5** c What does your family do on the weekend?

GRAMMAR D **1** do **2** does **3** does **4** do **5** do **6** does

GRAMMAR E **1** Where do you **2** What do you **3** When does the class **4** When do you start **5** How much does the class

Lesson 2

LISTENING A train station

LISTENING B **1** correct **2** incorrect: turn right **3** incorrect: second left

LISTENING C There's a big **hotel on the right**. The train station is **next to the hotel**.

VOCABULARY A **1** c It's on Top Street. **2** g It's on the right. **3** e The store is across from the park. **4** f My place is between the big store and the restaurant. **5** b The hotel's on the corner of Fifth Avenue and Tenth Street. **6** a The college is next to the bus station. **7** d The ATM is on the left.

VOCABULARY B **1** on, between **2** corner **3** on, the, next **4** across

GRAMMAR A **1** c give directions and instructions. **2** a in sentences with directions. **3** b the start of a sentence.

GRAMMAR B **1** Go straight up this street. **2** It's between the store and the restaurant. **3** Excuse me, where is the bookstore? **4** Turn left and take the second right. **5** The coffee shop is on the corner of Fourth and Main. **6** The ATM is across from the college.

GRAMMAR C **1** b **2** a **3** b **4** b

GRAMMAR D **1** A: **Excuse** me, is there an ATM **near** here? B: Yes, it's on the **corner** of Main and Tenth. **2** A: **Where's** the Grand Hotel? B: **Go** straight up this road. **Turn** left. It's on **the** right. **3** A: Excuse **me**, where's the language school? B: **Turn** right. **Take** the second left. It's across **from** the park.

GRAMMAR E Welcome to the city! You are at the train station. Where do you want to go? City park: Go straight up the road. **Turn** left. **Take** the second right. The park is on **the** right. National Museum: Turn right. **Take** the first left. The museum **is between** the big store and the parking lot. Shopping mall: Take the #101 bus. The bus stop is across **from** the train station. The trip is about 10 minutes.

Lesson 3

LISTENING A bag, boots, dress, jeans, shirt, shoes, skirt. **Not mentioned:** pants, suit

LISTENING B **1** cheap, 10 **2** shoes **3** yellow **4** beautiful **5** blue **6** expensive

VOCABULARY A boots, dress, jacket, jeans, pants, shoes, skirt, suit

VOCABULARY B **1** jeans, pants, skirt **2** jacket **3** boots, shoes **4** dress, suit

VOCABULARY C **1** casual **2** cheap **3** tight **4** short

GRAMMAR A **1** this, that **2** these, those **3** this, these **4** that, those

GRAMMAR B *this/that:* dress, jacket, skirt, suit, T-shirt *these/those:* boots, jeans, pants, shoes

GRAMMAR C **1** that **2** these **3** that **4** Those **5** This

GRAMMAR D **1** these **2** that **3** Those **4** that **5** Those **6** this

GRAMMAR E **1** these **2** this **3** this **4** these **5** these **6** that **7** those **8** that

Language and Life

FUNCTIONAL LANGUAGE A **1** $30 **2** $250 **3** $2

FUNCTIONAL LANGUAGE B **1** Excuse **2** much **3** cheap **4** take **5** please **6** Here

WRITING A **1 beautiful** jewelry **2 old** book **3 modern** apartment **4 interesting** book **5 small** coffee shop **6 expensive** clothes **7 busy** store **8 cheap** shoes

WRITING B **1** This is an **interesting** book. **2** Those shoes are **cheap**! **3** It's a **modern apartment**. **4** This shop sells expensive **clothes**.

UNIT 5

Lesson 1

VOCABULARY A **1 drive** a car **2 bake** a cake **3 do** karate **4 play** an instrument **5 dance** salsa **6 swim**, 1,500m **7 ride** a horse **8 draw** pictures **9 ride** a motorcycle

VOCABULARY B **1** ride a horse **2** bake a cake **3** do karate **4** drive a car **5** dance salsa

VOCABULARY C **3** swim 1,500 meters; **4** ride a motorcycle; **6** play an instrument; **7** draw pictures; **8** dance

LISTENING A **1** True **2** True **3** False

LISTENING B **1** Abbie **2** Manuel **3** Manuel, Abbie **4** Abbie

GRAMMAR A **1** things **2** questions **3** statements **4** short answers

GRAMMAR B **1** Can you drive a car? Yes, I can. **2** Can they play the guitar? No, they can't. **3** Can she ride a motorcycle? Yes, she can. **4** Can your mom bake a cake? No, she can't. **5** Can he do karate? Yes, he can.

GRAMMAR C **1** she can't **2** I can **3** they can't **4** he can **5** they can **6** he can't

GRAMMAR D **1** f I can dance salsa, and I can sing. **2** a I can ride a horse, but I can't ride a motorbike. **3** e I can't play the guitar, but I can play the piano. **4** c I can draw pictures, and I can write stories. **5** b I can speak English, but I can't understand Chinese. **6** d I can bake a cake, and I can cook pasta.

GRAMMAR E A: What do you do? B: I'm a teacher. I teach karate. A: Wow! I can't **do** karate. Can you do other sports? B: Yes. I can swim **and** I can ride a horse. I love music, but I **can't** dance salsa. Can you dance salsa? A: No, I **can't**. My brother is a dancer. He studies at a dance school. He can dance, **and** he can sing. He's amazing! B: What do you do? Are you a student? A: No, I'm a chef. B: So you **can't** dance, but you can cook delicious meals. A: Yes, I **can**!

Lesson 2

VOCABULARY A **1** art **2** math **3** music **4** paint brush **5** safety glasses **6** calculator

VOCABULARY B **2** art **3** science **4** Chinese **5** creative writing **6** guitar **7** dance class

READING A online profile

READING B **1** Spanish **2** China **3** cartoons **4** paint brushes **5** draw **6** car **7** dictionary **8** shoes **Extra:** guitar, music

READING C **1** Chinese **2** artist **3** college **4** dictionary, dance

GRAMMAR A **1** things we own or people we are connected to **2** name or noun **3** doesn't mean

GRAMMAR B My **friend's** brother is a teacher. His name is Tommy and he teaches music. I go to his music class on the weekend. **Tommy's** classes are very popular. I play the piano and I sometimes play my **friend's** guitar.

GRAMMAR C **1** Emily's **2** father's **3** teacher's **4** Amanda's **5** college's

GRAMMAR D **2** These are Jon's books. **3** This is my friend's phone. **4** This is Colin's calculator. **5** These are the teacher's paint brushes.

GRAMMAR E **2** The college's new library is open. **3** This is my sister's bag. **4** Where are my brother's pens? **5** The teacher's safety glasses are on the table. **6** The city's parks are beautiful.

Lesson 3

VOCABULARY A **1** sunny **2** snowy **3** rainy **4** cloudy **Extra word:** windy

VOCABULARY B **1** b /uː/ **2** a /aʊ/ **3** b /iː/ **4** a /ɒ/ **5** a /eɪ/ **6** a /eʊ/ **7** a /ʌ/ **8** a /ɪ/

LISTENING A **1** Jason isn't in the office. **2** Diana isn't in the office. **3** Lulu is in the park.

LISTENING B **1** b Jason's having coffee because the weather is freezing. **2** a Diana isn't working in the office because there's a problem in the building. **3** c Lulu's walking because there are no cabs.

LISTENING C **1** False. **Jason's brother** is talking to Angelica. **2** True **3** True **4** False. Diana **is** very busy today. **5** True **6** False. Kim is playing soccer in the park.

GRAMMAR A **1** d talk about activities that are happening now. **2** c before the main verb. **3** a the end of the main verb. **4** b for irregular verbs.

GRAMMAR B **2** We **aren't** eating dinner. **3** He **isn't** shopping at the mall. **4** You**'re** playing the guitar. **5** They**'re** speaking Chinese. **6** She **isn't** sleeping in her bed.

GRAMMAR C **2** They **aren't doing** their homework. **3** She **isn't watching** a movie. **4** The girls **are getting** coffee. **5** It's **raining** today. **6** I**'m not having** fun.

GRAMMAR D **1** They're swimming in the ocean. **2** She isn't studying at college. **3** I'm not riding a motorcycle. **4** He's playing the piano. **5** You're not eating your lunch.

GRAMMAR E Hey! What's up? Here we are at home. We're busy students because **we're** studying to be doctors! We **aren't** studying tonight. We're relaxing. Sean's **eating** pizza. **David's** talking on his phone. Karen's **sleeping** now! What are you all doing?

Functional Language

FUNCTIONAL LANGUAGE A **1** b Don't go in the morning. **2** c Eat at BB's restaurant. **3** a Get a cup of coffee. **4** e Go to the city park. **5** d Visit the museum.

FUNCTIONAL LANGUAGE B **1** Visit, Eat, Don't go **2** Go, Get, Don't go

WRITING A **1** or **2** because **3** and

WRITING B **1** because **2** and **3** or

UNIT 6

Lesson 1

VOCABULARY A **1** ears, mouth, teeth **2** heavy, legs, blond/brown **3** dark, tall, slim **4** tall, eyes, dark **5** gray, short, blue

VOCABULARY B **Color:** gray, blond **Face:** eyes, mouth, nose, ears **Body:** tall, short, slim, arm, leg

VOCABULARY C 1 f /eɪ/ 2 e /iː/ 3 g /ai/ 4 c /aʊ/ 5 b /oʊ/ 6 d /ɑr/ 7 a /e/

LISTENING A Photo 1: Francesca Photo 3: Sebastian

LISTENING B 1 slim 2 blond 3 nose 4 gray 5 ears 6 heavy

GRAMMAR A 1 c a person's face and body. 2 a *I/You/We/They*. 3 d *He/She*. 4 b *don't* or *doesn't* before *have*.

GRAMMAR B 2 don't have 3 doesn't have 4 have 5 don't have 6 has

GRAMMAR C 1 doesn't 2 have 3 is 4 has 5 are 6 don't

GRAMMAR D 1 He **has** brown eyes and brown hair. 2 They **are** tall and heavy. 3 I **don't** have gray hair. 4 She **has** a very big nose. 5 Fiona **is** young and beautiful.

GRAMMAR E 1 is 2 has 3 has 4 have 5 are 6 have 7 have 8 don't have 9 has 10 is

Lesson 2

VOCABULARY A Across 2 egg 5 cereal 7 salad 8 sandwich **Down** 1 vegetables 3 chicken 4 fish 6 juice

VOCABULARY B **one syllable:** eggs, fish, juice, tea, toast **two syllables:** chicken, coffee, pasta, salad, sandwich **three syllables:** cereal, vegetables

READING A social media page

READING B 1 sunny 2 lunch 3 four 4 cups 5 quiet 6 usually 7 chef

READING C Students' own answers

GRAMMAR A 1 b number of different things 2 a any 3 b some

GRAMMAR B 1 some 2 any 3 a 4 any 5 an 6 some

GRAMMAR C 1 A: Let's have **a** cup of tea. B: Oh no, I don't like tea. Do you have **any** coffee? A: No, sorry. Would you like **some** orange juice? B: OK, thanks. 2 A: Is there **any** pasta? B: Yes, there is. There is **some** fish, and there are **some** vegetables, too. A: OK. Is there **any** bread? B: No, there isn't. 3 A: Do you want **some** cereal for breakfast? B: No, thanks. A: How about **an** egg and **some** toast? B: Yeah. Thanks.

Lesson 3

VOCABULARY A 1 bored 2 hungry 3 tired 4 excited 5 sad 6 happy

VOCABULARY B 1 tired 2 hungry 3 bored 4 excited 5 sad 6 happy

LISTENING A 1 radio show 2 person from the city

LISTENING B 1 Mina's family 2 Mina's job 3 when Mina cooks 4 Mina's favorite stores 5 Mina's favorite place to eat

LISTENING C 1 San Diego 2 math, science 3 across from, next to 4 piano, swim 5 always, in the evening 6 often, on the weekend 7 pants, cheap 8 the UK, granddaughter 9 gray, nose 10 an egg, some, some

GRAMMAR A 1 can 2 prepositions of place 3 to be 4 adverbs of frequency 5 present progressive

GRAMMAR B 1 Is the tall man your grandfather? 2 There are two museums in the city. 3 They can't/can speak French, but they can/can't speak English. 4 The ATM is between the restaurant and the coffee shop. 5 He always gets up at 5:30 a.m. 6 There's some pasta, and there are some eggs.

GRAMMAR C 1 d simple present information questions 2 f plural nouns 3 e prepositions of time 4 b possessive 's 5 c present progressive 6 a *yes/no* questions with simple present

GRAMMAR D 1 We're from Mexico. We **live** in Mexico. 2 I **usually** start work at 8:00 a.m. 3 **We're** watching a movie because it's cold and rainy. 4 He can ride a horse, but he **can't** ride a motorcycle. 5 **Does** your sister go to college?

GRAMMAR E 1 Good 2 I'm 3 my 4 and 5 a 6 goes 7 studies 8 can 9 weekend 10 's

Language and Life

FUNCTIONAL LANGUAGE A 1 e What can I get you? 2 h Can I get a coffee, please? 3 g What size: small, medium, or large? 4 a Any other drinks? 5 c Is that coffee for here or to go? 6 b Can I get you some food? 7 d That's $4.50, please. 8 f Here's your change.

FUNCTIONAL LANGUAGE B **Drinks:** tea—medium **Where:** to go **Food:** egg sandwich **Total:** $9.50 **Change:** 50 cents

WRITING A 1 capital letter 2 wrong word 3 punctuation 4 spelling 5 word order

WRITING B 1 I like **coffee**. 2 The food is **delicious**, **but** the waiters aren't friendly. / The food is delicious, and the waiters are friendly. 3 Do you like tea? 4 One black **coffee**, please. 5 This is a **busy restaurant**.

Workbook Audio Script

Unit 1

Track 01

Max: Hello, I'm Max. I'm here for the English class. What's your name?
Francesca: I'm Francesca. Nice to meet you, Max.
Max: Sorry? Can you repeat that?
Francesca: Francesca. Fran-ces-ca.
Max: Francesca. Nice to meet you, too. Ah, here's the teacher.
Mrs. Wood: Good evening! Welcome to the first English class! I'm your teacher. My name's Mrs. Wood.

Track 02

1 They're from Japan. They **aren't** from China. Their first language **isn't** Chinese.
2 **He's** from Canada. He **isn't** from the UK. His first language is French.
3 My first language is Spanish. **I'm not** from Spain. **I'm** from Mexico.

Track 03

Jeff: My name's Jeff. Here is a photo of my family, and here's a photo of my friends.
So here are my parents, Seth and Nancy. My father is 54. My mother is 49. And here is my grandfather. His name's Bill. He's 78 years old.
OK, and this is Benji, Tonya, Jake and Jenny. Benji is my friend. He's a student. I'm a student, too. This is Tonya. She's my sister. She's 17. And Jake is my brother. He's 25. And Jenny is his wife.

Track 04

Mark: Mark. My last name is Peterson.
P-e-t-e-r-s-o-n.
I'm from the US. I'm American.
My major is English.
markp21@me.com
My cell number is 555-716-4300.

Unit 2

Track 01

1 Oh, look at this! Hmmm. Oh, it isn't a nice room. I like big places. I like modern places. This room is very small and it's very old. It isn't modern.
2 Wow, look at this! Where is it? I'm not sure. Well, it's in a big city. And the building is big. It's big and it's modern. I don't like small or old buildings. This building isn't small or old. It's beautiful, and I love it!

Track 02

1 I like big places. This room is very small and it's very old. It isn't modern.
2 It's big and it's modern. This building isn't small or old. It's beautiful, and I love it!

Track 03

Nathan: Hey, Mom!
Mom: Nathan? Are you OK? Aren't you at school? Where are you?
Nathan: Yes, Mom; I'm at school! But, Mom? Um, where's my black school bag? Is it at home?
Mom: Oh Nathan! It's your bag! I don't know. Hang on. It isn't here. No, sorry! Yes! Here it is!
Nathan: Oh, good! What's in my bag? Is my laptop in my bag?
Mom: Hold on. Yes, your laptop and … your umbrella … three or four pens … your sandwiches! Your lunch is in the bag!
Nathan: Oh …
Mom: And two notebooks … and your wallet! Nathan! Everything you need is in your bag!
Nathan: My phone isn't in the bag. My transit card isn't in the bag.
Mom: No, not your phone or transit card! I'm on my way to school now!
Nathan: Thanks Mom! Sorry …

Track 04

1 phone, watch, brush, pen
2 wallet, notebook, laptop
3 umbrella, transit card, ID card

Track 05

There are two rooms in the apartment. The small room is my favorite. There is a window. There's a bed behind the door. There's a desk next to the bed. There are two bags under the bed.

Track 06

Hotel worker: Yes? Park Hotel?
Kellie: Good afternoon. I want to book a double room for Saturday night, please.
Hotel worker: OK. Let me see. Yes. There's a double room.
Kellie: Good. Thank you. How much is it?
Hotel worker: It's $175 and guests pay at the hotel, miss. Could you please give me your name and email?
Kellie: Can you repeat that, please?
Hotel worker: $175. Guests pay at the hotel; name and email?
Kellie: Kellie, K-E-L-L-I-E, Black, B-L-A-C-K. My email is kellieb1234@mymail.com.
Hotel worker: Thank you. That's one double room for Saturday.
Kellie: Thank you for your help. Goodbye.
Hotel worker: You're welcome, have a good day! Goodbye.

Track 07

1 Yes? Park Hotel?
2 Guests pay at the hotel, miss.
3 Name and email.
4 You're welcome, have a good day! Goodbye.

Unit 3

Track 01

chef	pilot
doctor	teacher
lawyer	waiter/waitress
manager	

Track 02

Sarah: I'm a student. I study languages. I speak English, French and Spanish. I don't speak Chinese. I don't have a job. I live in Lima. I live with my parents and my grandfather. My brother doesn't live in Lima. He works in the UK.

Track 03

Linda: Hi Elly!
Elly: Hey Linda! How are you?
Linda: I'm fine, thanks.
Elly: Where are you?
Linda: I'm at work.
Elly: Work?
Linda: Yes! I work in my friend's coffee shop in the evening. I'm a waitress.
Elly: Yeah, but today is Thursday. You work in the coffee shop on Tuesday. You work at the store on Thursday, right? So, where are you, Linda?
Linda: I'm in the coffee shop! I work at the store on Tuesday and I work at the coffee shop on Thursday. The coffee shop doesn't open on Tuesday.
Elly: Oh, OK, OK. Sorry! Hey I wanted to ask: do you drive to work?
Linda: Well, I go to college in the afternoon. My last class finishes at 5:00 p.m. …
Elly: I know. We're in the same class, Linda!
Linda: … and then I go to work by bus. So, I don't drive to work. I start work at 6:00 p.m. I finish at about 10:00 p.m. It's a long day!
Elly: It is indeed! Hmmm. Well, never mind … see you at school! Our class starts at 8:00 a.m.!

Track 04

Sammy: I always get up at 7:00 a.m. I usually eat breakfast. I rarely drink coffee or tea.
I never go to work by bus. I sometimes drive my car. I start work at 8:00 a.m. I'm a doctor. I finish work at 9:00 p.m. I often work late. I love my job.

Track 05

Beth: Hey Amber, how are you?
Amber: I'm good. And you?
Beth: OK, thanks. Are you free on Saturday? Let's go to the park.
Amber: No, sorry. I work on the weekend. How about Friday? I don't work in the afternoon.
Beth: Great. Let's go on Friday. How about 2:00 p.m.?
Amber: OK. See you!
Beth: Bye!

Track 06

1 Let's go to the park.
2 Let's go on Friday.

Unit 4

Track 01

Geraldine: Hello, I'm Geraldine. I work with Jon. Are you his sister?
Chloe: Yes, I am. Nice to meet you. I'm Chloe. Do you work at the museum?
Geraldine: Yeah, that's right. I'm a teacher, too.
Chloe: Are you? Where do you teach?
Geraldine: At the new sports center. The big sports center by the train station.
Chloe: Ah, yes, I know. So, what do you teach?
Geraldine: cycling, fitness classes, swimming … I teach everything! The fitness class is always fun. Come and try a class!
Chloe: OK, thanks. When does the class start?
Geraldine: The class starts at 7:00 p.m. It's on Monday and Thursday,
Chloe: Oh no. I usually finish work at 7:00 p.m.
Geraldine: Ah, when do you start work?
Chloe: I start work at 10:00 a.m.
Geraldine: Well, there's a class at 7:00 a.m. It's on Wednesday.
Chloe: Great! How much does the class cost?
Geraldine: The class is $10 for students.
Chloe: OK great, see you there!

Track 02

A: Excuse me, is the train station near here?
B: The train station? Sure. About five minutes. So go straight up this road. Turn right.
A: Go straight … turn left.
B: No. Go straight, turn right.
A: Sorry, yes, right. I'm late. My train is in ten minutes.
B: Ten minutes! OK, take the second left. There's a big hotel on the right. The train station is next to the hotel. It's easy! Good luck!
A: Second left … big hotel on right … entrance next to hotel. Thank you!

Track 03

Conversation 1

A: Look at this store! There are awesome clothes here! Hey! Look at this skirt!
B: Yes! It's long … and it's cheap. It's $10! Oh, and look at these shoes! They're $20. Wow, they're cheap, too. Do you like them?
A: Yes, I love them!
B: Do you like that bag?
A: Uh, where?
B: The yellow bag … by the window. Do you like that bag?
A: No, sorry.
B: Me neither. I don't like the color yellow. Ugh. I Immm. Do you like those boots? The boots by the blue bag?
A: Yeah! Oh yes, they're great!

Conversation 2

C: I like your dress. It's beautiful. Is it new?
D: Oh, thank you. No, it's old. But it's my favorite. I like your jeans. And your shirt is nice. It's a great color! Blue? Purple?
C: Blue, I think. Thanks. My jeans are new. My shirt is new, too.
D: You look great! The shirt is very dressy … and very expensive?
C: Uh, yeah. $200.
D: Excuse me? $200? That is expensive!
C: Yeah, I know … but I love it!

Track 04

Conversation 1

Buyer: Excuse me, how much are these boots?
Seller: They're $30.
Buyer: OK. Could I take those, please?

Conversation 2

Buyer: Excuse me, how much is this laptop?
Seller: It's $250.
Buyer: Oh, OK. No, thank you.
Seller: Sure, no problem.

Conversation 3

Buyer: Excuse me, how much are the books on this table?
Seller: They're $2 each.
Buyer: They're cheap! Could I take these four books, please?
Seller: Sure. That's $8, please.
Buyer: Thanks. Here you are.

Track 05

Buyer: Excuse me, how much are the books on this table?
Seller: They're $2 each.
Buyer: They're cheap! Could I take these four books, please?
Seller: Sure. That's $8, please.
Buyer: Thanks. Here you are.

Unit 5

Track 01

1 I can swim 1,500 meters. Can you?
2 I don't like motorcycles. I can't ride a motorcycle.
3 Can you play an instrument?
4 My friend can draw pictures. She's great!
5 He likes music, but he can't dance salsa.

Track 02

Abbie: Manuel! Look at this!
Manuel: What is it, Abbie?
Abbie: It's an ad on the city website. It's for an activity day in the city park. It's on Saturday.
Manuel: An activity day? What does that mean?
Abbie: You can try different sports and activities. Look! Look at the list of activities—do karate … dance salsa … draw pictures … ride a horse! I love horses, but I can't ride. Can you ride a horse, Manuel?
Manuel: No, I can't. My sister can ride a horse. She's a teacher.
Abbie: Really? Wow!
Manuel: It's a great job! What about salsa? I can't ride a horse, but I can dance salsa. Can you?
Abbie: No, I can't. I love salsa music.
Manuel: Me too! You can play the piano. You're very good!
Abbie: Thanks! Can you play an instrument?
Manuel: No, I can't.
Abbie: What are the other activities?
Manuel: Bake a cake, ride a motorcycle, draw pictures.
Abbie: Draw pictures? Yes, please! I can't draw. I want to draw.
Manuel: Let's go! How much does it cost?
Abbie: Tickets are $30 for the day. All the activities are free. There's a big lunch with international food. Mmm. There's music in the evening.
Manuel: Awesome!

Track 03

1 Where is my dictionary?
2 I love my art class. The teacher is great.
3 I think science is my favorite subject. It's very interesting.
4 Can you speak Chinese? I can't.
5 Stefan likes creative writing. He writes funny stories.
6 Mr. Jones can play the guitar.
7 My sister goes to a dance class on Monday.

Track 04

1 Are these Pablo's shoes?
2 The college's new library is open.
3 This is my sister's bag.
4 Where are my brother's pens?
5 The teacher's safety glasses are on the table.
6 The city's parks are beautiful.

Track 05

Conversation 1

Jason: Hi Terry, Jason here! I'm in the café. Where are you, buddy? I'm having a cup of coffee because I'm cold. It's freezing today! Are you driving here, or are you getting the bus? My brother is here. He's talking to Angelica. They're laughing about something. Oh, and he's wearing new jeans. He isn't wearing those ugly jeans today! See you soon!

Conversation 2

Diana: Good morning Matthew. This is Diana speaking. Thank you for your help with the report. I'm reading the report now. I think it's *very* good. I'm making some notes now … and I'm changing one or two parts. I'm here with Ryan, and he's reading the report too. He's helping me today because I'm very busy. Please call 555-582-0244. This is a different number. We aren't working in the office today because there's a problem in the building.

Conversation 3

Lulu: Hello Kim! It's me, Lulu. I'm late! I'm sorry. I'm very sorry! I'm walking up Main because there are no cabs. I'm running across the street. Sorry! Oh my, I'm near the park. So, OK. I'm at the park. I'm looking for you. Where are you? You aren't answering your phone. Ah! There you are! You're playing soccer with two people. Who are they? I'm here! Hello!

Unit 6

Track 01

/e/ /aʊ/ /iː/ /ai/
/oʊ/ /ɑr/ /eɪ/

Track 02

This is my mom, Francesca. She's young in this photo. I think the photo's old. She has gray hair now, but she has blond hair in the photo. There are her big brown eyes. She has a small nose and a small mouth. She's beautiful.
And this is my friend, Sebastian. He's tall. I think he's very tall. He isn't heavy. He's slim. He has dark hair and blue eyes. He has small ears. He has a big nose.

Track 03

Conversation 1

A: Excuse me, I'm looking for Dwayne. Is he here?
B: Yeah, he's over there. He's talking to that group of people. He's short and slim.
A: Uh, is he the man eating a sandwich?
B: No, no! That's Kris. Dwayne is drinking coffee. He has blond hair and a big nose.
A: Ah, OK. Thanks.

Conversation 2

C: Excuse me, where's Jane?
D: Oh, sorry. She isn't working today. Can I help you?
C: Yes, please. There's a problem with my laptop.
D: Ah, ask Dan for help. He's at the desk across from the door.
C: Is he the man with gray hair?
D: That's right. He has gray hair and big ears. He's tall and heavy.
C: OK, thanks for your help.
D: No problem.

Track 04

cereal	fish	sandwich
chicken	juice	tea
coffee	pasta	toast
eggs	salad	vegetables

Track 05

Conversation 1

A: Let's have a cup of tea.
B: Oh no, I don't like tea. Do you have any coffee?
A: No, sorry. Would you like some orange juice?
B: OK, thanks.

Conversation 2

C: Is there any pasta?
D: Yes, there is. There is some fish, and there are some vegetables, too.
C: OK. Is there any bread?
D: No, there isn't.

Conversation 3

E: Do you want some cereal for breakfast?
F: No, thanks.
E: How about an egg and some toast?
F: Yeah. Thanks.

Track 06

Tony: Welcome back, listeners! Now, it's 11:30 a.m., so … it's time for "Two minutes with Tony." That's right, guys; it's time for the very quick—only two minutes—interview with a famous person from our beautiful city, San Diego.
Our guest is Mina Anderson. Mina is the winner of Channel One's popular program, "Super Chef." Welcome, Mina!
Mina: Hello, Tony! Thank you. Nice to meet you.

Track 07

Tony: Nice to meet you, Mina. So, let's start! Where are you from?
Mina: Well, I'm from San Diego! I'm American. My parents and my grandparents are from this city. We're all American. We all love San Diego! My brother lives in the UK. He works there.
Tony: And what do you do?
Mina: I'm a teacher. I teach children. I teach math and science. In fact, the school is near the radio station. It's across from the park and next to the old museum. My class is very excited about this radio interview. They're listening now. Say hello, Tony! They like you!
Tony: Sure! Hey, kids! What's up?
Mina: Thank you! That's a very happy class now!
Tony: So "Super Chef!" Congratulations! What a competition! When do you cook?
Mina: Every day. It's my favorite activity. Oh, I can play the piano, so I like that, too. I can't swim and I don't like sports, but … I can cook! Anyway, I always make a big meal in the evening. My husband often cooks on the weekend, too. We love cooking.
Tony: OK. So, what's your favorite store in San Diego?
Mina: Oh, that's an easy question! The Old Boot. It sells old clothes, and they're beautiful! There are a lot of shoes, jackets, and pants. And it's cheap!
Tony: Where's your favorite place to eat?
Mina: Oooh, difficult question. The Full English. It's a very small restaurant. The manager, Steve, is great. Steve's granddaughter is in my class. I teach her. Yeah, so Steve's from the UK. He's from London. He's short and heavy. He has gray hair and a big nose … and a very big smile. The food is delicious!
Tony: Oh, time's up! Thank you and …
Mina: Hang on! I have a present for you Tony. Where is it? Ah, yes, here it is in my bag. Here's your lunch. It's an egg salad with some pasta. And here's some juice. And here's some cake!
Tony: Oh, thank you so much, Mina. Let's pause for a break and then …

Track 08

Waiter: Hello. What can I get you?
Customer: Hello. Can I get a cup of tea, please?
Waiter: No problem. OK. What size: small, medium, or large?
Customer: Medium, please.
Waiter: Sure. Any other drinks?
Customer: No, thanks.
Waiter: OK. Is that tea for here or to go?
Customer: To go, please.
Waiter: Can I get you some food? There are some nice sandwiches here, and there's some delicious cake.
Customer: OK. An egg sandwich, please.
Waiter: Sure. That's $9.50, please.
Customer: Here you are.
Waiter: Thank you. Here's your change. 50 cents.